OECD ECONOMIC SURVEYS

1999-2000

United States

OECD

ORGANISATION FOR ECONOMIC CO-OPERATION AND DEVELOPMENT

ORGANISATION FOR ECONOMIC CO-OPERATION AND DEVELOPMENT

Pursuant to Article 1 of the Convention signed in Paris on 14th December 1960, and which came into force on 30th September 1961, the Organisation for Economic Co-operation and Development (OECD) shall promote policies designed:

- to achieve the highest sustainable economic growth and employment and a rising standard of living in Member countries, while maintaining financial stability, and thus to contribute to the development of the world economy;
- to contribute to sound economic expansion in Member as well as non-member countries in the process of economic development; and
- to contribute to the expansion of world trade on a multilateral, non-discriminatory basis in accordance with international obligations.

The original Member countries of the OECD are Austria, Belgium, Canada, Denmark, France, Germany, Greece, Iceland, Ireland, Italy, Luxembourg, the Netherlands, Norway, Portugal, Spain, Sweden, Switzerland, Turkey, the United Kingdom and the United States. The following countries became Members subsequently through accession at the dates indicated hereafter: Japan (28th April 1964), Finland (28th January 1969), Australia (7th June 1971), New Zealand (29th May 1973), Mexico (18th May 1994), the Czech Republic (21st December 1995), Hungary (7th May 1996), Poland (22nd November 1996) and Korea (12th December 1996). The Commission of the European Communities takes part in the work of the OECD (Article 13 of the OECD Convention).

Publié également en français.

Table of contents

• • • • •

Tables

Annexes

Figures

BASIC STATISTICS OF UNITED STATES

THE LAND

Area (1 000 sq. km)	9 373	Population of major cities, including their metropolitan areas, July 1996:	
		New York	19 938 000
		Los Angeles-Anaheim-Riverside	15 495 000
		Chicago-Gary-Lake County	8 600 000

THE PEOPLE

Resident population, November 1st 1999	273 866 000	Civilian labour force, 1999	139 368 833
Number of inhabitants per sq. km	29.2	of which:	
Annual net natural increase		Health services	9 972 600
(average 1994-98)	1 599 600	Unemployed	5 876 417
Natural increase rate per 1 000 inhabitants		Net immigration	
(average 1994-98)	6.1	(annual average 1994-98)	906 800

PRODUCTION

Gross domestic product in 1999		Origin of national income in 1999	
(billions of US$)	9 256.1	(per cent of national income[1]):	
GDP per head in 1999	33 797.9	Manufacturing	15.9
Gross fixed capital formation		Finance, Insurance and real estate	18.6
Per cent of GDP in 1999	20.3	Services	24.2
Per head in 1999 (US$)	6 849.6	Government and government enterprises	12.8
		Other	28.6

THE GOVERNMENT

		Composition of the 105th Congress as of December 7, 1998:	House of Representatives	Senate
Government consumption 1999 (per cent of GDP)	14.4			
Government current receipts, 1999 (per cent of GDP)	31.1			
Federal government debt helded by the public (per cent of GDP), FY 1999	39.9	Democrats	206	54
		Republicans	228	55
		Independents	1	–
		Total	435	100

FOREIGN TRADE

Exports:		Imports:	
Exports of goods and services as per cent of GDP in 1999	10.4	Imports of goods and services as per cent of GDP in 1999	13.3
Main exports, 1999 (per cent of merchandise exports):		Main imports, 1999 (per cent of merchandise imports):	
Food, feed, beverages	6.5	Food, feed, beverages	4.3
Industrial supplies	21.1	Industrial supplies	21.6
Capital goods	44.7	Capital goods	29.0
Automotive vehicles, parts	10.7	Automotive vehicles, parts	17.5
Consumer goods	11.6	Consumer goods	23.4

1. Without capital consumption adjustment.
Note: An international comparison of certain basic statistics is given in an annex table.

This Survey is based on the Secretariat's study prepared for the annual review of the United States by the Economic and Development Review Committee on 15 March 2000.

•

After revisions in the light of discussions during the review, final approval of the Survey for publication was given by the Committee on 21 April 2000.

•

The previous Survey of United States was issued in May 1999.

Assessment and recommendations

The growth potential of the US economy has increased markedly...

The US economy seems to have shifted to a higher potential growth path, having recovered a considerable amount of the dynamism lost in the 1970s and 1980s. It has now been expanding continuously for longer, albeit not more rapidly, than at any time in modern history. Such a durable increase in output is linked to a significant economic transformation. At the aggregate level, trend labour productivity growth has probably doubled from the rate seen in the 20 years prior to the mid-1990s, helped by a surge in the capital equipment and software available for each worker. Central to this development has been the extraordinarily robust technical progress in the computer and communications industries. Advances in information technology have resulted in a sharp fall in the price of investment goods, boosting the growth of the capital stock and thus of labour productivity in the high-technology parts of the economy. These gains appear to be spreading into other sectors, and, if the decline in price of investment goods continues, may offer the possibility of maintaining, or even further boosting, the higher overall growth of labour productivity and hence of average real incomes for some time to come.

... but demand has increased even more rapidly...

While the economy's ability to supply goods and services has improved significantly, demand continues to increase even more quickly. Financial markets have anticipated future income gains and capitalised them to a very full extent. Consequently households, as well as benefiting from improved employment prospects and gains in real income, have seen a continuing substantial increase in their net worth. The personal sector has translated a part of this rise into higher consumption, which has accounted for a growing share of domestic demand in recent years. Investment, too, has been buoyant because of the prospects for persistently buoyant sales and ample availability of low-cost capital. Moreover, from the middle of 1999, exports too have been adding to demand, as the world expansion has become increasingly robust.

... provoking wider private-sector and external imbalances,...

Such high demand has resulted in the intensification of a number of tensions over the past year. Household saving has fallen further, with personal indebtedness rising swiftly. Companies, too, have been borrowing heavily, and credit has risen rapidly. Investment capital has also been readily available to the booming Internet sector of the stock market – recently capitalised at around 12 per cent of GDP – although few of these companies make profits at the moment. However, as yet, the debt-service ratios for both households and companies have not returned to the levels seen at the end of the 1980s. Moreover, while these sectors no longer have financial surpluses, their identified net borrowing remains small. Nonetheless, their deterioration has helped to generate a large current-account deficit that, at 4.2 per cent of GDP in the fourth quarter of 1999, was the largest since the Second World War. This growing imbalance has led the nation's net foreign liabilities to rise to an estimated 20 per cent of GDP, up from an average of 5 per cent of GDP in the first half of the 1990s.

... as well as tighter labour market conditions

In addition to the external imbalance, the labour market has become more stretched. Indeed, at around 4 per cent of the labour force, the overall unemployment rate is the lowest in 30 years, and the corresponding rates for minorities have fallen to record lows. The economic expansion has brought with it a fall in the poverty rate, and, possibly in combination with welfare reform, has contributed to a shortening of the welfare rolls. It has also stemmed the long-standing trend to a more uneven distribution of income. At the same time, faster productivity gains and tight labour market conditions have pushed up real wages more generally.

While wage pressures have remained limited so far...

Even so, nominal increases in salaries and benefits were quiescent for much of 1999, little changed from previous years. This raises the question of whether there has been an underlying improvement in the functioning of the labour market. Certainly, the changing demographic composition of the labour force – with fewer young people and more middle-aged workers – would account for some fall in structural unemployment, though much of this effect occurred in the 1980s. More recently, however, improved job matching from temporary help agencies and the Internet job market may have resulted in a further fall. Nevertheless, for the time being, there is little empirical evidence to indicate an equilibrium unemployment rate below 5 per cent, suggesting an eventual pickup in inflation.

... signs of price tensions have emerged in product markets...

Some signs of inflationary pressure have emerged elsewhere in the economy. World oil prices have more than doubled. Indeed, higher petroleum prices have helped push the increase in the consumer price index above 3 per cent over the past twelve months. Moreover, other commodity prices have been increasing, notably in the area of metals and other primary materials. Such moves have led to some increase in prices at the early stages of production. Furthermore, with the dollar no longer strengthening, overall non-oil import prices have stopped falling for the first time in four years.

... which, as economic activity is expected to remain buoyant,...

Considerable momentum now exists in final demand, suggesting that there may be no slowdown in the pace of the expansion this year. The reduction in real incomes stemming from the substantial increase in oil prices over the past year has not left an appreciable mark on consumer spending. Moreover, the increase in personal wealth is sufficiently large that a further fall in the saving ratio can be expected. At the same time, outlays on information technology equipment continue to be driven by falling relative prices and seem likely to recover from their Y2K-induced slowdown at the end of 1999. Although part of the increase in demand is projected to be met by another widening of the current-account deficit, output seems set to grow faster than potential for the year as a whole, with GDP probably expanding by some 4½ per cent against an increase of just over 3½ per cent in estimated potential output. The resulting enlargement in the output gap points to the likelihood of a modest rise in core inflation and some upward creep in wage increases.

... bring the risk of a general pick-up in inflation

With the considerable changes that have occurred in the economy in the past few years, uncertainties surround the projections of both inflation and output. Faster demand growth than is currently projected risks higher inflation, particularly if the recent moderation in wage growth turns out to have been driven by temporary factors, rather than a further fall in the structural unemployment rate. In a pessimistic scenario there could be a falling-off in the foreign demand for US assets that would lower the dollar exchange rate and reinforce the pressures on inflation. This could end the "exuberance" in equity markets. In such a case, recent levels of borrowing could be seen as excessive and so generate a pervasive slowdown in demand as private-sector balance sheets are restructured. A similar outcome could occur if there were a spontaneous fall in the stock market generated by investors returning to earlier more conservative valuation rules that might adversely affect the technology sector, just as occurred at the end of the 1960s bull market.

Against this background, overall financial conditions still appear relatively easy,...

Over the past year policy makers have sought to ensure that inflation remains low and stable. In 1998, when international instability led to adverse movements in financial markets, short-term interest rates were lowered. These cuts were gradually unwound during 1999. By November, three quarter-point increases had restored the level of nominal interest rates to that of the summer of 1998. However, even after the latest increase in March, some measures of real short-term rates are still below their pre-crisis levels. Overall credit growth remains rapid, though the surge in money and bank credit seen at the end of 1999 may be unwound as the liquidity injected to deal with potential Y2K problems is progressively withdrawn. Thus, with little change in the effective exchange rate and continuing equity-price gains, overall financial conditions do not yet seem tight.

... so that monetary policy needs to be more restrictive...

Increases in the inflation trend, however slow and apparently innocuous, will eventually become entrenched in expectations, making its ultimate reversal that much more difficult. With output increasing by 6½ per cent annual rate in the last two quarters of 1999, inflation expectations were, once again, moving towards 2½ per cent per year at the beginning of 2000. Such conditions warrant a further progressive increase in interest rates this year. The full extent of the increase that will be necessary is as yet uncertain, as underlying equilibrium real interest rates may have risen with the improvement in returns to capital. If the projected further 1 percentage point increase in the Federal funds rate, to 7 per cent by the end of this summer, proves to be sufficient to slow growth to less than 3 per cent in 2001, as projected by the OECD, that should not cause undue problems in financial markets, as such an increase in rates has now been largely discounted. In any case, a modest decline in stock prices would help to restore the balance between supply and demand in the economy as a whole by lowering private consumption more quickly than could be achieved by movements in short-term interest rates alone.

... and further changes in the communication strategy of the Federal Reserve should be considered

The clear transmission of the intentions of the monetary authorities can aid the smooth functioning of financial markets. The Federal Reserve has signalled its intentions to markets in a number of ways: the announcement of biases to policy, together with speeches and testimony before the Congress. But confusion over the appropriate interpretation of such biases led it rightly to reconsider its procedures. As from the beginning of 2000, all interest rate decisions have been accompanied by a set of standard phrases to describe the risks facing the economy over a period that extends beyond the next meeting of the Federal Open Market Committee (FOMC). It remains to be seen whether such a step is a sufficient increase in transparency. Earlier publication of the minutes of the FOMC meetings might also be considered in order to provide a fuller appreciation of the future stance of policy.

At the same time, the impetus to higher budget surpluses appears to be fading...

The need for a tighter monetary policy has, in any case, become more pronounced with the recent change in the underlying thrust of fiscal policy. After a seven-year period when the general-government sector improved its balance by an average of 1 percentage point of GDP per year, the structural surplus appears to have stabilised. The saving in expenditure brought about by the end of the Cold War has ceased, and federal discretionary spending is expected to rise in real terms in 2000, exceeding agreed, albeit unrealistic, budgetary caps. Moreover, the extent to which federal tax revenues are rising faster than GDP has diminished. State and local governments have also used unexpected revenue increases to lower tax rates. Nonetheless, the general government sector is projected to have a surplus of 1¼ per cent of GDP in 2000, and gross general government debt may fall to 61 per cent of GDP, a decline of almost 15 percentage points in the past seven years.

... and needs to be renewed in order to prepare more fully for the longer-term consequences of ageing

Medium-term budget projections point to increasing surpluses. Already questions are being raised as to whether these should be used to raise expenditure or lower taxes. However, these projections are very sensitive to the assumptions used. For instance, just a modest increase in the pace of government spending would be sufficient to eliminate all projected on-budget surpluses. Moreover, there is not as much room for manoeuvre as the surpluses for the next decade would suggest, given the ageing of the population that is likely to boost spending on Social Security and Medicare thereafter. Accordingly, from a longer-term perspective, it would be wise to use the surpluses to continue to pay down debt. On the other hand, official projections are based on what may eventually be conservative estimates about the potential growth rate of the economy. Nevertheless, unless it becomes clear that the economy is on a faster growth trajectory, it would be unwise to jeopardise future surpluses by new spending and taxation plans. In any case, some further reform of the old-age pension system, will be necessary to ensure the sustainability of social security.

Longer-term growth prospects could be enhanced by innovative policies

Securing growth over the longer-term will require more than just continuing to follow sound fiscal, monetary and regulatory policies. Social and environmental policies, in particular, need to be reviewed in the light of achieving sustainable development. At the same time, there are markets where economic efficiency could be improved further.

The social agenda has a role to play in this area

In the social area, better long-term economic prospects could be achieved through government policies with respect to education and health. Increasing the quality of the nation's schools is essential to maintaining the supply of highly skilled workers, so vital to the continued surge in high-technology sectors. Progress has been made in recent years in setting output standards for schools. By 1999, nearly all states had adopted standards for basic subjects, and most now assess school performance, revealing some improvement. Yet much still needs to be done to meet the agreed standards. The growing number of charter schools reflects efforts to improve performance; more funding could be made available to them. Federal subsidies for the hiring of additional public school teachers create opportunities for higher overall educational achievement and allow for a more equitable distribution of resources. Nonetheless, some youths are bound not to obtain highly valued skills. It is important to avoid pricing them out of jobs through too-rapid increases in minimum wages. It would be preferable to aid low-wage workers through raising the earned income tax credit. Health outcomes remain poor in the United States, given the scale of expenditures, perhaps reflecting imperfect access to medical care. Although the State Children's Health Insurance Program has improved coverage for children in poor families, the share of the poor with health insurance coverage has declined slightly in recent years. More complete coverage for poorer people in general should remain a priority.

But future growth has to be achieved in an environmentally sustainable fashion...

Despite the undeniable environmental progress made in recent years, many question whether high growth is sustainable, not only in conventional economic terms but also in terms of accompanying effects on our surroundings. The natural environment is difficult to manage efficiently because of the lack of price signals – there are few markets in environmental benefits, as they accrue to all. Furthermore, the full cost of any damage is generally not borne by the entity that caused it. As in other countries, the authorities' initial response to this problem was to introduce command and control regulations. Indeed, much of this approach remains, frequently in the form of rules that are complicated and expensive to administer. The government is aware of these costs and has been experimenting under Project XL with more flexible implementation of such command and control regulations, though the early results are disappointing.

... which could be facilitated by the use of tradable pollution permits

There has accordingly been a move away from regulation towards market solutions. Trading in permits for sulphur dioxide emissions began in 1995, and their prices have been lower than expected. By limiting the overall quantity of such emissions and allowing a uniform price to be established, the overall costs of meeting the aggregate emissions ceiling have been minimised and incentives given to find efficient abatement techniques. Such pollution has fallen markedly. In 1999, permit trading was introduced for emissions of nitrogen oxides in a number of north-eastern states; further benefits should accrue to this programme following its extension to neighbouring states in 2004.

Energy use could be limited either through such permits or taxation...

The tendency towards greater use of economic instruments has not, however, been uniform. One such area where little progress has been made is transport. Quite apart from its importance as a contributor to greenhouse gas emissions, the road transport sector has many other externalities. The costs of reducing some of these is borne by the sector itself (e.g. accident insurance and safety regulations, catalytic converters and emission regulation). Where the externality is closely related to fuel consumption, measures to increase fuel costs directly, whether through taxation or otherwise, would be both more effective and less costly than the imposition of average fuel economy standards on new car sales. Due to its high energy consumption, the United States is by far the largest per capita contributor to greenhouse gas emissions. Along with most other OECD countries, it seems unlikely to meet its original aim under the United Nations Framework Convention on Climate Change to keep greenhouse gas emissions in the year 2000 to no higher than their 1990 level. Meeting the more stringent emissions target for 2008-12 set out in the Kyoto Protocol using only domestic measures, would require considerable increases in carbon-based energy prices (either through taxation or through a cap-and-trade system). The introduction of a scheme involving international trading of emissions permits could substantially reduce the scale of the price increase necessary to reduce carbon emissions. The government is thus justified in seeking approval of such a scheme. But price increases should be adopted sooner rather than later, in order to allow adjustment to begin quickly, thereby lowering its ultimate cost.

... while there should be increased use of economic incentives to deal with pollution in the areas of agriculture and water

The achievement of sustainable growth and economic incentives to avoid pollution are also notably absent in the area of agriculture and water use. The extensive use of nitrogenous fertilisers and intensive animal rearing have contributed to the continued growth of food production, but they have also caused deterioration in water quality and other kinds of environmental degradation in some regions. At the same time, agricultural subsidies generally contribute to higher output and intensive production methods that help create these problems, even if some of the subsidy programmes have significant environmental conditionality attached. A consistent application of the polluter pays principle in agriculture would imply, for example, taxing nutrient application in fertiliser and feeds in areas where water quality is compromised. Agriculture is also a major user of water for irrigation, often supplied at prices that are well below those paid by other users. It would appear that the structure of water use rights is frequently a barrier to its rational use. A way of either trading such rights or charging resource rents on water extraction needs to be found so as to try to enhance sustainability, even of agriculture itself, in areas where aquifers are being rapidly depleted.

More generally cost-benefit analysis should be used in policy formulation more heavily...

The impact of regulation can also be made more favourable by the more widespread use of cost-benefit analysis. Rules and procedures governing the use of such analysis are inconsistent, with some legislation actually preventing its use in areas where it would obviously be beneficial. Such restrictions should be removed, and guidelines and quality control for its use shouldbe strengthened, with similar requirements for its use in both regulatory impact assessments and environmental impact statements. Of course, many of the benefits and some of the costs of environmental regulation are uncertain and difficult to quantify. While the use of cost-benefit studies should be the norm, policy should not be rigidly constrained by their results, especially where non-quantifiable effects are important. Clear principles should be established under which non-quantifiable effects can influence the balance of net costs and benefits.

... perhaps tempering the role of the courts

Heavy use of the courts is probably inevitable in the area of environmental law, where the use of market mechanisms to mediate conflicts – whether over environmental damage or protection of property rights against "takings" – is difficult. However, a recent OECD study, *Regulatory Reform in the United States*, concluded that the degree of litigation generally imposes considerable costs on society and the economy. Improved drafting of laws and regulations could probably reduce these costs. The tendency for legislation to provide only the broad targets of policy, with the details and some elements of strategy left to the executive branch of the government to interpret, increases the likelihood of costly litigation, however. Establishing the basic principle that the benefits of a measure must exceed its costs should at least focus attention on the essence of problems rather than procedures.

Elsewhere, economic efficiency could still be improved in the financial sector...

In the financial sector, the reduction of the Depression-era barriers between banking and other financial activities has been a long-standing concern. After many failed attempts at revision, these barriers have finally been abolished through the welcome enactment of the Gramm-Leach-Bliley Act. The legislation should prompt a further integration of capital markets and allow greater efficiency in the provision of banking and insurance services, though it also increases the demands on the regulatory structure. Financial modernisation needs to continue with a reduction in the relatively large number of regulatory authorities for deposit-taking institutions: the Office for Thrift Supervision could usefully be merged with the Office of the Comptroller of the Currency, for example. The market could also be given a greater role in applying discipline to financial institutions. Finally, the role of government-sponsored financial enterprises should also be reconsidered. Commercial markets no longer need implicit government guarantees provided to these enterprises, and policy should be oriented to reducing, or even severing, their links to government.

... and sustained by putting electronic commerce on a level playing field with traditional forms of trade

In the newer sectors of the economy, electronic commerce is already a powerful agent of growth, offering significant new business opportunities and greatly expanded consumer choice. It is also serving to transform many business models, by streamlining business processes. However, in terms of the fiscal regime, electronic commerce should be put on an equal footing with conventional commerce so as to avoid evident market distortions. There seems every reason to bring electronic commerce, and indeed the mail-order business, into the sales tax net, especially as emerging technology is making the attribution of such taxes that much easier. Such a move would also safeguard future state and local government revenues that depend heavily on such taxes.

Open product markets also have a vital role to play

There is also a need to maintain a constant vigil to ensure that product markets remain open. To that end, to the extent that official discretion is involved, it is crucial that recourse to contingency measures be kept to a minimum. But perhaps most important is the position of the United States in the ongoing efforts to initiate another round of global trade liberalisation. The world's largest economy, as well as its partners, stands to benefit handsomely from opening up trade in goods and services, especially in agriculture and textiles where intervention, which harms the interests of consumers and reduces efficiency, remains the order of the day.

Overall, the nation seems set to continue to enjoy first-rate economic performance, so long as policy is set in a far-sighted way

The US economy now appears to be in a position to supply faster medium-term growth of living standards to households than has been achieved at any time since the 1960s. The upswing seems likely to continue this year, with growth of about 4½ per cent. The prolonged surge in activity, along with welfare reform, has increased employment of less-favoured groups, and reduced welfare rolls, while poverty rates have fallen. The movement to greater income inequality has been checked, though it remains high relative to other OECD countries. Higher investment in information technology has been the one of the keys to the step-up in productivity gains. At the same time, prudent economic policies have prolonged the expansion. Abstracting from energy price increases, inflation has been low and fairly stable. But demand continues to outstrip supply, generating a very tight labour market, a widening external deficit and the risk of higher underlying inflation, raising the economy's vulnerability to business cycle risks. To safeguard a continued, if slower, expansion, at just under 3 per cent in 2001, further increases in short-term interest rates are needed. Fiscal policy should focus on the longer term, using prospective budget surpluses to pay down debt, thereby securing future pension benefits as the population ages. Policy-makers also need to ensure that growth is ultimately sustainable. Here, improving the education and health of the least advantaged is crucial, as is maintaining the quality of the environment through a further expansion of economic incentives in this area. A far-sighted orientation to policy can only benefit the nation.

I. Economic conditions and the maintenance of faster growth

The economy's improved supply-side performance

Real GDP has grown at a surprisingly fast pace – about 4 per cent annually – for four consecutive years in an economic upturn that started nine years ago, surpassing projected growth rates year after year. This expansion is now the longest since records began to be kept around 1850, and recent indicators point to continued strength in activity in the near term. The US economy appears to be operating above potential – even with significant improvements on the supply side that reflect strong investment in technology (Figure 1). Labour markets remain very tight, with a record employment-to-population ratio and the lowest unemployment rate in 30 years. Nonetheless, labour compensation slowed last year. Combined with rapid productivity growth, unit labour cost increases slowed as well, but they remained above those in product prices. Overall inflation picked up, reflecting higher energy prices, but core inflation, as measured by the evolution of prices excluding food and energy, remained fairly subdued.

The central issue in evaluating this performance is to what extent the economy can continue to grow so rapidly over the medium term. The first part of this Chapter looks at the factors that may have generated the recent improvement and concludes that the medium-term growth rate of the economy appears to have increased and may have scope to rise further. However, as the rest of the Chapter points out, demand has been growing even faster, and a number of imbalances have emerged that may lead to a slowdown in growth, as discussed at the end of the Chapter.

Generated by favourable productivity developments...

The unexpectedly rapid expansion of the economy in the past four years has its origin in the rapid growth of labour productivity that has helped to keep costs under control and to boost expectations of future profits. Until recently, it appeared that the average increase of whole-economy labour productivity in the period since 1972 had been slightly below 1 per cent annually, a markedly slower rate than had been achieved in the previous 20 years.[1] The precise number

Figure 1. **Aggregate economic indicators**

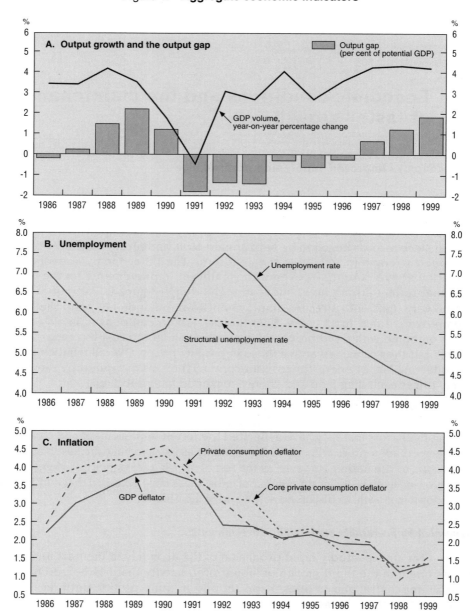

Source: Bureau of Economic Analysis and OECD.

Box 1.   The 1999 comprehensive revisions to the national accounts

In October, the Bureau of Economic Analysis (BEA) released its comprehensive revision of the National Income and Product Accounts, revising GDP, national income and their components back to 1959. In addition to incorporating revised and more complete source data for recent years into the accounts, a number of methodological changes were made.[1] On balance, the level of nominal GDP in 1998 was revised up by about $250 billion, 3 per cent of the previous estimate. Changes to real GDP were larger on average, as prices were revised down somewhat. Since 1959, the annual growth rate of real GDP was 0.2 percentage point higher on average but was raised by 0.4 percentage point since the beginning of the current expansion in 1991. Revisions were widespread across components.

A major source of revision to the level of GDP was a definitional change that treated business and government expenditures on software as fixed investment rather than as an intermediate input. This change boosted the level of nominal GDP in 1998 by $160 billion, or two-thirds of the overall upward revision. The boost to average real GDP growth from software was about 0.2 percentage point per year.

In recent years, real GDP growth was raised roughly ¼ percentage point per year by the incorporation of information from new input/output accounts and economic censuses and revisions to source data. Revisions here were particularly large for private investment in non-residential buildings, private consumption of food and other non-durable goods and consumption by state and local governments.

In earlier years, real GDP growth was raised by the introduction of new source data – the research consumer price indexes – to deflate personal consumption expenditures, as these data show lower inflation.[2] Since the BEA had already included estimates of these (geometrically weighted) indexes in its consumption prices starting in 1995, most revisions affected data between 1978 and 1994. Over this period, average annual growth of real consumption was boosted (and consumer inflation was lowered) by about ¼ percentage point on average and real GDP by 0.15 percentage point.

Another important definitional change, dealing with a shift in the treatment of government pensions, had no affect on GDP or national saving but a large effect on personal income and saving. The personal saving rate was revised up by 3.2 percentage points in 1998. About half of the upward revision was attributable to a change in the treatment of contributions to government employee pension plans, which are now considered personal income, the same as contributions to private pension plans. Government net saving was lowered by a comparable amount, so the definitional change left national saving unchanged.

Overall, the revisions raised the OECD's projections of potential growth by 0.3 percentage point.

---

1. For more details on the definitional and technical changes made, see Moulton *et al.* (1999), Moulton and Seskin (1999) and Seskin (1999).
2. A discussion of the research CPI is provided in Box 4.

depended on the time period chosen for the comparison and the measure of employment or output that was used. Evidence of a faster rate of labour productivity started to become evident in 1998, but it was difficult to disentangle cyclical from trend effects. An extra year of rapid growth and a marked revision to economic data (Box 1) now strongly suggest that there has, indeed, been more than a cyclical upturn in productivity. For example, the growth of productivity usually slackens in a mature economic expansion, as happened at the end of both the 1960s and the 1980s booms (Figure 2). In this cycle, labour productivity growth has, if anything, accelerated. A simple statistical analysis, which allows for cyclical effects, suggests that a significant break in the growth of labour productivity appears to have occurred after 1995 (around quarter 18 in Figure 2). This increase far exceeds the gain in productivity that has been generated by improved measurement of GDP – that factor only adds 0.2 percentage point to the historic growth of productivity. On average, labour productivity has increased by 2.0 per cent annually since 1995, when measured for the whole economy and has grown even faster in the non-farm sector of the economy (Table 1), or if measured using the income measure of GDP. All of these measures show faster productivity growth in the past four years than on average in the period 1960 to 1995.[2]

The improvement in labour productivity trends is closely linked to the surge in the growth of the capital stock (Figure 3). Specifically, there has been a

Figure 2. **Labour productivity growth in three extended business cycles**
Output per hour, non-farm business sector
Year-on-year percentage change

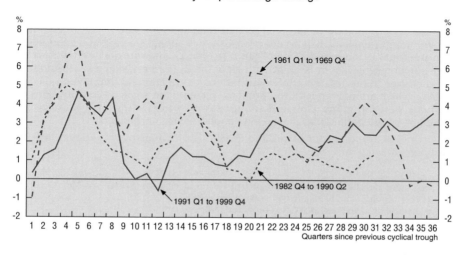

Table 1. **The estimated sectoral distribution of hourly labour productivity growth**

Annual average percentage changes

	1960-95	1972-95	1995-99	Change between 1995-99 and	
				1960-95	1972-95
Overall economy					
GDP (expenditure based)	1.8	1.2	2.0	0.3	0.8
GDP (income based)	1.7	1.3	2.5	0.7	1.2
Non-farm sector	2.1	1.5	2.7	0.6	1.2
Non-financial corporate sector	2.0	1.8	3.4	1.3	1.6
Excluding the computer sector					
GDP (expenditure based)	1.6	1.1	1.6	0.0	0.5
GDP (income based)	1.6	1.1	2.0	0.4	1.0
Non-farm sector	1.9	1.2	1.9	0.0	0.7
Non-financial corporate sector	1.8	1.4	2.6	0.8	1.2
Computer sector	22.8	25.8	42.0	19.2	16.2

Note: As the real GDP data is chain linked, sectoral components of GDP do not add to total GDP. Consequently, the difference between aggregate and sectoral productivity includes a measurement residual as well as true sectoral differences. Productivity is measured as output per hour.

Source: Output data for overall sectors and the computer sector from the Bureau of Economic Analysis. Employment data is from the Bureau of Labor Statistics. Output data for sectors excluding the computer sector estimated by the OECD, taking into account the chain-linked nature of the source data.

Figure 3. **Growth of the estimated business sector capital stock[1]**

Year-on-year percentage change

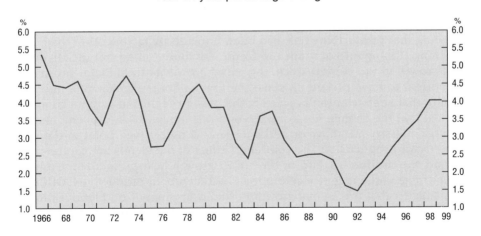

1. Estimates based on post-revision investment data, including software outlays.
Source: OECD.

particularly marked increase in the stock of information technology products. Between 1994 and 1998, such equipment (hardware only) accounted for 59 per cent of the increase in gross equipment investment. A further factor that has boosted capital stock growth has been the adoption of new national accounting standards that count purchases of software as investment (see Box 1), whereas previously such expenditure had been counted as a cost of production and written off in its year of acquisition. The depreciation rate of such outlays is high. So, even though such outlays represented over 12 per cent of private non-residential capital formation during 1999, OECD estimates suggest that the cumulated value of net software investment was only 2 per cent of the capital stock by 1999, while the inclusion of software has boosted the growth of the capital stock by about 0.1 to 0.2 percentage point annually in recent years.[3] As a result of faster hardware and software outlays, the capital stock is now growing faster than in the previous two decades.

... linked to an acceleration in capital deepening

Increased capital formation has brought about faster labour productivity growth through an increase in the amount of capital per unit of labour input (capital deepening). The extent of capital deepening has been increasing during this business cycle, with capital per hour worked rising as quickly as at the peak of the cycle in the high-growth period of the 1960s, given that labour inputs are increasing somewhat less rapidly than in the 1960s (Figure 4, panel A). There also seems to be some statistical evidence of a slight acceleration in total factor productivity, though confirmation of this movement will have to await the availability of capital service data.[4] In the latest revisions to the national accounts, output and investment were revised up, but output was revised by even more, suggesting that productivity has also been boosted by factors other than capital deepening. Taking into account the trend movement in labour inputs and the actual growth in the capital stock, the trend growth of total factor productivity does appear to have picked up since the first half of the 1980s, to a rate that is similar to that seen over the average of the past 40 years, but without compelling evidence that the change has gone beyond this. Recently, improvements in the computer industry may have added a further 0.2 percentage point to the growth of total factor productivity. The combined effect of the significant capital deepening and the modest pickup in the trend growth of total factor productivity explains most of the recent acceleration in actual labour productivity. OECD estimates suggest that the annual growth in whole-economy trend labour productivity is now above 2 per cent (Figure 4, panel B) and that this trend, itself, has been increasing by close to 0.2 percentage point per year since 1995. If maintained over the longer term, even the former change would have a profound impact on the medium-term growth of living standards.

Figure 4.   **Productivity growth**
Year-on-year percentage change

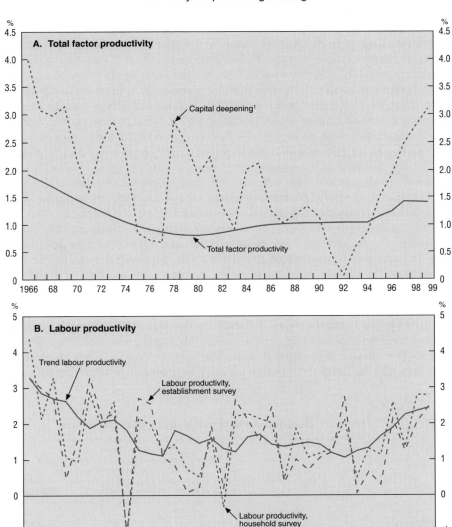

1.   Capital deepening is change in the real capital stock per hour worked.
Source: OECD calculations based on Bureau of Labor Statistics data.

While the breadth of the productivity gains are not yet fully clear,...

The acceleration in productivity growth has been evident throughout the economy, but has been particularly marked in the computer sector. In this area, the change in the growth of productivity has been spectacular, with annual average growth increasing by 16 percentage points in the four years ending 1999, according to OECD estimates (Table 1). Even though this sector is small (representing 1.1 per cent of nominal GDP in 1999), it was nevertheless responsible for 30 per cent of the acceleration in productivity. The remaining increase in productivity growth was spread throughout the rest of the economy, with growth in the private non-farm, non-housing, non-computer sector increasing by 0.7 percentage points, according to OECD estimates. Such an increase is the reflection of the amount of real investment that has been undertaken outside the computer producing sector of the economy, as can be seen in the growth-accounting studies such as Oliner and Sichel (2000) and Whelan (2000). Indeed, a recent study (Council of Economic Advisers, 2000) found that one-third of the increase in labour productivity could be accounted for by capital deepening outside the computer sector (Table 2). This factor could not however explain all of the acceleration in productivity outside the computer sector. Some part may have been cyclical[5] and some could be possibly related to an increase in total factor productivity. If the rapid growth of the capital stock outside the computer sector persists, then a significant part of the acceleration in productivity may turn out to be a permanent phenomenon.

The assessment of the recent movement in labour productivity in the non-computer sector is made more difficult by the fact that the most computer-intensive industries are in the service sector. Measurement problems abound in this area. The service industries that are the most intensive users of information technology (IT), as judged by the share of IT equipment in total capital or by IT

Table 2. **Decomposition of productivity movements**

	Non-farm business sector (average of income-and expenditure-bases) Annual average percentage change		
	1973 to 1995	1995 to 1999	Change[1]
Output per hour	1.43	2.90	1.47
Capital deepening	1.06	1.53	0.47
Labour quality	0.26	0.31	0.05
Computer sector total factor productivity	0.16	0.39	0.23
Other factors[2]	−0.06	0.65	0.70

1. Percentage points.
2. Other factors reflect cyclical and trend movements in total factor productivity in the non-computer sector of the economy.
Source: Council of Economic Advisors (2000).

capital per worker, account for 43 per cent of non-farm business output. Despite their high and presumably growing IT intensity, the level of measured productivity in these industries fell by 0.3 per cent annually on average between 1990 and 1997[6] (Department of Commerce, 1999). Of the 16 service industries identified as belonging to this sector, half exhibited productivity growth in line with expectations (averaging growth of 4.8 per cent annually), while the other industries averaged a decline in the level of productivity of just over 1 per cent annually. At the extreme, business services have seen one of the fastest increases in IT capital per worker, with such goods representing almost half of the equipment used in that industry, but measured productivity fell by just over 2½ per cent annually on average between 1990 and 1997. Equally striking is the dispersion of measured growth of productivity between financial brokers and the banking industry. Much of this differential may disappear when new methods of measuring banking output are incorporated into the sectoral output data. There is every reason to believe that other IT-intensive service industries would also be found to have better productivity numbers if output were measured directly, rather than by using inputs. However, since they largely concern sectors that produce intermediate inputs, the difficulty in measuring sectoral productivity should not impact to a great extent on the measurement of economy-wide productivity trends.

... they appear to be sustainable

The increase in the capital stock could continue at its recent pace without undue burden on company finances because technical progress is likely to continue to push down the prices of capital equipment. No direct estimates are available for the growth of total factor productivity in the semiconductor and computer industries, due to the absence of sufficiently disaggregated capital stock data. However, the pace of technical progress in those aggregates of which these two are part (industrial machinery and equipment and electronic and other electric equipment) has been particularly rapid, with annual TFP growth of 8.9 per cent and 4.6 per cent, respectively, between 1990 and 1996 (Department of Commerce, 1999). Moreover, the pace of such advances appears to have accelerated and has resulted in a rapid decline in the prices of computer and peripheral equipment (by upward of 22 per cent annually in the past five years when measured by quality-adjusted price indices – see Box 2). Indeed, based on these price developments, multifactor productivity in the semi conductor and computer industries increased at a pace of 45 and 16 per cent respectively between 1996 and 1999 (Oliner and Sichel, 2000). This movement has generated a marked decline in the relative price of investment goods. As a result, while the real capital stock growth so measured has been rapid, the growth of the nominal capital stock has been slower. Hence net business investment as proportion of GDP is significantly lower than at previous cyclical highs (Figure 5) – imposing less of a financial burden on companies for a given increase in the real capital stock.

Box 2. Hedonic price indices and chain weighting

Changes in the prices of a number of high-technology goods are difficult to measure by conventional matched-model techniques, given their short product cycle. New products with different and generally more desirable characteristics are introduced at a rapid pace, making it difficult to price an identical product over time. Hedonic price estimation is a technique that attempts to create an identical product over time – for example, computing power – out of different goods – say, computer boxes.[1] The purchase price of a typical new computer system has declined somewhat in recent years and average computing capabilities (real outputs) have increased dramatically. As a result, the price of computing power, measured by the hedonic price index, has dropped tremendously over the same period. The average pace of price decline nearly doubled during the 1995 to 1999 period, compared with the average over the previous 10 years.

Prices of computers and other equipment
Year-on-year percentage change

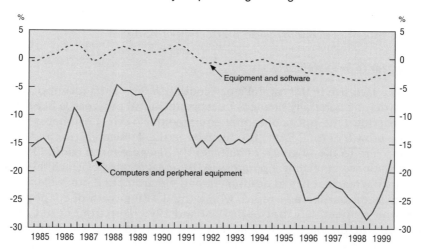

Source: Bureau of Economic Analysis and OECD.

Such rapid decline in prices boosts the volume of outlays and would quickly generate a very rapid increase in real output if spending were aggregated using fixed weights. However, annual changes in prices and quantities in the national accounts are calculated using a Fisher formula that uses weights from two adjacent years.[2] These annual changes are chained (multiplied) together to form time series of price and quantity (volume) indexes. An important advantage of this index formula is that it isconstructed using weights that change over time as expenditure patterns change. As

---

Box 2. Hedonic price indices and chain weighting (*cont.*)

a result, a chain Fisher quantity index reflects shifts in demand, including, but not restricted to, those induced by falling relative prices. When applied to price indexes the Fisher formula eliminates so-called "upper-level substitution bias" in the measurement of inflation. By contrast, price indexes with fixed weights, such as the CPI, do not pick up shifts in demand adequately, and, even worse, the weight in measured inflation for products with falling relative prices, such as computers, drops quickly in years following the base period. Other features of the Fisher index include the fact that percentage changes are not affected by the choice of base year and are symmetric – that is, the product of the quantity index and the price index yields the current-dollar index. However, it is important to note that chained-dollar values for components generally will not sum to overall GDP or to intermediate aggregates. For components for which prices and volumes are changing rapidly, such as computers and some other high-tech capital goods, the residual (between chain-weighted aggregates and the sum of their components) can become quite large within a few years of the base period.

---

1. In addition to computers, the consumer price index, which is the source for most consumption prices in the national accounts, uses hedonic procedures to adjust the observed prices of a number of products for quality improvements, including televisions, video cameras, a variety of audio products, apparel, and rent. In particular, hedonic procedures decompose observed prices into implicit prices for each important feature and component. This provides an explicit mechanism for replacing obsolete products with current ones without counting the value of quality improvements as price increases.
2. Using fixed 1996 weights instead of chained weights, real GDP would have grown about $2/_3$ percentage point faster per year in 1998 and 1999 than in the official statistics, and real private investment in equipment and software would have risen 3¼ percentage points faster on average per year. These differentials grow larger the greater the time that has elapsed since the base year. In the pre-revision data that used 1992 as the reference period, the difference between GDP growth in 1998 calculated with 1992 fixed weights and using chain weights was 2¾ percentage points.

The decline in the price of computer equipment has driven down the cost of computer capital and boosted its demand, adding to the prospect of sustained growth of the capital stock. Typical aggregate investment equations find only a small role for the cost of capital. Many researchers find the behaviour of investment to be dominated by changes in the rate of growth of output. However, such models of investment fail to explain the current continued acceleration in the growth of the capital stock at a time when the rate of growth of output has been quite stable. On the other hand, a disaggregation of equipment investment into computers and other products suggests that the falling user cost of capital for computer products has been significant factor in boosting the capital stock (Tevlin and Whelan, 2000). The estimated effect of the cost of capital on computer investment is almost nine times as large as that on aggregate investment. Moreover, most of it

Figure 5. **Gross and net investment**

Per cent of GDP in the business sector at current prices

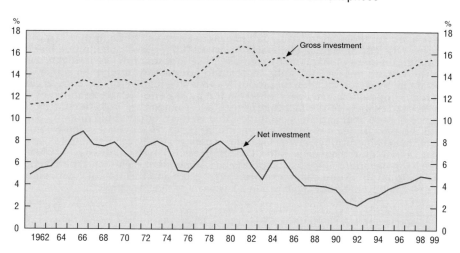

Source: OECD.

occurs because of the large impact of the decline in the relative price of computers. Tevlin and Whelan (2000) suggest that a possible interpretation is that information technology products are better substitutes for other factor inputs than are
other types of equipment.

The digital economy is raising growth more in the United States than elsewhere...

The contribution of the stock of computers to output growth has become
significant in recent years. By 1999, computers and peripheral goods represented
8.4 per cent of private non-residential nominal investment but only accounted for
1.7 per cent of total nominal business sector physical capital in 1997 (the last date
for which detailed data is available). On the assumption that computer equipment
earns a competitive rate of return, the computer capital stock generated growth of
between 0.15 and 0.38 percentage point per annum in the late 1980s and early
1990s (Sichel, 1997 and Jorgenson and Stiroh, 1995), reflecting the small share of
computers in the overall capital stock in that period. Recent work by the OECD
indicates that the average annual contribution of the IT capital stock has grown to
0.40 percentage point in the period 1990 to 1996 (Schreyer, 2000). Since then, the
contribution of IT capital has increased markedly to more than a percentage point
from 1996-99 (Oliner and Sichel, 2000).

The contribution of IT capital to overall economic growth has been significantly larger than in most other major countries. As long ago as 1985, the US economy exhibited a relatively high level of computer investment (Table 3). With the growth in investment in such equipment outpacing that in all other major countries in the 1990s, the United States had drawn well ahead of other countries in the use

Table 3. **The role of information technology in the growth of output and productivity: an international comparison**[1]

	United States	Japan	Germany	France	Italy	United Kingdom	Canada
	Per cent						
Share of information and communication technology (ICT) equipment in the nominal capital stock							
1985	6.2	1.2	2.9	2.4	1.3	3.6	4.3
1996	7.4	2.3	3.0	3.2	2.1	5.2	5.0
Annual growth of investment in IT equipment							
1985-90	19.6	23.6	18.8	16.2	20.8	25.5	17.2
1990-96	23.8	14.5	18.6	11.0	12.9	17.6	17.6
	Percentage points per year						
Contribution of ICT equipment to growth of output							
1985-90	0.34	0.17	0.17	0.23	0.18	0.27	0.31
1990-96	0.42	0.19	0.19	0.17	0.21	0.29	0.28
	Per cent						
Share of economic growth attributable to growth of ICT equipment							
1985-90	10.6	3.5	4.7	7.2	6.0	6.9	10.7
1990-96	14.0	10.6	10.6	18.9	17.5	13.8	16.5
	Per cent of GDP						
Production of ICT goods 1997	3.3	4.8	1.5	2.1	1.3	2.7	1.5
Value added in ICT industries 1997 (or latest year)	4.4	n.a.	3.8	3.5	2.5	n.a.	2.9
Sales of IT goods and services 1997	4.0	2.3	2.1	2.4	1.4	2.7	3.3

1. Capital stocks and investment are not official data. They are based on a common price index for ITC equipment that is applied to all countries.
Source: Schreyer (2000) and OECD (2000).

of IT equipment by 1996. Consequently, the absolute contribution of such equipment to growth in the United States was substantially greater than seen in other major countries in the same period, with the US performance only being matched in the United Kingdom.[7] Other indicators confirm the greater IT intensity of the US economy. Domestic sales of such equipment are much higher than in other major countries. Production of IT goods is also higher, but to a lesser extent than sales, as the United States imports a large amount of components from Asian countries. The US lead is not, however, universal in the use of information and communication technology: for example, the spread of mobile telephony has fallen behind that in a number of countries in Asia and Europe in recent years (see Chapter III).

... and could generate further gains...

Some analysts have asserted that the revolution in computers will generate more than a normal return to capital and hence eventually lead to improved total factor productivity growth. The process is seen as being slow to occur, as was the case with other major technological breakthroughs such as the use of electricity whose price fell in relative terms by an average of 7 per cent per year between 1899 and 1948[8] In that case, it was not until the spread of electric motors reached 50 per cent of the total installed power in factories that the growth of total factor productivity started to move higher (David, 1999). Such a process took some 40 years from the introduction of the first central generating systems. Overall, the speed with which the electric motor intensity rose between 1899 and 1914 was similar to the rate at which the computer intensity of the stock of producers' equipment rose between 1979 and 1987. As yet, though, the acceleration of total factor productivity has been limited. One reason for this, as yet, limited impact may be the costs of adapting organisations to the use of computers. Aggregate studies suggest that adjustment costs are substantial (Kiley, 1999). Moreover, microeconomic studies suggest that the returns from computerisation are maximised only if the company has a decentralised structure (Brynjolfsson and Hitt, 1998). In any case, the opportunities for the reorganisation of economic processes that are being generated are not limited to the company sector: the diffusion curve for residential use of personal computers is following a similar path for the acquisition of the other household durables that are now almost universally owned (Cox and Alm, 2000).

... as intermediation costs fall

The spread of computers into the home offers the possibility for improvement in the distribution of goods over the Internet that could increase productivity and reduce both costs and the relative price of certain products. At present such sales are a relatively small proportion of retail sales,[9] though growing very rapidly[10] (see Chapter II). While the potential for lower prices exists, they do not appear to be lower yet on average (OECD, 1999a). Certainly, electronic commerce offers the possibility of slashing the cost of retail outlets, but these costs represent a form of marketing expense and have to be replaced by other forms of publicity to attract consumers. At the same time, distribution becomes relatively expensive as it switches from high-density channels (warehouses to shopping centres) to lower-density routes (factories to residential areas). The greatest possibilities for price reduction may occur in the areas where the product is not consumed in the house or can be digitised in some form – thereby allowing the reductions in property and labour costs to flow through into the prices charged to the consumer. Examples abound in the financial and travel industries. In these sectors, Internet delivery of services has reduced the commissions paid to purchase shares and airline tickets by a compound annual rate of 40 to 50 per cent between 1993 and 1998 (OECD, 1999a). The savings on share purchases have been realised directly by consumers, and have contributed to a tripling of on-line stock trading between 1997 and 1999 in the United States. Until recently, much of the savings on airline commissions has been absorbed by airlines or passed on only indirectly to consumers. However, some carriers now offer direct discounts to customers using that company's web site to purchase tickets. In the banking industry, Internet transaction costs are estimated at only 9 per cent of the costs of branch banking. The gains in this area are still in the future, though, as the most successful US commercial bank in this area appears still to have less than one million on-line clients (Merrill Lynch, 1999). In the broader retail market, cost savings are harder to achieve. Initially, at least, supermarkets appear to have been charging similar prices for online and normal sales. Customers may, however, gain through convenience and delivery.

Falling computer and communication charges are also enhancing the appeal of business-to-business use of the Internet. At present, such transactions account for 70 to 85 per cent of all electronic sales, but most still occur over closed networks. The United States leads in this market both in the size of transactions and in readiness to use more open networks. The software for this market is largely produced by US companies; they had a global market share of 63 per cent in 1999 (OECD, 1999a). The electronic medium provides a faster, more information-intensive and less error-prone way to connect firms. Consequently, it offers a way to make business processes more efficient. As yet, though, it is not clear whether greater retail and business Internet usage offers a way to increase the growth of total factor productivity or whether it merely represents a way to maintain its growth, as the potential of previous innovations is exhausted over time.

Labour markets have adapted to changing demands

None of the recent improvement in economic performance has come through an acceleration in the use of labour inputs. The growth of the working-age population has been quite stable, at around 1 per cent annually, while earlier increases in the participation rate appear to be easing off. At the same time, the average length of the working week has remained stable. Indeed, the growth of the labour force between 1995 and 1999 was less rapid than in the period 1972 to 1995. It should be noted though that the increase in the labour force for the whole economy is based on the household survey estimate of employment. This has been increasing less rapidly than the establishment-based counterpart. If the latter ultimately turns out to have been the best measure of employment, then the increase in the labour force will be more than suggested above. However, even using an essentially establishment-based broad measure of employment, the growth in the labour force would be slower in the period 1995 to 1999 than in the period 1972 to 1995. An upward revision to the household employment data would require either an upward estimate of participation rates or, perhaps more likely, an upward revision to population growth.

The surge in the output of the IT sector and the increasing use of IT has generated a significant change in the structure of US labour markets. Employment in the computer sector of the economy has grown rapidly, most noticeably in the software and service industries rather than the hardware industry. The growth in these sectors has been so rapid (on average over 8 per cent annually between 1989 and 1997) that their relative wages have been pushed up by an average of 2½ per cent per year.[11] Employment in this sector, however, accounted for only 1.4 per cent of total employment in 1997. Overall employment growth has been oriented to the IT-using sectors of the economy in this period, with over 55 per cent of employment growth in this area. However, unlike in the software industry, this increase in employment has been achieved without any increase in relative wages.

With some fall in the structural unemployment rate

The performance of the labour market in the recent past suggests the level of unemployment consistent with a stable rate of inflation has declined. The entry of the baby-boom generation into the labour market may have pushed up the structural unemployment rate by about three-quarters of a percentage point between 1963 and 1977. By 1990, this increase had been reversed as the labour force progressively aged. Whether the fall in the structural rate has gone beyond this is still uncertain and depends very much on the econometric estimation methods that are used to identify the fall. A few researchers have attempted to quantify the factors that may have led to a decline in the structural unemployment rate over the 1990s. In particular, Katz and Krueger (1999) argue that the structural unemployment rate has declined since the late-1980s due to a number of factors. They estimate that about one quarter of the decline in structural unemployment is the result of the demographic shift toward older workers, with other factors, such as the increased use of temporary help agencies in hiring and the rise in the incarceration rate to 0.7 per cent of the population by mid-1998, up from 0.3 per cent in 1985, responsible for the remaining portion. Other research also suggests that the rise in the share of employment at temporary help agencies has reduced the structural unemployment rate (Otoo, 1999).[12] Estimates of the structural unemployment rate by government and private-sector analysts tend to range from 4½ to 5½ per cent for 1999 (Meyer, 2000). In any case, in the recent past favourable movements in other short-term economic variables such as import prices, price expectations and possibly unexpected productivity shocks have meant that actual unemployment could remain below the long-run structural unemployment rate without pushing up the growth of nominal wages (see below).

Permitting a significant acceleration in potential output

The overall consequence of the rapid growth in the stock of information technology goods and a slight pickup in the growth of total factor productivity has been to generate a progressive increase in the potential growth rate of the economy. The growth rate of potential would appear to have risen to around 3.6 per cent from a low point of slightly over 2½ per cent at the beginning of the 1990s (Figure 6).[13] Moreover, provided that the fall in the relative price of computers continues at its recent pace, there would appear to be scope for potential growth to move up further. Maintaining the current growth of the capital stock requires a

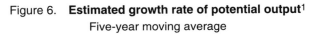

Figure 6. **Estimated growth rate of potential output[1]**
Five-year moving average

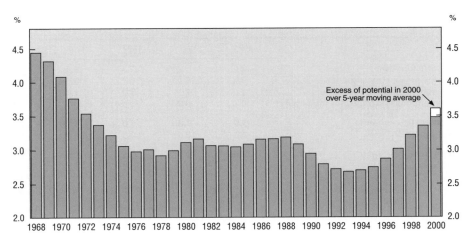

1.   For more information on the construction of potential output see Giorno, *et al.* (1995).
Source: OECD.

continued increase of about 5¼ per cent in real business investment, but a rise in nominal outlays of only some 4½ per cent – less than the increase in nominal potential output. Thus, if nominal investment remained constant as a share of potential GDP – which is currently growing about 3½ per cent annually – the growth of the capital stock would continue to increase, bringing a rise in trend labour productivity growth, other things being equal.

Over-rapid demand growth brings some imbalances

Demand continued to increase more rapidly than potential output in 1999

While potential growth has surged, economic activity continued to expand even more rapidly than potential in 1999. Real GDP rose 4.2 per cent for the year, about the same as in the previous two years (Table 4). Final domestic demand advanced 5½ per cent, nearly the same as in 1998. Though the composition of demand shifted toward consumption, the increase in real private investment spending nonetheless far exceeded that of output, further boosting the growth rate of the capital stock. Net exports continued to hold down growth for the year by a substantial amount, but the negative contribution was smaller in the second half of the year when foreign sales picked up. With GDP growth above the OECD estimates of potential, the output gap edged up further – to an estimated 1¾ per cent on average in 1999.

Table 4. **Contributions to GDP growth**

Percentage points, volume terms, chain 1996 prices

	1995	1996	1997	1998	1999
Private consumption	2.0	2.2	2.3	3.3	3.5
Private residential investment	−0.2	0.3	0.1	0.4	0.2
Private non-residential investment	1.0	1.1	1.2	1.5	0.8
Government consumption and investment	0.1	0.2	0.4	0.3	0.8
Final domestic demand	**3.0**	**3.8**	**4.0**	**5.5**	**5.3**
Stockbuilding	−0.4	0.0	0.5	0.1	0.0
Total domestic demand	**2.6**	**3.8**	**4.5**	**5.6**	**5.3**
Net exports	0.1	−0.1	−0.3	−1.2	−1.1
GDP	**2.7**	**3.7**	**4.2**	**4.3**	**4.2**
Memorandum:					
Growth rate of:					
Private consumption	3.0	3.3	3.4	4.9	5.3
Private non-residential investment	9.8	10.0	10.7	12.7	8.3

Source: Bureau of Economic Analysis.

Led by strong consumption boosted by rising wealth...

Real consumption expenditures accelerated to 5¼ per cent in 1999, with large increases posted for a wide variety of goods and services. Spending on durable goods continued to outpace the growth of expenditures on non-durable goods and on services. Increases were particularly notable for household furnishings and motor vehicles, as consumers filled their newly acquired homes and garages. Spending on recreational goods and brokerage services also rose swiftly. Overall consumer spending surged ahead of income growth again in 1999, bringing the personal saving rate to a record low of 1.8 per cent in the fourth quarter, down from 3½ per cent a year earlier. Households' borrowing accelerated in 1999, and their debt-service burden edged up, primarily reflecting rising mortgage loans.[14] Despite this increase in indebtedness, delinquency rates on credit cards and other consumer loans dropped considerably, and the number of people filing for bankruptcy protection declined from the very high levels reached in 1998. Indeed, non-mortgage debt remained constant relative to disposable income in 1999.

The economic fundamentals for the household sector have remained extremely favourable. Real incomes moved up swiftly again with strong growth in employment and compensation, and household net worth climbed higher largely because of gains in stock market wealth (Figure 7). In addition, the share of families that own equities has continued to rise.[15] With falling unemployment and

Figure 7. **Net worth of households**
Ratio to disposable personal income

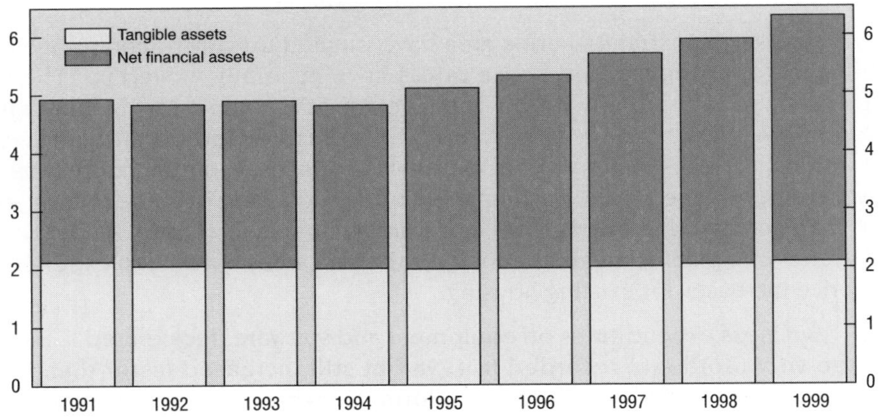

Source: Board of Governors of the Federal Reserve System and Bureau of Economic Analysis.

rising wealth, consumer confidence has risen to an all-time high. The extraordinary run-up in stock prices over the past four years, which has pushed up the share of stock market wealth to roughly one-third of household assets, has given a substantial boost to household net worth. Rising stock market wealth has boosted consumption growth – possibly by about 1¼ percentage points per year over the past three years.[16] In addition to soaring stock prices, the extraction of housing equity – the realisation of capital gains through sales of existing homes and the extraction of unrealised capital gains through mortgage refinancing and home equity loans – boosted households' liquid resources, particularly in 1998. Households likely channelled some of this additional liquidity into consumption, especially households with small amounts of other liquid assets. As mortgage interest rates moved up in 1999, refinancing and the associated extraction of home equity dropped off considerably. Nonetheless, mortgage debt continued to expand rapidly (reflecting robust housing sales), rising to an estimated 45 per cent of the value of the housing stock from 44 per cent the previous year.

... and brisk investment, especially in high technology areas...

While consumption has so far been resilient to rising interest rates, housing demand slowed in the second half of 1999 from the highs reached earlier in the year. Average interest rates for 30-year fixed-rate mortgages moved up over 100 basis points in 1999, but their effect on housing demand was blunted to some extent by a shift toward adjustable-rate loans, where rates were slower to increase. The share of adjustable-rate mortgages rose to about 30 per cent of originations in December, up from 9 per cent at the end of 1998. For the year as a whole, residential housing investment increased 7½ per cent, still quite brisk but down from the 9¼ per cent pace seen in 1998. The homeownership rate reached 67 per cent last year, up from about 64 per cent in the first half of the 1990s.

Capacity constraints in this area have pushed up construction wages and building materials prices, and house prices have generally moved up. The four-quarter change in the quality-adjusted price of new homes was 4½ per cent in 1999, up from 3½ per cent in 1998. A trend toward larger and better homes, coupled with rising prices resulting from materials shortages, is putting more pressure on average new-home prices, pushing them up 12¼ per cent over the four quarters of 1999. By contrast, the average price of existing homes increased 5¾ per cent in 1999. However, a significant number of metropolitan areas have been experiencing large price increases for existing housing.

Business expenditures on equipment and software decelerated somewhat from the very rapid rate recorded in 1998 but still increased faster than in any other year since 1984. Purchases of information-processing equipment and software continued to rise at 1998's brisk pace (about 22 per cent). Over the past five years, investment in information-processing equipment has accounted for about two-thirds of the contribution of all equipment investment to GDP growth. The rapid pace of business output growth has boosted the desired increase in the capital stock of all investment goods, including high-technology equipment, and the trend shift toward high-technology capital goods, which depreciate faster than traditional equipment, has increased the amount of replacement investment required to maintain the capital stock (see Figure 4). Some of the investment in information-processing equipment in recent years was associated with end-of-millennium (Y2K) upgrades, and the rapid rise in expenditures on communications equipment reflects structural changes in the telecommunications sector (discussed in Chapter III). For firms with access to equity markets, cheaper equity finance may have offset some of the impact of the recent interest rate increases on the cost of capital. In contrast to equipment spending, business spending on non-residential structures fell 2½ per cent in 1999, after solid increases in the previous three years. Still, the level of investment remained sufficiently high to further boost the stock of non-residential structures last year.

... though the pace of stockbuilding slackened

In 1999 as a whole, the increase in stocks was less rapid than the previous year. But there was a turnaround in the pace of stock building in the third and fourth quarters of the year, when the accumulation of private inventories added nearly 1¼ percentage points to GDP growth on average. Still, sales increased much faster than inventories, pushing inventory-sales ratios to even lower levels. Indeed, after remaining stable in 1997 and 1998, total business inventories fell to only 1.3 months of sales in December 1999. Retailers and wholesalers added to their inventories over the year, while those of manufacturers were nearly unchanged on balance. The decline in the inventory-sales ratio through December suggests that firms may have been surprised once again by the strength of sales. While some of the build-up in inventories late last year was probably intended to be temporary Y2K-related stockpiling, firms are unlikely to need to slow dramatically the pace at which they increase stocks early in 2000.

From mid-year, exports picked up...

After several years of slowing market growth, the external demand for US products improved somewhat in 1999. After increasing only 2¼ per cent in 1998, real exports of goods and services rose 3¾ per cent in 1999. Growth was concentrated in the second half of the year, when exports advanced more than 9 per cent at an annual rate. Foreign sales picked up for a wide variety of products, but renewed strength was particularly notable for semiconductors and capital machinery. Exports to Canada, Mexico and Asia accelerated, with most of the latter increase going to Korea.

... but the continued strength of imports helped widen the current account deficit

The rapid rise in aggregate demand has fuelled import growth. Purchases from foreign suppliers accelerated in 1999 despite a large increase in overall import prices. The hike in world petroleum prices was responsible for most of the import price surge, and oil import volumes do not tend to respond significantly to short-term price movements. Prices of most imported goods other than oil continued to decline on average in 1999, albeit at a slower pace than in recent years. Increases in the volume of purchases were particularly large for high-tech imports (telecommunications equipment, semiconductors and computers), whose prices have dropped rapidly. Brisk demand also pushed up imports of autos, furniture and appliances, and a wide variety of other consumer goods. Imports increased from most areas of the world, but the rise in demand was largest for products originating from Canada and Mexico, reflecting in part auto trade between the United States and its neighbours. Overall, the negative contribution of net exports to GDP eased in the second half, owing entirely to the strength in export growth.

Nonetheless, with the terms of trade deteriorating, the current account deficit continued to increase, reaching nearly $400 billion (annual rate), over 4 per cent of GDP, in the fourth quarter of 1999, compared with a deficit of 2½ per cent of GDP in 1998 (Table 5). A large increase in the deficit on goods accounted for nearly all of the widening in the overall account. Despite the large and growing current account deficit, the deficit on the investment income account has deteriorated

Table 5. **Current account**
$ billion, seasonally adjusted, annual rate

	1997	1998	1999	1999			
				Q1	Q2	Q3	Q4
Current account balance	−143	−221	−339	−276	−325	−356	−399
of which:							
Exports of goods, services and income	1 197	1 192	1 234	1 182	1 204	1 253	1 297
Imports of goods, services and income	1 299	1 369	1 526	1 416	1 484	1 564	1 641
Net unilateral transfers abroad	42	44	47	41	45	45	56
Balances:							
Goods	−197	−247	−347	−298	−338	−368	−385
Non-factor services	92	83	80	81	77	77	83
Investment income	3	−12	−25	−17	−18	−21	−42
Private transfers	−25	−27	−29	−28	−29	−30	−30
Official transfers	−17	−17	−17	−13	−15	−15	−25
Memorandum:							
Current account as share of GDP	−1.7	−2.5	−3.7	−3.0	−3.5	−3.8	−4.2

Source: Bureau of Economic Analysis.

surprisingly little in recent years, reflecting higher average rates of return earned on US foreign investments.

Labour markets remain tight...

The supply of workers has expanded considerably since the 1990-91 recession. Strong labour demand and structural changes (including welfare reform and the expansion of the earned income tax credit) have encouraged a growing number of people to join the work force. The overall labour force participation rate climbed to about 67 per cent in 1997 and remained there in 1998 and 1999 (Table 6).[17] The recent stability of the overall figure masks offsetting changes in the participation rate for men, which is falling, and for women, which continues to rise.

Employment, as measured by the establishment survey, has increased nearly 2½ per cent on average per year since 1991, when the current expansion began, and the employment-population ratio has risen to an all-time high. In contrast to the view that job creation in the United States is concentrated on poor jobs, job growth has been strongest for relatively high-wage occupations. Services

Table 6.   **Labour market outcomes and compensation**

Per cent

	1991-95	1996	1997	1998	1999
Population growth (16 years and older)	1.0	1.0	1.3	1.0	1.2
Labour force participation rate	66.4	66.8	67.1	67.1	67.1
Employment-population ratio	62.1	63.2	63.8	64.1	64.3
Private employment growth[1]	2.2	2.4	2.9	2.8	2.3
Average weekly hours[2]	34.5	34.4	34.6	34.6	34.5
Share of employed part-time for economic reasons	4.7	3.4	3.1	2.8	2.5
Unemployment rate	6.6	5.4	4.9	4.5	4.2
Share of potential workers[3]	7.1[4]	6.5	5.9	5.4	5.0
Share of unemployed over 26 weeks	18.2	17.4	15.8	14.1	12.3
Share of unemployed who quit	10.8	10.7	11.8	11.8	13.3
Median duration of unemployment (weeks)	8.3	8.3	8.0	6.7	6.4
ECI[5] for private industry (December/December)	3.4	3.1	3.4	3.5	3.4
ECI wages (December/December)	3.0	3.4	3.9	3.9	3.5
ECI benefits (December/December)	4.4	2.0	2.3	2.4	3.4
Non-farm compensation per hour (Q4/Q4)	3.1	3.2	4.2	5.3	4.4

1. Establishment survey.
2. For production or non-supervisory workers.
3. Unemployed plus those out of the labour force who want a job as a per cent of the sum of the labour force plus those out of the labour force who want a job.
4. Average 1994 and 1995.
5. Employment Cost Index.
Source: Bureau of Labor Statistics.

industries account for about half of the job growth during this expansion, with three-quarters of those jobs in managerial and professional occupations. Job growth for professionals and managers has also been widespread in other industries. However, there have also been significant employment gains for blue-collar workers, especially in construction. Individuals who had been working part time for economic reasons (due to slack work conditions or because they could only find part-time work) have been able to move into full-time jobs. Lay-off rates have dropped, and, possibly with them, workers' fears of job loss. In addition, the cost of becoming unemployed has declined; the median duration of unemployment fell considerably in 1998 and drifted down to less than 6½ weeks on average in 1999.

In 1999, employment growth slowed from the torrid pace of the previous two years, but continued to push down the unemployment rate, which ended the year at 4.1 per cent, the lowest rate in nearly 30 years. The pool of available labour (the number of unemployed plus the number of people who are currently out of the labour force but want a job) also fell to a historical low. The decline in unemployment rates has been widespread, notably with record low rates recorded for minorities (see Chapter III). The share of long-term unemployed continued to drop, and the share of the unemployed who quit their last job increased considerably last year. Recently, almost a third of small businesses reported hard-to-fill job openings to the National Federation of Independent Businesses (2000), nearly a record high for the survey and up considerably from only 10 per cent in 1991.

... bringing rapid real wage growth...

Temporary factors have allowed the unemployment rate to fall below the NAIRU without putting much upward pressure on inflation. Workers' real wage demands have responded to the rise in productivity with a lag, and until last year favourable supply shocks held down price inflation – thus boosting real wage growth without requiring comparable nominal wage gains. Nonetheless, the decline in the actual unemployment rate has outpaced the effective decline in the NAIRU, and real wages accelerated through 1998 (Figure 8).

... but a slackening in nominal pay increases

The annual change in nominal compensation slowed somewhat in 1999 when measured by hourly compensation in the non-farm business sector and, to a lesser extent, by the employment cost index (Table 6). The deceleration in hourly compensation last year reflected a decline in the growth of wages and salaries. The change in benefits costs picked up to the fastest pace in five years, partly reflecting an acceleration in employers' cost of health insurance. The deceleration in wages last year also likely reflects some adjustment to the surprisingly low price

Figure 8. **Growth in real compensation**
Percentage change in a four quarter moving average

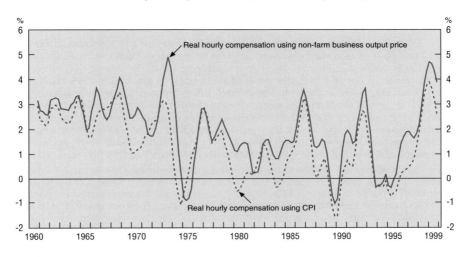

Source: Bureau of Labor Statistics.

inflation (and, consequently, high real wage growth) recorded in 1998. Some of the recent swing in compensation increases also reflect the surge in bonuses and commissions earned on financial transactions in 1998. While compensation of workers in the finance, insurance and real estate industry continued to rise more rapidly than for the average worker in 1999, the differential narrowed as the pace of real estate transactions and mortgage refinancings slowed from 1998's torrid pace. Despite the slowing in nominal compensation increases, real compensation continued to grow fairly rapidly last year, especially in terms of the business sector output deflator.

Since 1996, the increasing use of stock options and other forms of flexible pay has boosted the growth rate of compensation. This has contributed to the gap between the increase in the employment cost index and hourly compensation in the non-farm business sector as the former does not capture certain forms of compensation, such as stock options and hiring, retention and referral bonuses. (The impact of stock options is discussed in Box 3). Part of the difference, though, may be cyclical. The ECI is fixed-weighted by industry and occupation, and measures the change in the cost of a specific job free of the influence of shifts in employment and hours (including overtime hours). On the other hand, hourly compensation picks up the effect on costs of shifts in the mix of employment and changes in overtime hours.

Box 3.   **Stock options and their impact on wage measurement
and profitability**

Estimates of the value of options granted by large firms in 1998 range from 10 to 19 per cent of reported earnings, several times larger than their value in the mid-1990s (Liang and Sharpe, 1999). In a sample of 125 of the largest non-financial corporations in the S&P 500, the value of stock options granted in 1998 averaged $1 725 per employee in the firm, about three times the average amount granted in 1994. The rate of stock option exercise rose faster than grants, reflecting a tendency for employees to exercise their options following stock-price run-ups. Gains per employee from exercising their options reached about $3 700 per worker in 1998, more than eight times their value in 1994. Anecdotal evidence suggests that the share of stock options in compensation may be even larger in financial firms.[1]

Options granted do not show up on the income statements or tax returns of firms. They are only reported in the footnotes of company annual reports (the source of the above figures). As a result, options do not lower reported corporate profits or raise measured employee compensation when they are granted, and are not reflected in the national accounts. When stock options are exercised, their value shows up in tax data, which is incorporated with a lag into the construction of compensation and profits in the national accounts and into non-farm compensation per hour from the Bureau of Labor Statistics' productivity and cost figures. By design, the Employment Cost Index never picks up the value of stock options, which are considered recruiting costs rather than labour costs associated with a specific job. The ECI also excludes hiring, retention and referral bonuses on the same grounds.[2]

Based on the per-employee values discussed above, Lebow et al. (1999) estimate that if grants of stock options by publicly traded firms had been included in (measured) private compensation, compensation growth would have been ¼ percentage point higher per year between 1994 and 1998. They estimate that the exercising of stock options over the same period boosted non-farm compensation growth by about ¾ percentage point, introducing a significant wedge between wage inflation measured by the ECI and non-farm compensation per hour. Stock options are reportedly also granted in privately held firms, but these are not included in this calculation. The Bureau of Labor Statistics is currently conducting research on the incidence of stock option plans and their impact on compensation.

1. Furthermore, according to Liang and Sharpe, when their sample is expanded to include the largest financial firms, the value of stock options granted per employee in 1998 rises somewhat to $1 943 from $1 725.
2. In June 2000, the ECI will begin to include such bonuses.

The share of profits in income has been pushed down...

Despite rapid productivity growth, the pickup in nominal compensation growth since 1996 has pushed up unit labour costs (Figure 9). As a result, inflation – as measured by the output deflator – has only declined on balance since

Figure 9.   **Corporate costs and profits**

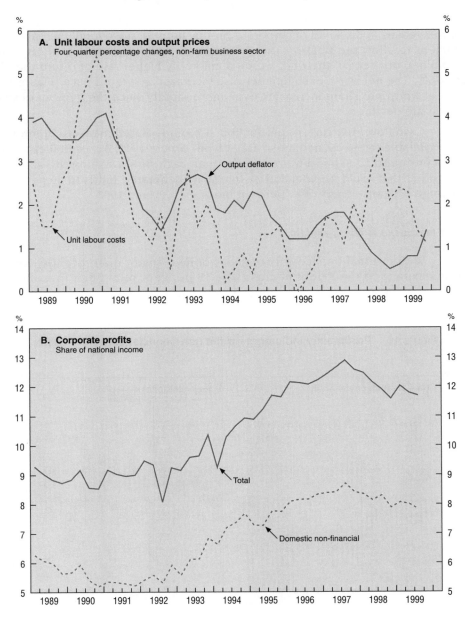

Source: Bureau of Economic Analysis and Bureau of Labor Statistics.

1997 as a result of falling non-labour costs and some compression in profit margins that generated a fall in the share of profits in national income. As yet, the fall in margins has been slower than the growth of overall sales, permitting continued increases in the level of corporate profits. Indeed, the overall increase was sufficient to allow the post-tax rate of return for non-financial corporations to remain at 6 per cent of their net worth, a markedly higher rate of return than in the 1980s. The net worth of companies also increased at a rapid pace (Figure 10), with net worth per share increasing even more rapidly since the number of shares in issue declined.

Cash flow from current production, a profits-related measure of internal funds available for investment, rose about 6 per cent in 1999. But capital expenditures continued to expand more rapidly than cash flow, pushing the share of investment that could be financed by internally generated funds to 80 per cent, compared with an average of 85 per cent between 1990 and 1998.

... but borrowing is rising rapidly...

With internal finance covering less of investment than recently, corporations expanded their debt at close to a 10 per cent rate. Seen in isolation,

Figure 10.   **Profitability indicators for the non-financial corporate sector**

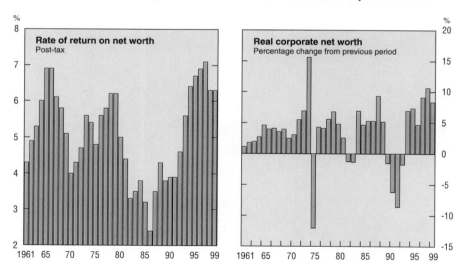

Source: Board of Governors of the Federal Reserve System and OECD estimates.

such a trend would not be sustainable, but companies have been borrowing substantially more than was required to cover their financial deficit. In 1999, the absolute increase in credit market borrowing of non-financial non-farm corporate business, at $444 billion, was almost five times their net financial requirement. Put another way, the deficit of these companies represented only 2.3 per cent of their initial debt, compared with an actual increase in debt of 11.6 per cent. The excess borrowing of companies has been used to finance a number of financial rather than tangible investments, most noticeably $270 billion of net share retirement. The bulk of these buybacks resulted from mergers and acquisitions. Part of these net share repurchases appear to have been used to offset the issuance of new stock options (Liang and Sharp, 1999). Gross buybacks were even larger as 555 companies raised a total of $73 billion in initial public offerings, almost half of which were in the technology sector. Consequently, the net financial deficit (or net lending) of the non-financial corporate sector has been modest by historical standards (Figure 11). Moreover, the overall indebtedness of companies had, up to 1998, been increasing only slightly faster than either net worth or total assets and interest payments are moderate by historical standards (Figure 12).

Figure 11.   **Company borrowing relative to total assets and net worth**

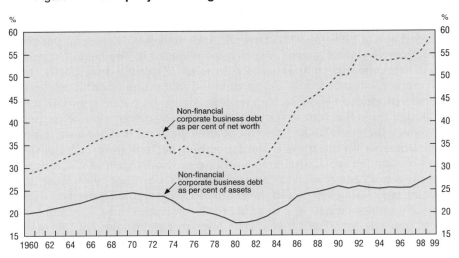

Source: Board of Governors of the Federal Reserve System.

Figure 12.   **Net financial investment**
Per cent of GDP

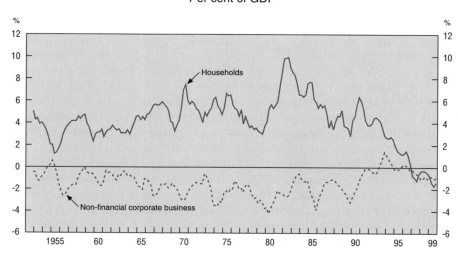

Source: Board of Governors of the Federal Reserve System.

... and equity markets remained strong

The relatively high rate of return on assets and rapid growth of net worth helped keep equity markets were very strong during most of 1999. Between the end of 1998 and of 1999, the widest overall stock market index rose 22 per cent, the fifth consecutive year of growth at such rates (Figure 13). The market sectors related to new technology companies rose even more rapidly during 1999 than the overall market. Internet stocks almost doubled in the same period, while technology stocks produced almost as high returns (Figure 14, panels 1 and 2). It is difficult to judge the full extent of the size of these two sectors relative to the whole market, given their overlap and the compilation methods that are used in different indices. However, on the basis of the Bloomberg sectoral index, capitalisation of Internet companies (which excludes hardware providers such as Cisco) represented nearly 8 per cent of market capitalisation in December 1999. Most of these companies are making losses and those that do make returns traded on extremely high price-earnings ratios – in a sample of 242 companies, only 37 made profits in the third quarter of 1999 and traded on a price-to-earnings ratio of 190. Moreover, two established companies accounted for 60 per cent of earnings. The other 35 companies traded on a price-earnings ratio of 270. In broad terms, such a multiple was discounting 75 per cent compound growth in earnings per share by these com-

Figure 13. **Overall stock market price index**
Wilshire 5000, 2 January 1997 = 100

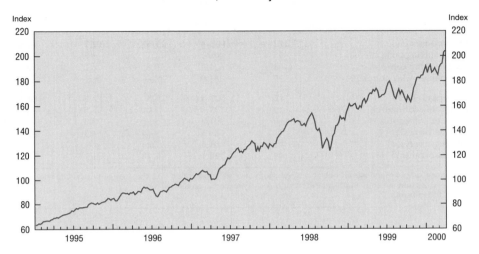

Source: Bloomberg.

Figure 14. **Stock prices in the technology sector**
31 December 1998 = 100

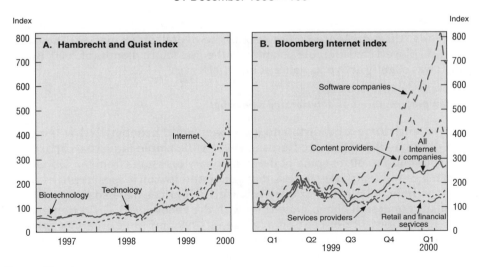

Source: Bloomberg.

Table 7. **Financial indicators for Internet companies**

Third quarter 1999, except for capitalisation in January 2000, $ billion

	Number	Market capitalisation	Gross sales	Net sales	Net income
All companies	**242**	**1 103.4**	**25.5**	**12.2**	**−10.4**
Profit-making companies	37	400.1	11.7	6.2	2.0
Loss-making companies	168	621.4	13.8	6.0	−12.4
Companies with no results	37	81.9	n.a.	n.a.	n.a.
All companies	**242**	**1 103.4**	**25.5**	**12.2**	**−10.4**
Electronic commerce	49	137.0	7.0	2.8	−3.2
Internet software	110	391.2	5.7	3.3	−2.4
Service providers	21	184.3	9.8	4.3	−2.7
Financial services	13	61.8	n.a.	n.a.	0.3
Internet content	49	327.1	3.1	1.9	−2.1

Note: Gross sales are measured net of returns. Net sales are gross sales less the cost of purchasing the goods or
services that are sold. Third-quarter results are expressed at an annual rate.
Source: Bloomberg.

panies for a decade. The remaining 205 companies made losses. For the 168 for which data was available, total losses in the third quarter amounted to $12½ billion (annual rate), while their market capitalisation was $621 billion (Table 7). The value of shares in this sector continued to rise during the first quarter of 2000, reaching an all-time high that was some 20 per cent higher than end-1999 values. However, by late-April such stocks had fallen some 30 per cent below their December 1999 values and 40 per cent from their all-time high, as fears rose that losses would exhaust the cash balances of some of these companies. Internet companies still represented 6 per cent of the overall stock market. The overall market displayed considerable volatility in the first fourth months of 2000. By late-April, it was slightly above its value at end-1999.

Inflation performance has deteriorated somewhat

Rapid domestic growth and a stronger world economy led to the emergence of some inflationary pressures in 1999. While ample industrial capacity has likely continued to offset some of the inflationary pressures from the labour market, many of the temporary factors that generated low increases in prices during 1998 have been eliminated or even reversed. Oil prices have soared and prices of industrial materials have moved up with the recovery in world demand. Oil prices rose about 38 per cent on average in 1999 and in February of this year were roughly 50 per cent higher than 1999's average. As a result, unless oil prices fall considerably, energy will boost average annual inflation this year as well. After rising for three years, the dollar was broadly stable in trade-weighted terms

Figure 15. **Inflation performance**
Year-on-year percentage change

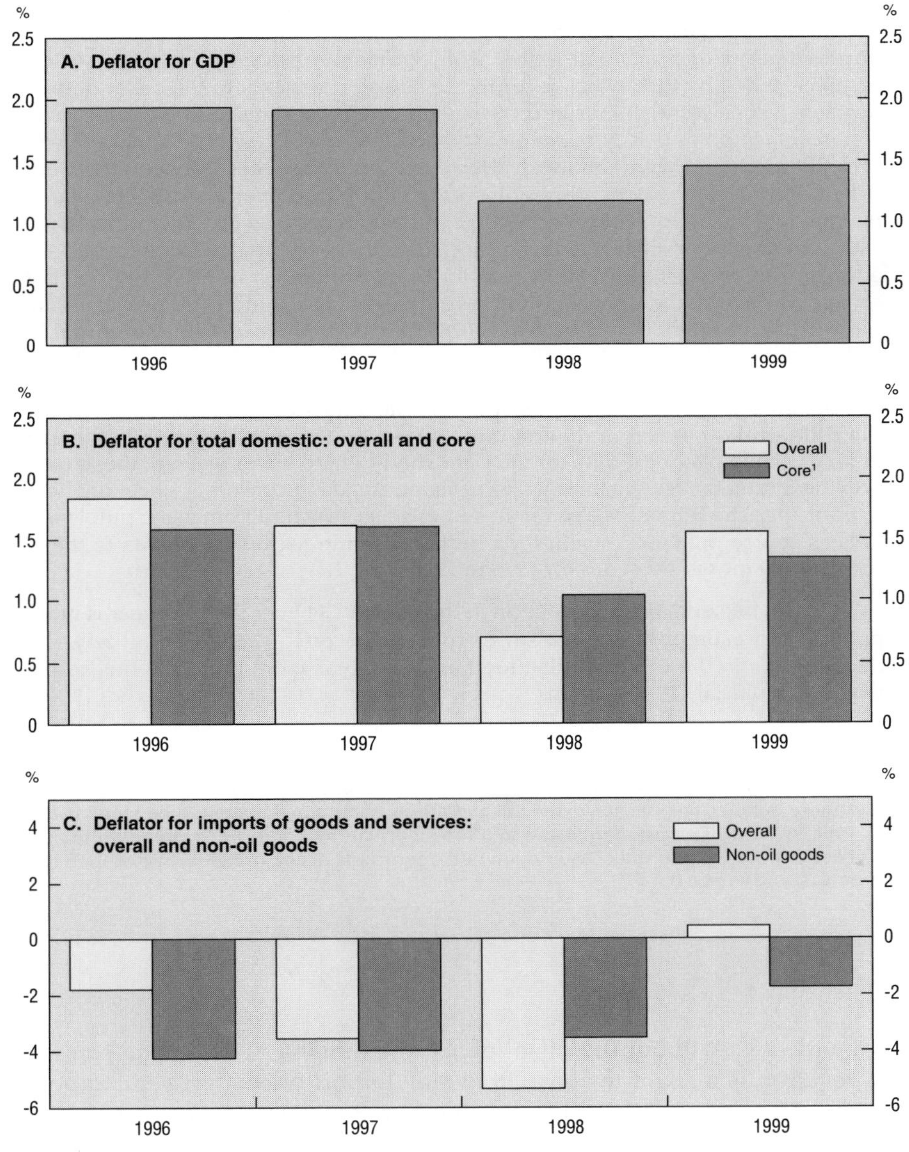
%
2.5
2.0
1.5
1.0
0.5
0
A. Deflator for GDP
1996
1997
1998
1999
B. Deflator for total domestic: overall and core
Overall
Core[1]
C. Deflator for imports of goods and services: overall and non-oil goods
Overall
Non-oil goods
4
2
-2
-4
-6

1. Excludes all domestic expenditures on food and energy.
Source: Bureau of Economic Analysis.

Box 4. What is the rate of inflation?

In recent years, the Bureau of Labor Statistics (BLS) has made a number of improvements to the construction of the consumer price index (CPI).[1] A new research series by BLS, which incorporates these changes into historical data to produce a consistently measured series, indicates that the CPI would have risen ½ percentage point less per year on average between 1978 and 1998 had the current CPI methodology been used.[2] However, the differences between the published and research series were not evenly distributed over time. While a large number of adjustments were made to the published data to make them consistent with current methodology, the technical change that had the largest effect was the adoption of owners' equivalent rent for homeownership in 1983. Before that change was made, the published CPI rose 1 percentage point faster per year than the current methods index; between 1983 and 1998, the average differential in annual inflation using the two measures was about $1/_3$ percentage point. In recent years, the extension back in time of geometric mean weighting for the detailed components of the CPI was the most influential adjustment, accounting for most the differential between inflation rates based on the published and research indexes. While historical data for the published CPI are never revised, these data provide alternative series in which to evaluate trends in consumer price inflation. In particular, the Bureau of Economic Analysis has switched from using published CPIs as source data for consumption deflators in the national accounts to these consistently measured series for 1978 to 1998.[3]

As can be seen, the acceleration in the overall CPI over the past year is more pronounced using the research series to measure price changes. Similarly, the deceleration in the CPI excluding food and energy is more muted in this series than in the official CPI.

---

1. These changes were discussed in Chapter I of OECD (1997).
2. The construction of this series is discussed in Stewart and Reed (1999).
3. A more detailed comparison of the CPI and the consumption deflator can be found in the 1998-99 OECD *Economic Survey* and in a recent article by Clark (1999). Key differences between the CPI and the consumption deflator include scope, weights, aggregation formulas, and source data.

in 1998 and 1999. Without the offset of a strengthening dollar, rising commodity prices resulted in a slight increase in overall import prices last year. Import prices of non-oil goods continued to decline but at a slower pace. Combined with rising unit labour costs, these factors led to acceleration in a range of price measures in 1999 (Figure 15). However, price measures that exclude energy have been more subdued. The annual change in the deflator for total domestic

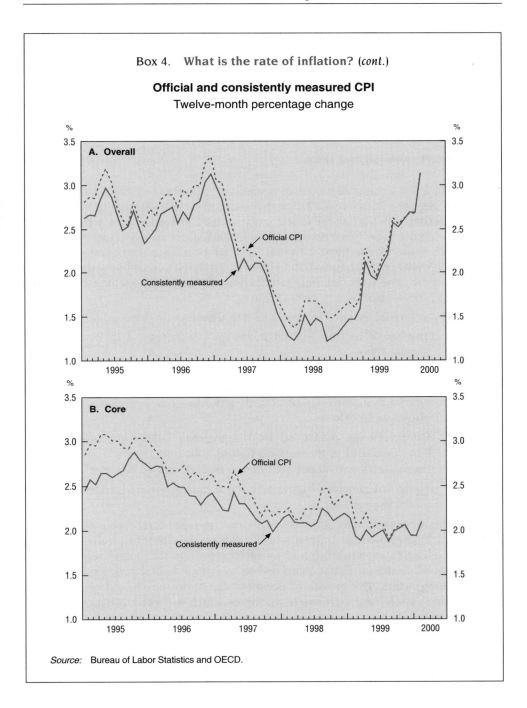

Box 4.   What is the rate of inflation? (*cont.*)

Official and consistently measured CPI
Twelve-month percentage change

A. Overall

Official CPI

Consistently measured

B. Core

Official CPI

Consistently measured

Source: Bureau of Labor Statistics and OECD.

demand was 1.5 per cent in 1999, double the rate in 1998. More than half of this increase in inflation was due to the turnaround in energy prices. Among the components of domestic demand, core consumption inflation only edged up slightly last year, while prices of capital equipment fell by less and construction costs surged. However, by March 2000, core inflation was beginning to show more pronounced signs do increasing.

The near-term outlook and risks

For 2000, economic growth is projected to increase slightly, bringing output to 4.5 per cent above its 1999 level. A marked further tightening of monetary policy, together with a small fall in the stock market, should ensure a slowdown in growth during the year.[18] As a result, growth in 2001 should drop to just below 3 per cent, which should be sufficient to start reducing the extent of excess demand. However, with the level of output still above potential, it seems likely that inflation (as measured by the GDP deflator) will continue to increase, reaching 2.2 per cent in 2001, up from 1.5 per cent in 1999 (Table 8).

The principal assumptions on which this projection is based are:

- The target for the federal funds rate is increased to 7 per cent by August 2000.

- The effective exchange rate of the dollar remains constant at its 3 March level of 125.1 (when measured by the OECD's nominal index against the currencies of 39 trading partners), a level that is ¼ per cent above its 1999 level.

- Oil prices (as measured by the average OECD import price) are $24 per barrel in the second half of 2000 and constant in real terms thereafter, some 40 per cent above their average 1999 level.

- Fiscal policy moves in line with the Administration's budget proposals for fiscal year 2001.

The recent strength of the US economy has been based on a combination of buoyant household consumption and private investment in non-residential assets. The former was underpinned by rapid growth in real wages, employment and wealth, while the latter has been driven by falling capital goods prices, especially for computers. The growth of personal consumption should be adversely affected this year by the increase in oil prices which will generate a much larger terms-of-trade loss than occurred in 1999. At the same time, the rate of increase of private-sector wealth is projected to be much slower this year than last, and the stock market component of wealth is assumed to actually fall in 2001, which would represent the first year-on-year drop in such wealth since 1988. Consequently, the growth of household spending may slacken slightly this year, before slowing more

Table 8. **Near-term outlook**

Percentage change over previous period, volume terms
(chain 1996 prices, seasonally adjusted at annual rates)

	1999	2000	2001	1999 I	1999 II	2000 I	2000 II	2001 I	2001 II
Private consumption	5.3	4.8	2.7	5.7	5.2	5.4	3.3	2.6	2.2
Government consumption	2.6	3.0	2.3	2.0	4.3	2.7	2.1	2.3	2.3
Gross fixed investment	8.2	6.7	4.2	9.8	6.2	8.2	4.4	4.2	4.0
Private residential	7.4	0.5	−1.1	10.2	−0.2	2.6	−3.0	−0.8	0.0
Private non-residential	8.3	8.5	5.9	9.4	7.9	9.8	6.6	5.9	5.3
Government	9.0	7.2	3.4	11.1	7.6	8.5	4.3	3.2	3.0
Final domestic demand	**5.5**	**4.9**	**3.0**	**6.0**	**5.3**	**5.6**	**3.3**	**2.9**	**2.6**
Stockbuilding[1]	−0.4	0.0	0.0	−1.0	0.5	−0.1	−0.1	0.1	0.1
Total domestic demand	**5.1**	**4.9**	**3.0**	**5.0**	**5.7**	**5.4**	**3.2**	**3.0**	**2.7**
Exports of goods and services	3.8	8.5	8.2	1.9	9.2	8.2	8.3	8.2	8.1
Imports of goods and services	11.7	10.7	7.2	12.6	13.2	10.6	8.4	7.1	6.3
Foreign balance[1]	**−1.2**	**−0.6**	**−0.2**	**−1.5**	**−0.9**	**−0.7**	**−0.4**	**−0.1**	**0.0**
GDP at market prices	**4.2**	**4.5**	**2.9**	**3.8**	**5.1**	**5.0**	**3.0**	**3.0**	**2.7**
GDP price deflator	1.5	2.0	2.2	1.6	1.4	2.3	1.9	2.3	2.3
Price consumption deflator	1.6	2.3	2.2	1.6	2.1	2.7	2.0	2.3	2.4
Unemployment rate	4.2	4.0	4.3	4.3	4.2	4.0	4.0	4.2	4.4
Three-month Treasury bill rate	5.4	6.7	7.0	5.0	5.8	6.2	7.1	7.1	7.0
Ten-year Treasury note rate	5.6	6.3	6.2	5.3	6.0	6.3	6.3	6.3	6.1
Net lending of general government									
$ billion	92.5	117.9	119.7	81.3	103.7	108.7	127.0	122.2	117.3
Per cent of GDP	1.0	1.2	1.2	0.9	1.1	1.1	1.3	1.2	1.1
Current account balance									
$ billion	−340.8	−437.3	−459.2	−301.4	−380.2	−429.6	−445.0	−455.9	−462.5
Per cent of GDP	−3.7	−4.4	−4.4	−3.3	−4.0	−4.4	−4.5	−4.4	−4.4
Personal saving rate[2]	2.4	1.4	1.7	2.8	1.9	1.4	1.3	1.7	1.8

1. Contribution to GDP volume growth.
2. OECD definition.
Source: OECD.

markedly next year. The pace of expansion in business investment is expected to slacken as well but to continue to remain above that of private consumption. The deceleration of business investment is projected to be concentrated in traditional investment goods and structures – the growth of outlays in the computer and information technology sector should hold up well.

With average growth in other OECD countries moving slightly above that in the United States from the second half of 2000 onwards, the current account deficit – after rising in the first half of 2000 – is expected to stabilise at 4.4 per cent of GDP, nearly $460 billion in 2001. Real exports should pick up markedly, to rates of increase that were only exceeded twice in the 1990s when the Asian economy was booming, while the growth in volume of imports should slow, reflecting a slackening in the growth of the final domestic demand and a stable nominal effective exchange rate. As the level of imports is almost one-third greater than of exports, the contribution of the foreign balance to changes in real GDP will remain negative in 2000 and 2001, despite exports rising faster than imports, but to a lesser extent than in 1999.

With the net foreign balance offsetting some of the deceleration in domestic demand, the growth of output should slacken next year from 4.5 to 2.9 per cent. This latter figure, though relatively rapid by the standards of the 1970s and 1980s, is likely to be sufficient to reduce the output gap from 3 per cent in the first half of 2000 (the highest since 1979) to under 2 per cent by the end of 2001. The impact of this slower growth may also be evident in the labour market, with unemployment rising to 4.4 per cent of the labour force in the second half of 2001 from 4.0 per cent this half year. Such a rise though would be insufficient to prevent compensation per employee accelerating by about 0.4 percentage point per year between the second half of 1999 and the same period in 2001. A similar acceleration may occur in the GDP deflator which is projected to rise at annual rate of 2.3 per cent by the end of 2001. However, with less upward pressure from oil prices, consumer price increases may actually edge down somewhat next year to about the same rate as inflation measured by the GDP deflator.

Risks

While the monetary tightening assumed in the projections is expected to lead to a soft landing, there are important tensions and imbalances in the US economy that point to risks that would require substantially different policy responses. Faster demand growth in the United States than elsewhere over the past several years has generated a substantial widening in the US current account deficit. That deficit is constrained by the willingness of foreign investors to accumulate dollar assets. In addition, inflation has remained remarkably quiescent in the face of an extremely tight labour market. A sharper rise in interest rates than assumed in the central projections might be called for if labour market pressures and higher oil prices were to translate into a faster pickup in wage inflation, or the dollar were to decline sharply, possibly in response to the mounting current account deficit. On the other hand, US equity prices remain at very high levels, and concerns about the consequences of over-valuation persist as the average household's portfolio is more exposed to changes in stock prices than ever before. An easier monetary stance might be warranted if a substantial correction of equity prices were to put strong downward pressure on private spending.

The extent to which there is a risk of a correction in the stock market is difficult to judge. On the basis of past earnings yield (or its reciprocal, the price-earnings ratios), the market is expensive. There are factors though would tend to support share prices. The current expansion has seen a markedly higher profit rate than the 1980s upturn, at 6.0 against 3.6 per cent, and even slightly higher than that of the 1960s (Figure 16, panel A). Such an increase would normally be reflected in changes in equilibrium price-earnings ratio (Kopke, 1997). This gain has allowed the company sector to expand its real net worth at a pace faster than that which occurred in the 1960s, especially after allowing for the fall in the number of shares that has occurred in this upturn (Figure 16, panel B). The total expected return on net worth, measured as the sum of the rate of return and the growth of net worth – as a proxy for future earnings growth – has risen to 14 per cent since 1994, against 8¾ and 7¾ per cent in the 1960s and 1980s expansions, respectively (Figure 16, panel A).

If the returns seen in 1999 were expected to continue indefinitely, the market would value equities markedly higher in relation to underlying assets than in previous expansions. Prices would rise in proportion to the increase in returns, jumping to 145 per cent of the underlying value of assets from 87 per cent in the 1960s expansion (Figure 16, panel B). However, this ratio for end-1999 was 201 per cent. Such a high price for the underlying assets could nevertheless be justified if the risk premium that investors' demand for share purchases had fallen over 3 percentage points.

Figure 16. **Equity prices and estimated total returns**

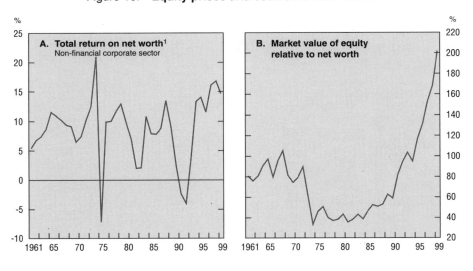

1.   Calculated as sum of post-tax rate of return on net worth and real growth of net worth.
Source: Board of Governors of the Federal Reserve System and OECD estimates.

There must be some doubt about whether the real net worth per share of the non-financial corporate sector can continue sufficiently rapidly to boost real earnings by around 8 per cent per year, when the annual potential growth of the economy is only around 3½ per cent. Some recovery in net worth of the company sector is possible, as it is currently low relative to GDP, as is the post-tax share of profit for the non-financial corporate sector. In addition, labour productivity has been growing more rapidly in this sector than elsewhere in the economy (at an annual rate of 4 per cent in the past two years).

II. Monetary and fiscal management

During the past year, monetary and fiscal policy makers have been faced with the issue of how to respond to a continuation of economic growth at rates well above those that which would have been normal any time since the early 1970s. Such rapid growth has not to date provoked a major increase in underlying inflation as a result of some temporary factors and an acceleration in the trend of labour productivity. With a tight labour market and uncertainty about whether a possible increase in wage inflation would be offset by a further pickup in productivity growth or persistent declines in non-labour costs, the cuts in interest rates made in 1998 to deal with financial instability were reversed during 1999. Against this, fiscal policy played less of a role in restraining demand in 1999 than in previous years, with government outlays on goods and services rising at their most rapid rate since 1986. To be sure, the federal budget surplus has increased once again and debt is on a falling path, but the earlier tight restraint on discretionary spending has ended, and the rate of increase of the estimated structural budget surplus has slowed. Over the longer term, faster economic growth would improve the solvency of the social security system somewhat, but not by enough to obviate the need for further reform.

Monetary policy

The rise in interest rates

During 1999, monetary policy was marked by a gradual reversal of the rapid cuts in interest rates that had been undertaken in response to turbulent financial market conditions in the fall of 1998. The target rate for federal funds had been reduced from 5½ per cent in August to 4¾ per cent in November, as stock markets fell and liquidity dried up in the face of a flight to quality (Figure 17). From November 1998 onwards, financial markets recovered quite quickly, lessening the need for such low nominal rates. Moreover, with an increase in overall inflation as from the spring, real short-term rates continued to fall. Yet despite this, there was some reluctance to reverse previous cuts, reflecting mounting evidence that sustained demand growth was being combined with an increase of the rate of produc-

Figure 17. **Nominal and real overnight rates**

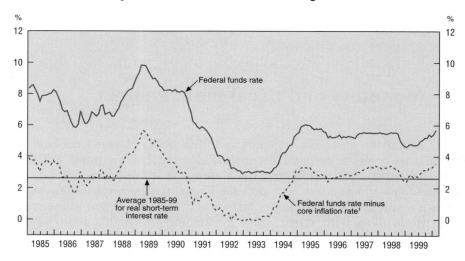

1.   CPI, non-food, non-energy.
Source: Board of Governors of the Federal Reserve System, Bureau of Labor Statistics and OECD.

tivity growth. Moreover, a slowdown in spending was foreseen in the second half of 1999 and 2000, given that the stock market was expected to stabilise, thereby reducing the favourable impact of higher wealth on private consumption. However, a step-up in headline inflation (linked to higher energy and tobacco prices) and further tightening in labour markets contributed to a change in climate among policy makers. The risks of a gradual increase in the core inflation rate were seen as rising, with the danger that pressures would spill over into labour markets. Official rates were increased in June and, with demand continuing to expand at a substantial pace in the second half, twice later in the year. By November, all of the rate decreases made in the autumn of 1998 had been reversed, leaving the target federal funds rate once again at 5½ per cent. With spending still surging at the end of 1999 and the core inflation rate stabilising, the federal funds rate was raised in both February and once again in March 2000, to 6 per cent.

Despite these increases, real short-term interest rates are not overly high. However, the recent increase in energy prices makes judgement about their movement particularly difficult, as overall and core inflation have evolved differently. By March 2000, the overall inflation rate remained above the upper end of the central tendency that the Federal Reserve projected for the inflation rate in 2000 (Figure 18), the first time the inflation rate had exceeded the Federal Open Market

Figure 18. **Actual inflation and Federal Reserve expectations[1]**
Consumer price index

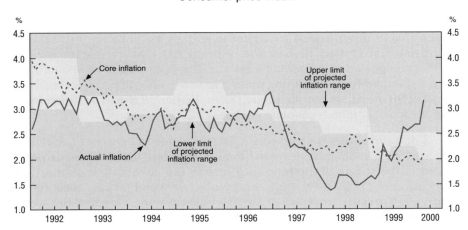

1. The projections refer to the central inflation tendency for a given year identified by the Federal Open Market
    Committee in the summer before the start of the year.
Source: Board of Governors of the Federal Reserve System, Bureau of Labor Statistics.

Committee's (FOMC) prediction for the current year since the beginning of 1997. On the other hand, core inflation was at the bottom of the range and was broadly stable. As a result, by March, the level of real short-term interest rates was at around its average for the past 15 years when measured using overall inflation but about 75 basis points higher when measured with the core CPI.

The past year has also seen a move by the Federal Reserve to increase the transparency with which it communicates its policy orientation to financial markets. The authorities use a number of channels to influence financial markets, ranging from speeches by policy makers and the publication of the minutes of meetings of the FOMC to giving directions concerning the bias in interpreting incoming data before the next Committee meeting. During 1999, in order to increase transparency, the Federal Reserve decided to announce the direction of its bias for the inter-meeting period at the same time as it announced the decision on the target federal funds rate, rather than delaying the announcement as had been customary in the past. It was not clear, though, whether this procedure was successful in reducing uncertainty. In part, this may have been due to confusion over the period to which the bias referred. As the minutes of the FOMC meeting have indicated, markets have misinterpreted the statements concerning bias. For instance, a shift to a neutral bias in June was interpreted as indicating an end to tightening, while it was revealed later that many members of the FOMC had expressed the view that there were still risks of a gradual pickup in inflation. On the other hand, in November the FOMC switched to a neutral bias because it wanted to show that no further increase in short-term rates was likely over the year-end period. It knew, however, that in the previous summer the market had interpreted the bias as referring to a much longer time period, with the risk that the market might conclude that the period of tightening was over. The FOMC has now decided that it will use a standard form of wording when it issues its interest rate decisions, indicating whether members see the prime risk in the period ahead as stemming from "higher inflation" or from "economic weakness".

Capital markets registered a marked change in sentiment during 1999 that generated a substantial increase in nominal bond yields that was partially reversed in the spring of the following year as the government started to buy back its own debt (Figure 19). Between October 1998 and January 2000, the yield on ten-year Treasury notes rose by 210 basis points, close to the average increase in nominal rates that occurred in the six previous bear markets for bonds (excluding that which occurred at the end of 1970s). Most of this increase appears to be consistent with a reversal of the fall in inflation expectations that had pushed the difference in yields between nominal and indexed bonds to as low 90 basis points (Figure 19, panel 2). This low differential in the autumn of 1998 was undoubtedly the result of an increase in the liquidity premium demanded on less liquid issues such as indexed bonds. By the middle of 1999, this gap had bounced back to close to 200 basis points. With the subsequent increases in official short-term rates, this gap stabilised until the beginning of 2000 when it rose to close to 2½ per cent, as the continued strength of demand in the economy became evident. The remainder of the increase in nominal rates can be attributed to an increase in real interest rates that jumped 90 basis points, to slightly over 4¼ per cent. A marked change in the government debt market occurred from the middle of January 2000. The Treasury first announced its intention to start buying back longer maturities of its own debt and reduce issuance of new longer-term securities. The government followed up this announcement with a buyback plan that led, in March, to the repurchase of $2 billion of debt, with an average maturity of almost 18 years. Coupled with the increase in short-term interest rates, the planned repurchase of debt led to a fall in 10-year interest rates of around 75 basis points to 6 per cent by the mid-April. The gap between the yield on nominal and indexed government securities also fell back towards 2 percentage points. The fall in the yield on 30-year bonds (that had peaked on the day before the announcement of the buyback programme) was slightly greater than that on 10-year bonds. With short-term rates rising and long-term yields falling, the yield curve (measured as the difference between the yield on 2- and 10-year bonds) inverted. Such inversions have sometimes preceded past recessions, as in 1981 and 1989.

Figure 19. **Bond market yields**

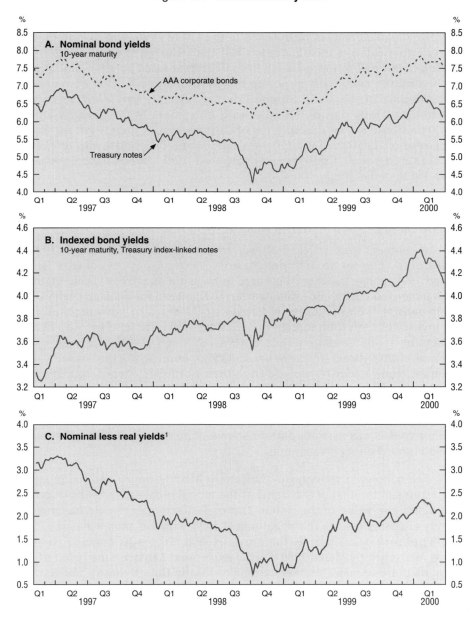

1.   Measured as the difference in yields between nominal and indexed bonds.
Source: Board of Governors of the Federal Reserve System and Bloomberg.

The corporate sector was not hit by as large an increase in real rates during 1999 as the government sector but did not see such a large fall at the beginning of 2000. Corporate borrowing rates had been particularly badly affected by the financial market turbulence in the fall of 1998. The margin on corporate over government interest rates fell back during the subsequent year, offsetting about half of the increase in real interest rates on government bonds. Nonetheless, the margin on corporate bonds remains somewhat above the average of the past 20 years and widened during February and March as corporate bonds followed only part of the downward movement in the government bond yields. The frequency of downgrades of corporate debt increased, but such re-ratings were concentrated in below-investment-grade bonds, with few changes for better-rated bonds. Consequently so-called "junk" bonds have not shared in the narrowing of margins.

The dollar remains strong

Foreigners were particularly active in US financial markets in 1999. The increase in the current account deficit, from 2.5 to 3.7 per cent of GDP between 1998 and 1999, partly matched this surge in investment activity (Table 9). In addition, an increased outflow of capital added to the need for financing, with US residents increasing their purchases of foreign stocks and also boosting their foreign direct investment. All told, foreign private investors increased their purchases of US assets by 1½ percentage points of US GDP. Much of this surge represented additional inward direct investment, as foreign enterprises purchased large US companies. Non-residents also added to their portfolios of corporate stocks, but the scale of purchases of bonds diminished. Official holders also, once again, became net purchasers of US assets in 1999, in contrast to 1998 when they had exceptionally reduced their holdings of official assets. Indeed, overall the swing in official purchases was as an important source of increased capital inflow, as were increased inward direct investments.

The continued widening in the current account deficit and the prospect of higher returns in the rest of the world as the global recovery spread played a role in stabilising the value of the dollar. The real effective exchange has now been relatively unchanged since the beginning of 1998, with the annual average for 1999 about ½ per cent below that for the previous year (Figure 20, panel 1). This slight loss was recovered by March 2000. Such a movement has been the result of offsetting trends in three major partner currencies for the United States: the yen, Canadian dollar and the Euro (Figure 20, panel 2). The first two currencies have appreciated against the dollar by 3 and 7 per cent respectively between the beginning of 1999 and late-April 2000. In contrast the Euro has depreciated by some 19 per cent against the dollar in the same period.

Table 9. **Capital market flows and net asset position**

	Assets/ liabilitie 1996	Assets/ liabilities 1997	Capital flow 1998	Assets/ liabilities 1998	Capital flow 1999	Assets/ liabilities[1] 1999 (estimated)
			Per cent of GDP			
Net US Assets	**−9.5**	**−15.9**	**−2.5**	**−17.5**	**−3.1**	**−19.7**
Official reserve assets	−8.2	−8.4	0.3	−7.9	−0.6	−8.0
Other US Government assets	−1.1	−1.4	0.0	0.9	0.0	0.9
Direct investment	3.8	1.7	−0.7	−0.6	−1.4	−2.0
Bonds	−8.8	−10.1	−2.1	−12.2	−1.3	−12.9
Corporate stocks	3.4	4.1	0.3	3.3	0.0	3.1
US net claims on unaffiliated foreigners	1.3	1.3	0.2	1.5	0.4	1.9
US net claims reported by US banks	0.4	0.2	−0.3	0.0	−0.1	−0.1
US currency	−2.4	−2.5	−0.2	−2.6	−0.2	−2.7
Total US assets	**55.6**	**63.7**	**3.3**	**67.9**	**4.0**	**68.3**
US official reserve assets	2.1	1.6	0.1	1.7	−0.1	1.5
Other US Government assets	1.0	1.0	0.0	0.9	0.0	0.9
Direct investment abroad	19.4	21.5	1.5	24.4	1.6	24.8
Bonds	5.2	6.5	0.3	6.4	0.0	6.1
Corporate stocks	11.2	14.5	0.9	16.1	1.1	16.3
US claims on unaffiliated foreigners	5.8	6.8	0.3	6.8	0.8	7.2
US claims reported by US banks	11.0	11.9	0.2	11.6	0.7	11.6
Total US liabilities	**65.2**	**76.3**	**5.7**	**85.4**	**7.2**	**88.3**
Foreign reserve assets in US	10.3	10.1	−0.2	9.5	0.5	9.5
Direct investment in US	15.7	19.8	2.2	25.0	3.1	26.8
Bonds	14.0	16.6	2.4	18.6	1.3	18.9
Corporate stocks	7.8	10.4	0.5	12.8	1.0	13.1
US liabilities to unaffiliated foreigners	4.4	5.5	0.1	5.3	0.3	5.3
US liabilities reported by US banks	10.6	11.7	0.5	11.6	0.7	11.7
US currency	2.4	2.5	0.2	2.6	0.2	2.7

1. The asset position for 1999 cumulates the capital flows for 1999 with the asset position at end-1998. It takes no account of revaluations due to price or exchange rate movements.
Source: Bureau of Economic Analysis and OECD.

Credit and money

The growth of debt aggregates became even more buoyant in 1999, with private-sector debt increasing at a double-digit rate, almost twice the growth rate of GDP (Table 10). Most of this increase in borrowing was financed through capital markets rather than through the banking sector. Indeed, following the major drawing on bank lines of credit during the period of financial instability in 1998, the growth of bank lending was subdued during most of 1999. As a result, the growth of all indicators of the money supply slackened during 1999 until the final quarter of the year. In that period, during the run up to the century date change, the monetary base surged by 8¾ per cent (actual rate). The broad money supply (M3) and bank lending – most notably for security operations – also rose rapidly (Table 11).

Figure 20.   **Exchange rates for the dollar**
January 1994 = 100

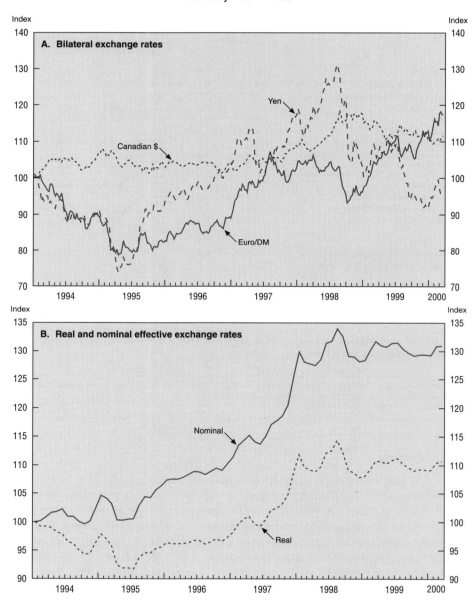

Source: Board of Governors of the Federal Reserve System.

Table 10. **Credit market debt outstanding by class of borrower**
Annual percentage change

	1996	1997	1998	1999	1999			
					Q1	Q2	Q3	Q4
All borrowers	7.1	7.2	7.1	9.8	11.5	8.3	10.3	9.1
Domestic non-financial	5.4	5.4	6.6	7.0	8.1	5.4	8.0	6.6
Federal	4.0	0.6	-1.4	-1.9	-2.0	-3.0	-2.2	-0.5
State and local	-0.6	5.3	7.2	4.4				
Private non-financial	6.6	7.2	9.5	10.3	11.7	8.4	11.7	9.3
Households	6.8	6.5	8.7	9.4	9.8	8.9	10.3	8.7
Business	6.4	8.1	10.5	11.2	13.9	7.9	13.2	9.9
Corporate business	6.3	9.0	11.9	12.6	16.8	8.2	15.2	10.3
Non-corporate business	6.8	6.0	7.2	7.9	7.0	7.3	8.2	9.1

Source: Board of Governors of the Federal Reserve System.

Table 11. **Growth in monetary aggregates**
Annual percentage change

	1996	1997	1998	1999	1999			
					Q1	Q2	Q3	Q4
M1	-4.0	-0.6	1.7	2.8	2.8	-0.4	-1.5	10.5
M2	4.8	5.8	9.0	5.3	5.8	6.2	5.2	5.6
M3	7.3	9.0	11.0	7.9	6.3	6.7	4.4	14.3
Bank loans	6.2	8.4	10.1	5.8	-2.1	4.8	2.2	19.4
GDP	5.6	6.2	5.5	5.6	5.7	3.3	6.8	9.1

Note: End-period data for monetary aggregates and period-average figures for GDP.
Source: Board of Governors of the Federal Reserve System and Bureau of Economic Analysis.

In addition to its normal open-market operations designed to accommodate such a demand for cash, as one element of its strategy to provide liquidity safeguards, the Federal Reserve also put in place a special Year 2000 borrowing facility, though banks only drew $124 million from this account by the end of the year. This surge in liquidity was progressively withdrawn from markets at the beginning of 2000, and the monthly growth of broad money slackened markedly thereafter (in January and February 2000).

Overall financial conditions

The evaluation of the impact of these different financial variables on the aggregate economy requires both an estimate of the consequences of each of

them on the economy and a judgement as to what is their neutral level. Econometric models can be of guidance in the former. The Federal Reserve model of the US
economy provides one set of estimates (Reifschneider *et al.*, 1999). These estimates show the impact of changes in the stock market, exchange rate and short-term
interest rates on the growth of economic activity after two years. As to the neutral
level of each variable, this has been set equal to its average value since 1986.[19]
The estimates of the impact of a change in each financial variable on the economy,
after a lag of two years, have been combined with the current level of each variable
relative to its neutral value. Of course, such a composite indicator is very sensitive
to this assumed neutral level, and so the indicator is perhaps best seen as measuring the change in stance of overall financial conditions. The indicator can be mis-
leading if the long-run rate of return on capital increases, pushing up the
equilibrium real interest rate above its previous average level. In that case, the
indicator would underestimate the extent of financial ease.

On the basis of this indicator, financial conditions have become markedly
more expansive since the autumn of 1998. The increase in real long-term interest
rates and the slight appreciation of the exchange rate will tend to dampen activity
in the future. On the other hand, the renewed rise in the stock market (see Chapter I)
has outweighed this restrictive effect. The rising value of the stock market appears
to have capitalised a substantial part of the future income that will flow from

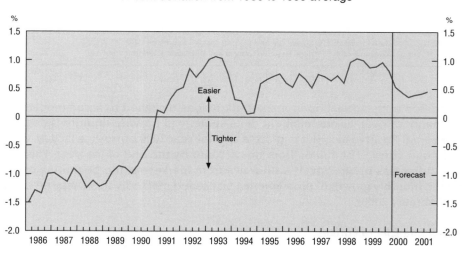

Figure 21. **Financial conditions indicator**
Per cent deviation from 1986 to 1999 average

Source: Board of Governors of the Federal Reserve System and OECD.

increased economic activity (see Chapter I). Such a one-off increase appears to have been one of the factors helping demand to surge faster than supply. Moreover, the growth of borrowing has been in excess of GDP. The increase in short-term interest rates has also failed to keep pace with inflation, adding to the easiness of overall financial conditions.

Summary

During 1999, the decreases in short-term interest rates made in the fall of 1998 in response to financial instability were reversed. Rates were finally moved above pre-crisis levels in February 2000. Overall financial conditions, though, have still not become appreciably tighter, though they have stopped becoming more expansionary. Higher short-term interest rates are now countering higher stock market values and the level of real long-term interest rates may eventually stop the growth of some components of demand. On the other hand, the exchange rate is no longer exerting any dampening influence on demand. With demand growth remaining well above the enhanced rate of growth of potential, some further tightening of monetary policy is needed. Indeed, at end-March financial markets assumed that by January 2001 the federal funds rate will be 100 basis points above its level then. The OECD assessment is that such a rise is indeed the minimum rise consistent with a gradual slowdown in growth in the absence of any major disturbances to the economy. Indeed, the projections assume that short-term interest rates will rise to 7 per cent by late summer 2000 and that the stock market will edge back from its high levels of March 2000. On this basis, financial conditions should become markedly less expansive during the next six months.

Fiscal policy

General government finances

The increase in the federal budget surplus has been mirrored by an improvement in the general government financial balance, which moved into a surplus of 1 per cent of GDP in 1999 (Table 12). A slight deficit at the state and local level, as measured in the national accounts, has partly offset the federal surplus. This latter surplus is somewhat lower than the surplus in the budgetary accounts due to a number of changes that have been made in the new version of the national accounts. In these accounts, the pension funds operated by all levels of government have been transferred to the personal sector, in line with the practice for the private sector. As the civil service pensions funds are entirely invested in government securities, the impact of the change is to raise government expenditure on interest – as previously the interest receipts of the funds were treated as a transfer between different branches of government that disappeared on consolidation. For state and local government, the impact is to mainly reduce their

Table 12.   **General government financial balances and debt**
Per cent of GDP

	1995	1996	1997	1998	1999	2000	2001
Budget basis							
Federal surplus (FY)	−2.2	−1.4	−0.3	0.8	1.4	1.8	1.8
National accounts basis							
Federal government	−2.6	−1.9	−0.5	0.6	1.1	1.5	1.6
State and local governments	−0.4	−0.3	−0.4	−0.2	−0.1	−0.3	−0.4
General government	−3.1	−2.2	−0.9	0.4	1.0	1.2	1.2
Cyclically adjusted	−2.9	−2.1	−1.1	0.1	0.5	0.5	0.7
Debt							
Gross general government	74.5	73.9	71.6	68.6	65.1	60.8	57.4
Net general government	59.3	58.9	57.0	53.7	49.7	45.4	42.0
Federal debt in hands of public (FY)	49.2	48.5	46.1	43.1	39.9	36.1	32.8

Source: OECD, except fiscal year data that are from the Congressional Budget Office.

income as the funds were mainly invested in private-sector securities. Overall, these new accounting procedures lowered the financial surplus of general government by an average of 1¼ percentage points of GDP between 1995 and 1998.

With revenue growth slackening and the volume of general government outlays on goods and services rising by close to 4 per cent (Figure 22), one of the

Figure 22.   **Government expenditures on consumption and gross investment**
Year-on-year percentage change, two-semester moving average, 1996 prices

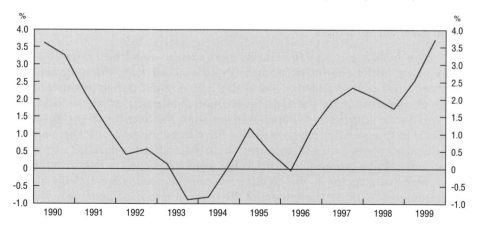

Source: Bureau of Economic Analysis.

fastest increases in the OECD area, the increase in the overall structural budget surplus was considerably less in 1999 than in 1998. This movement seems likely to continue, and the general government financial balance should stabilise at around ½ per cent of GDP in cyclically-adjusted terms. The combined effect of rapid output growth and a surplus should be sufficient to lower the gross and net debt-to-GDP ratios to 61 and 46 per cent, respectively, by 2000, down from peak levels of 75 and 55 per cent in 1994.[20] These figures exclude the present value of future social security liabilities that are increasing at the moment. The current cash surplus of the social security system represents nearly all of the general government surplus. However, if the social security accounts were placed on an accruals basis, the system would have a deficit.

Federal government finances

Fiscal 1999

The recent trend for federal budget surpluses to exceed previous budget forecasts continued in FY 1999, with the surplus rising to $124 billion or 1.4 per cent of GDP (Table 13). The extent of the overshoot was, however, reduced compared to previous years. The gain between the current services estimate of the surplus produced some eight months before the start of the financial year and the final outcome was $127 billion in 1999 against close to $180 billion in each of the previous two years. Both contributed, but the major gain came from the tax side. There was a marked decline in the growth of *tax receipts*, notably those from individual income taxes, which have been particularly buoyant in recent years. Corporate income taxes fell, reflecting weaker profit developments and, possibly, greater use of corporate tax shelters (see Chapter I). At the same time the growth of overall federal spending was broadly stable. A marked pickup in the growth of discretionary spending, in both defence and other areas was compensated by a drop in outlays in two areas. Spending on health care for the elderly, through Medicare, fell, albeit trivially, after growing by only 1½ per cent in the previous year, compared with an average annual increase of 9½ per cent in the previous decade. This unprecedented outcome reflected both a lower increase in the relative price of health care and the restrictive measures taken in previous budgets. In addition, net interest payments were reduced following the achievement of a budget surplus in FY 1998.

The growth in tax revenues in recent years has been driven by a number of factors, mostly related to changes in the distribution of income. The classic process of fiscal drag has played only a small part in the revenue increase. An analysis of a sample of individual tax returns suggests that between 1994 and 1998, the passage of individuals into higher tax brackets generated only slightly more than 22 per cent of the total gain (CBO, 2000). A number of other factors, such as the rapid growth of private pension contributions, withdrawals from tax-

Table 13. **Federal budgets and outcomes**

$ billion

	FY 1998	FY 1999		FY 2000		FY 2001
	Outcome	Current services	Outcome	Current services	Estimate	Current services
		February 1998	January 2000	February 1999	January 2000	February 2000
Total revenue	1 722	1 730	1 827	1 871	1 943	2 009
Individual income taxes	829	793	879	902	944	978
Corporate income taxes	189	194	185	187	189	190
Social insurance taxes	572	596	612	636	636	682
Excise taxes	56	71	70	65	65	69
Other	76	76	81	82	81	90
Total expenditure	1 652	1 732	1 703	1 775	1 767	1 838
Total discretionary	554	569	575	596	603	635
Defence	270	271	275	279	283	295
Other discretionary	284	298	300	317	320	340
Total mandatory	910	964	937	1005	980	1041
Social security	376	396	387	405	402	422
Medicare	193	208	190	215	199	218
Medicaid	101	108	108	115	115	124
Deposit insurance	−4	−4	−5	0	0	0
Other mandatory	244	256	257	270	264	277
Offsetting receipts	−55	−43	−39	−42	−40	−46
Total primary	1 409	1 490	1 473	1 559	1 543	1 630
Net interest	243	242	235	216	224	208
Surplus ($ billion)	**70**	**−3**	**124**	**96**	**176**	**171**
On budget	−29	−108	0	−33	23	11
Off budget	99	105	124	129	153	160
Surplus (per cent GDP)	**0.8**	**0.0**	**1.4**	**1.1**	**1.8**	**1.7**
On budget	−0.3	−1.2	0.0	−0.4	0.2	0.1
Off budget	1.2	1.2	1.4	1.4	1.6	1.6

Source: Office of Management and Budget and Congressional Budget Office.

exempt savings accounts, and the low growth of deductions due to a fall in interest rates, accounted for a slightly smaller gain (Kasten *et al.*, 1999). On the other hand, distributional factors were particularly important. Capital gains surged in the period to 1997 but appear to have been a less buoyant source of revenue in 1998 (Table 14). Other factors, including the growth of income from highly taxed sources and a shift in the distribution of income to those with higher tax rates also boosted receipts.

Table 14. **Sources of growth in individual income tax liabilities in excess of GDP growth, tax years 1994-98**

As a percentage of total growth

Sources of growth	1994-95	1995-96	1996-97	1997-98[1]	1994-98[1]
Taxable personal income (TPI) grows faster than GDP	21	12	14	26	18
Adjusted gross income (AGI) grows faster than TPI					
Capital gains taxes grow faster than TPI	21	52	29	16	31
Other AGI grows faster than TPI	14	4	12	9	9
Changes in the effective tax rate on AGI					
Effect of real growth on effective rate	21	17	25	27	22
Other changes in effective rate	23	15	21	22	20
Total	100	100	100	100	100
Memorandum:					
Growth of individual income tax liabilities in excess of GDP growth (billions of dollars)	27	39	36	33	134

1. The estimate for 1998 tax liability does not include the child and education credits enacted in the Taxpayer Relief Act of 1997.
Source: Congressional Budget Office.

The extent of the concentration of the increase in incomes amongst the highest earners was particularly marked between 1994 and 1997. The share of gross taxable income accruing to the top one percent of income earners had been practically stable between 1986 and 1994 (Petska and Strudler, 1998), though the various tax reforms had pushed up their share of tax payments. Starting in 1994 there was a renewed surge in the incomes of such well-off families.[21] This was mainly due to an increase in their number rather than in an increase in their average income. Indeed, between 1994 and 1997, nearly 60 per cent of the net increase in the number of tax returns was concentrated in the highest income group, with middle-income families accounting for most of the remaining increase (Table 15). With some increase in average incomes amongst high-income families, almost three-quarters of the increase in nominal income between 1994 and 1997 was concentrated amongst families with an income of over $100 000, despite this group accounting for less than 6 per cent of the number of tax returns in 1997. Even within this income category, the gains in nominal income were concentrated. Households with incomes of over $500 000 (0.3 per cent of the total number of tax returns) accounted for almost 30 per cent of the total increase in incomes, reflecting an 85 per cent increase in the number of households in this category in the period. Preliminary data for 1998 suggest that the pace at which taxable income is becoming concentrated may be slackening. The increase in the share of total taxable income that accrued to those with incomes over $500 000 dropped to 0.9 percentage points, against an average of 1.2 percentage points in the previous three years. By 1998 such taxpayers (0.4 per cent of the total) accounted for 25.6 per cent of income tax liabilities.

Table 15.   **The change in the distribution of income by fixed income class, 1994-97**

	Adjusted gross income by income class in the initial year $ per year				
	Less than 15 000	15 000 to 49 999	50 000 to 99 999	over 100 000	All
	Annual average increase, per cent				
Change between 1994 and 1997					
In average income	4.5	1.0	1.8	8.7	20.5
In number of returns	−4.3	3.9	21.2	58.6	5.7
In aggregate income	0.0	4.9	23.3	72.4	27.3
	Per cent				
Distribution of the change between 1994 and 1997					
In number of returns	−28.2	30.1	57.8	40.3	100.0
In aggregate returns	0.0	6.8	26.3	66.9	100.0
Capital gains					
As a share of income	2.1	0.4	2.2	15.1	3.2
As share of total gains	2.3	7.3	11.6	78.8	100.0

Source: Internal Revenue Service and OECD calculations.

Fiscal 2000

The principal plank of the Administration's budget for FY 2000, a proposal to "save social security", was not reflected in the final budget legislation. Congress did not pass any of the resulting proposed changes (a transfer from general revenues to the social security fund, a partial investment of the trust fund in equities and the creation of individual saving accounts outside social security). On the other hand, the proposals changed the climate of the budget debate and generated a broad consensus that both branches of government should try to limit spending and conserve tax revenues in order that the budget, excluding social security, should remain in balance and the social security surplus not be used to finance other expenditure. Nonetheless, the final spending plans resulted in extra spending of some $30 billion relative to the President's proposal and produced an initial slight deficit ($17 billion) in this measure of the budget balance, although the most recent estimates by the CBO project a small surplus. The compromise reflected the impossibility of agreeing on spending limits that remained within the spirit of the discretionary spending caps, which, from the outset, appeared unlikely to be met from 2000 onwards. Such a development was made all the more likely by the extent of emergency spending allowed in FY 1999. Overall, discretionary spending is now slated to rise by 5 per cent in FY 2000 (Table 16). Moreover, some of the earlier restrictive measures concerning Medicare were eased, helping to push mandatory spending up a projected 4½ per cent, compared to only 3 per cent the

Table 16. **Change in Federal government spending and revenue**

	FY 1998	FY 1999	FY 2000	FY 2001
	Per cent change from previous period			
Total revenue	**9.0**	**6.1**	**6.3**	**2.4**
Individual income taxes	12.4	6.0	7.4	3.6
Corporate income taxes	3.7	−2.1	2.2	0.5
Social insurance taxes	6.0	7.0	6.5	4.6
Excise taxes	−2.3	29.5	−2.9	1.5
Other	20.9	6.0	11.1	0.0
Total spending	**3.2**	**3.1**	**3.8**	**4.0**
Total discretionary outlays	**1.1**	**3.8**	**4.9**	**5.3**
Defence	−0.6	1.9	2.9	4.2
Other discretionary	2.7	5.6	6.7	6.3
Total mandatory outlays	**5.9**	**3.0**	**4.6**	**6.2**
Social security benefits	2.9	2.9	3.9	5.0
Medicare	1.6	−1.6	4.7	9.5
Medicaid	5.6	6.9	6.5	7.8
Other mandatory outlays	9.7	5.3	2.7	4.9
Offsetting receipts	**10.0**	**−29.1**	**2.6**	**15.0**
Total primary expenditure	**3.8**	**4.5**	**4.8**	**5.6**
Net interest	−0.4	−5.3	−2.6	−7.1

Source: OECD.

previous year. Total spending is likely to rise by 3¾ per cent (even though interest payments are falling), slower than the projected increase in revenues.

Comparing FY 2000 and FY 1998, the improvement in the budget surplus has come equally from the social security account and the remainder of government. Excluding social security, the budget was in slight deficit in 1998, in equilibrium in 1999 and is projected by the CBO to be in slight surplus of $23 billion in 2000. Despite the relaxation of the spending constraint, the CBO projects that the overall budget surplus will be higher in FY 2000 than the previous year at 1.8 per cent of GDP ($176 billion), reflecting a continued boost to the revenues from fast economic growth. Moreover, this projection was made on the basis of a projected growth of 3.3 per cent in 2000, a figure that is likely to be exceeded sufficiently to generate extra tax revenue of $25-50 billion.[22]

The movements in actual outlays and revenues so far this fiscal year do, indeed, suggest that some increase in the budget surplus is likely. Taxes on individuals (income tax and social insurance) were projected to run 5.7 per cent above

FY 1999 levels in July, but in the first three months of the fiscal year they had increased by 7.6 per cent. With spending likely to increase by less than this – despite a brisk start in the defence area and a renewal in the growth of Medicare spending – the budget surplus should improve. Indeed the deficit, in the first three months of the fiscal year, was slightly lower than in the corresponding period one year ago, after allowing for last year's shift in social security payments.[23]

Fiscal 2001

For the next fiscal year, the Administration's budget proposal gives similar results to those that would stem from keeping the current level of federal services unchanged in real terms. The Administration projects a budget surplus of $184 billion against an estimated $171 billion if the level of current services moves with inflation, and a Congressional Budget Office forecast of $188 billion if discretionary expenditure moves in line with inflation. As such, this budget marks the formal end of the spending limits enacted by the 1997 Balanced Budget Act (BBA). Total discretionary spending is put at nearly 11 per cent above the BBA limits for 2001. On the other hand, the Administration pledges to use emergency spending only for true emergencies.

Although the overall deficit figures are similar to those based on an inflation-adjusted projection of spending, this is the result of a number of offsetting changes, reflecting the priorities of the Administration. Notably, five areas of discretionary spending (Labour and Education, Interior, Transport, Energy and Housing) would see their allocations upped by an average 8¾ per cent, while in other areas rises average only 3 per cent, bringing the total increase in allocations to 5 per cent. This would be funded through increasing the Federal Reserve contribution to the budget, raising the excise tax on tobacco and a number of user fees. In addition, the budget makes provision for a number of new mandatory programmes and tax cuts. The effect of these could be felt mainly over the longer term (see below). In 2001, the principal tax changes relate to expanding the Earned Income Tax Credit and introducing tax credits for college education, together with limiting the marriage tax penalty (Table 17). All told, tax cuts of $5.9 billion would be funded by closing various tax loopholes. However, there must be some doubts about which parts of the budget will be passed by Congress. Already, the House has passed legislation that would quadruple the amount of tax cuts allowed for reducing the marriage tax penalty in the budget, though proposals for tax cuts in previous years were successfully blocked by the Administration.

Consequences of the surpluses for debt management

Over the next few years, the on-budget balance of the federal government seems likely to remain in broad balance, while social security may remain in surplus for about 20 years. Consequently, there will be a progressive shrinkage in the amount of government debt outstanding. This will pose a number of challenges for

Table 17. **The Administration's budgetary framework proposals**

	2001		2010	
	$ billion	Per cent of GDP	$ billion	Per cent of GDP
Prescription drugs in Medicare	0.0	0.00	31.4	0.20
Medicaid coverage widened	1.2	0.01	18.3	0.12
Retirement saving programmes	−0.1	0.00	12.5	0.08
Reduction of Alternative Minimum Tax for families	0.4	0.00	11.1	0.07
Limitation of the marriage tax penalty	0.2	0.00	7.5	0.05
Health care tax credits	0.1	0.00	5.9	0.04
Tax credit for college tuition	0.4	0.00	4.1	0.03
Tax credit for child/dependents care	0.1	0.00	5.0	0.02
Tax deductions for charity contributions	0.6	0.00	2.1	0.01
Total of above proposals	2.8	0.03	97.9	0.62

Source: Office of Management and Budget.

the government in meeting its objectives of minimising the cost of financing a given stock of debt, ensuring the availability of adequate cash balances and finally in promoting efficient capital markets. Already the Treasury has taken a number of steps to prepare the ground for a decline in the amount of outstanding debt. These actions have resulted in a marked fall in the extent of government debt rollovers, which seem likely to fall from $512 billion in 1998 to $400 billion by 2002. If debt issuance is maintained at the popular 10- and 30-year maturities and cut at shorter maturities, then, given the maturity pattern of existing debt, the average maturity of gross debt will rise from the current 5¾ years to 8 years by 2004. It is planned to avoid such a development, first by instituting a programme of debt buybacks and second by selectively re-opening the issue of existing securities. In this way, debt issuance can be concentrated in larger, more liquid issues. The buyback plan involves holding reverse auctions for all maturities. All told, the government plans buybacks of $30 billion this year.

However, despite these measures, the liquidity and depth of the Treasury market appears to have declined in the past two years. At first, this may have been the consequence of the market instability in the fall of 1998. Nonetheless, the worsening of liquidity appears to have been maintained well after the ending of the Long Term Capital Management and Russian crises. The deterioration can be seen in a number of measures: the difference in yields between the largest and most liquid recently issued bond and other bonds; the median difference between the price of a bond and its constituent parts when separately quoted as single coupon payments (STRIPS); and the difference between the yields on bills and notes with

Table 18. **Measures of liquidity in the government bond market in five large OECD countries**

	Canada	Italy	Japan	United Kingdom	United States
Bid-ask spread					
Fixed coupon[1]: 2 years	2	3	5	3	1.6
5 years	5	5	9[4]	4	1.6
10 years	5	6	7	4	3.1
30 years	10	14	16[5]	8	3.1
Volume outstanding (a)[2]	285	1 100	1 919	458	3 457
Yearly trading volume (b)[3]	6 243	8 419	13 282	3 222	75 901
Turnover ratio (b/a)	21.9	7.7	6.9	7.0	22.0

1. The table shows the bid-ask spreads of on-the-run issues, given in one-hundredth of a currency unit for the face amount of 100 currency units.
2. The figures are as of end-1997, in $ billion, converted at the exchange rates of end-1997 (US$1 = Can$ 1.43 = L 1 770 = Yen 130, £1 = $1.65).
3. The figures are for the 1997 calendar year, on a two-way basis.
4. Six-year bonds.
5. Twenty-year bonds.
Source: Bank for International Settlements (1999).

a similar maturity (Mitchell, 1999). At the same time, the volume traded and the quantities quoted at firm prices have also declined. Still, the market remains more liquid than those in other countries, with more turnover and lower bid-to-ask spreads (Table 18). Kambhu *et al.* (1999) have made a number of suggestions for improving the efficiency of the market. These hinge on allowing a greater degree of fungibility amongst stripped securities and a degree of substitution between bonds of nearby maturities. Such reforms would allow the market to use the component parts of relatively low-priced bonds to create artificial high-priced ones.[24]

It is noticeable, though, that the capital market is reacting to the growing shortage of large liquid Treasury issues. All of the major government-sponsored enterprises (see Chapter III) have come to the market with issuance of securities designed to be similar in structure to those of the Treasury. Indeed in the first nine months of 1999, these institutions issued $88 billion of securities with more than two-year maturity against an issuance $99 billion from the US Treasury, though the average issue size for government-sponsored enterprises was substantially less. Moreover, there has been a move by these agencies to pre-announced auction schedules that favours the development of a repurchase market. If the stock of agency issues increases in line with GDP, then their outstanding issue will exceed that of Treasury by 2006. This could generate a further pricing advantage for agency issues, though this will be limited by the extent of competition from swaps for the role of a benchmark security. Such fixed rate swaps trade twice as actively as agency securities, though they suffer from a greater degree of counterparty credit risk.

State and local government finances

The continued expansion of the economy produced a further improvement in the finances of state and local governments in FY 1999. Tax revenues rose substantially, increasing by over 6 per cent against the expectation of state budget officers when budgets were established that revenues would increase by only 2 per cent. Such buoyancy came despite some reductions in tax rates at the state level. Overall these amounted to only 0.2 per cent of total tax revenues, but in four states (Missouri, Ohio, Massachusetts and Wisconsin) there were cuts of between 5 and 10 per cent in the yield of state income tax. While the growth of current expenditure picked up slightly to just over 5 per cent, this was still less than the growth of GDP. Indeed, current state outlays have remained quite stable over the past 20 years, fluctuating in a narrow band relative to GDP, although there was a modest increase in the share of state transfer payments in GDP at the beginning of the 1990s. In 1999, investment expenditure was extremely buoyant, with net capital formation jumping 8 per cent, reflecting a surge in receipts from the federal government as the provisions of the 1999 revision to the Highways Act came into force. Capital spending financed at the state level grew more modestly. Consequently, the state and local government cash deficit continued its slight decline, reaching 0.3 per cent of GDP, down from 0.9 per cent of GDP in 1991.

In FY 2000, State general account budgets are likely to move further into surplus, though on a national accounts basis they will remain in deficit. Expenditure growth is projected to slacken. On the other hand, the pace of revenue growth should be maintained, as the scale of tax cuts has been reduced this year while the growth of nominal GDP should remain broadly unchanged. Such a surplus would represent a relatively rare occurrence and is likely to generate pressures for further tax cuts in the future, though electronic commerce is a longer-term threat to revenues (Box 5).

State finances will continue to benefit from the 1998 tobacco settlement but to a greater extent in 2000 than in 1999. Six manufacturers agreed to make annual payments which will amount to $207.9 billion over the next 25 years, as well as up-front payments of $12.7 billion. Such an income stream is equivalent to a one-off payment of just over $100 billion (1.1 per cent of GDP) if discounted at a risk-free long-term rate of interest. Payments in 2000 may total nearly $7 billion against $2.4 billion the previous year. The agreement will come into force on the earlier of 30 June 2000 or when 80 per cent of the states (by number and by size of financial allocation) have fulfilled two criteria. These are that they have passed legislation that requires non-participating manufacturers to pay into a reserve fund for future claims and that the state courts have approved the agreement. More

Box 5.   Electronic commerce and tax revenues

State and local governments depend on sales tax revenues for a significant part of their total income. The development of electronic commerce at the retail level could result in the erosion of the tax base. Individual states have the power to require collection of sales taxes only for transactions within their jurisdictions, unless the company has a physical presence in the state when sales tax is due even if the transaction took place out of state. Thus, electronic commerce offers the consumer the possibility of avoiding sales tax for many transactions. States do have the option of taxing the use of a good rather than its purchase, but enforcing this law is difficult for most goods, as they are unable to require notification of transactions from out-of-state sellers. The absence of taxation does appear to be one of the driving forces in the growth of electronic commerce. The residents of states with high sales taxes undertake more of such transactions than those living in states with low sales taxes (Goolsbee, 1999). Both in theory and in practice, the absence of sales tax on electronic sales – as well as mail-order sales – represents a distortion that could divert greater resources into such activities than would be justified on economic grounds.

At present the size of the distortion is small. Total retail e-commerce has been estimated at just under $15 billion in 1998 (Boston Consulting Group, 1999a) and, based on third quarter data, is likely to have reached $36 billion in 1999 (Boston Consulting Group, 1999b), representing less than 0.6 per cent of private consumption outlays. Over the holiday period, sales accelerated even further, quadrupling relative to the same period in 1999. Even so, retail e-commerce remains substantially less important than mail order sales which amounted to $55 billion in 1998. Seen from the perspective of taxing authorities, a large part of these sales would not in any case have been subject to sales tax. Financial, travel and entertainment services represent a significant part of on-line purchases, and, not being tangible goods, they are generally exempt from sales tax. Purchases of computer equipment represent a further significant part of electronic trade, and it is likely that a high proportion of such sales would have been conducted through mail-order or telephone call centres in the absence of e-commerce (Goolsbee and Zittrain, 1999). Overall, only 30 per cent of the total value of e-commerce seems likely to have resulted in a loss of sales tax revenues in 1998.

In the future, however, the distortion may grow. E-commerce is likely to penetrate more sectors, but on the other hand the movement into lower-value sectors, such as grocery sales, increases the probability that the selling company will have a physical presence in the state where the sale is made. Even allowing for an annual growth of 70 per cent in sales between 1998 and 2003 as in the projections made by Forrester (2000), the loss in tax revenue may still represent only $2.7 billion by 2003 (0.03 per cent of GDP). The benefit of ensuring that there is no discrimination between different retail sectors is, thus, relatively small. On the other hand the costs of ensuring compliance, in static terms, are also relatively low (Goolsbee and Zittrain, 1999). Although there are 30 000 different authorities that raise sales taxes in the United States and a plethora of exemptions and varying rates, information technology is at present able to generate appropriate sales tax bills for out-of-state customers at relatively low cost (Sullivan et al., 1999). The task would be easier, though, if postal codes were reworked so that a given code did not overlap tax jurisdictions. Compliance costs would also be relatively low, given that two-thirds of e-commerce sales are made by established retail firms and that the top 10 e-commerce outlets accounted for 50 per cent of on-line sales in 1998. Enforcing an out-of-state use tax by retail e-commerce vendors, though, would require specific Congressional action.

than half of all the state governors have recommended a segregated fund to receive the payments, the commonest uses for which would be funding child and adult health programmes. Some states propose to issue bonds whose interest and principal would be paid out of their future entitlements to settlement payments.

Medium- and longer-term fiscal projections

Medium term

Recent official medium-term projections of federal finances suggest that surpluses are likely to grow over the next decade. The CBO suggests that the surplus will rise to just over 3¼ per cent of GDP by 2010, with an average surplus of 2½ per cent of GDP (Table 19). Most of the surplus in this period is concentrated in the Social Security Fund, which is expected to register an average annual surplus of 1¾ per cent of GDP. With debt increasingly being held within the government, the Administration suggests that by 2013 the public may hold no net government debt. Some debt that had initial long-term maturities may still exist, necessitating the acquisition of some financial assets even with the buyback programme as the government is still issuing 30-year bonds and selling savings bonds and cannot

Table 19. **Medium-term federal budget projections**
Per cent of GDP

	2000	2001	2002	2003	2004	2005	2010
Unified budget							
CBO budget scenario	1.8	1.8	2.0	2.1	2.2	2.2	3.3
Administration, current services	1.9	1.7	1.9	1.8	1.8	2.0	3.0
Policy changes	−0.1	0.1	−0.1	−0.1	−0.2	−0.3	−0.6
Administration, budget proposal	1.7	1.8	1.8	1.7	1.7	1.8	2.4
Social security							
CBO budget scenario	1.6	1.7	1.7	1.8	1.8	1.9	2.0
Administration, budget proposal	1.5	1.6	1.6	1.7	1.7	1.8	1.8
On-budget							
CBO budget scenario	0.2	0.1	0.3	0.3	0.3	0.4	1.3
Administration current services	0.3	0.1	0.2	0.1	0.2	0.3	1.2
Policy changes	−0.1	0.1	−0.1	−0.1	−0.2	−0.3	−0.6
Administration, budget proposal	0.2	0.2	0.1	0.0	0.0	0.0	0.6
Debt in hands of public							
CBO	36.1	32.8	29.5	26.3	23.2	20.1	6.3
Administration, budget proposal	36.3	32.9	29.8	26.9	24.1	21.3	7.1

Source: Congressional Budget Office (scenario in which discretionary spending grows at the rate of inflation after 2000) and Office of Management and Budget.

force the sale of these instruments in the future. As a result, the government will have to either accumulate cash balances or purchase other financial assets (see above).

The Administration budget for 2001 already contains a number of proposals that could reduce the growth of the budget surplus. While initially having little cost (see above), these proposals gradually increase in size, reaching 0.6 per cent of GDP by 2010 (Table 19). The principal objective of these proposals is to increase both the depth and the breadth of the two government health plans. Thus, retired people would become eligible for assistance in the purchase of prescription drugs, while the parents of children eligible for Medicaid would themselves become eligible for care. On the tax side, the principal proposals are to introduce incentives for retirement savings by low- and moderate-income families, an expansion of the Earned Income Tax Credit, a tax credit for higher education tuition, reform of the Alternative Minimum Tax for families and to make the tax treatment of married couples closer to that of couples that are not married. Nonetheless, although these proposals halve the likely on-budget surplus in 2010, the unified budget surplus could be as high as 2½ per cent of GDP in that year.

Longer term

Over the longer term, the financial outlook for the federal government depends crucially on the movement of age-related expenditures, notably Social Security and Medicare, that will eventually more than absorb all of the projected budget surpluses. The last *Survey* dealt with the prospects for these types of outlays and concluded that long-term stability of Social Security would not be assured by its actual and prospective surpluses, nor by the prospective surpluses in the remainder of the government. In view of this situation, the President proposed that the general fund of the budget should transfer money to the Social Security Trust Fund and that a portion of the resulting Trust Fund balance should be invested in equities. This would have prolonged the breakeven point of the Fund but would not have avoided the need for structural reform. In the event, no action to improve the financial position of the Trust Fund was taken in 1999. However, in March 2000, legislation was passed that allowed people over 65 to continue working, without any reduction of social security benefits. People who draw benefits before 65 will still be subjected to a deduction from their earnings if they continue to work. The current budget proposes to allocate savings in debt interest payments from 2010 onwards to the Social Security Trust Fund.

Given the fact that the Social Security system remains actuarially underfunded, a target for fiscal policy is required that provides for the long-run stability of the public finances. It is clear that an objective of maintaining a zero "on-budget" balance will not suffice to generate a stable outcome for the future level of government debt in the very long run. The on-budget concept is arbitrary. There seems no good reason, for example, to include the surplus of the federal employee pension funds in the on-budget surplus while excluding the social security surplus on the grounds that its surpluses are needed to partially fund future pensions. Indeed, the ultimate ability of the government to pay social security pensions depends on the combined financial position of the Trust Fund and the rest of the government. Earlier work on the sustainability of fiscal policy points to using as an indicator a measure of the extent to which the current path for spending and revenues diverges from a path that would ensure the government eventually stabilises its debt at the current level, so remaining within its long-run budget constraint. This indicator (the fiscal gap) can be viewed as in the increase in taxes (or reduction in expenditure) as a per cent of GDP that would be needed to match the initial debt-to-output ratio with that at the end of a 75-year period. The CBO has estimated the fiscal gap on the base of a number of assumptions. If discretionary federal spending is kept constant in nominal terms between 1999 and 2002 and constant in real terms between 2003 and 2009 and then allowed to grow in line with GDP, then the fiscal gap would amount to only 0.5 per cent of GDP: a relatively small figure given the speed with which the federal budget surplus has been increasing in recent years.[25] Moreover, if discretionary spending were kept constant in real terms after 2010, then the fiscal gap would become negative, indicating no need for any adjustment in taxation or spending. Indeed, in this case, according to OMB projections, the overall Federal budget would remain in surplus until 2055.

Future uncertainties

Discretionary spending

One risk to such low estimates of the long-run fiscal gap is that the government will not be able to restrain the growth of discretionary outlays to the extent that it is incorporated in the CBO long-term projections. Indeed, in one of its January 2000 budgetary projections for the next decade, the CBO has such spending rising slightly faster than inflation. This growth reflects a real increase in federal civil service pay of just under 2 per cent annually (in contrast to the period in the past 20 years Federal pay has barely kept up with inflation), a constant number of employees and constant real purchases of other goods and services. Even with such a projection (that is less strict than the assumptions incorporated in the long-term projections), by the end of the decade discretionary expenditure would be 1.3 percentage points of GDP lower than in 1998. Such a decline would be in line with downward trend of such spending since 1960. However, most of that fall came from reduced defence spending. As a share of GDP, other domestic discretionary spending was lower than in 1999 only in the period 1962-64, suggesting further reductions may be difficult to achieve. Over the very long term, the assumption of constant real discretionary expenditure, as in the above OMB projection, is even more unrealistic, as it would imply discretionary spending falling to 1 per cent of GDP by 2055 and accordingly a large on-budget surplus. Indeed, if discretionary spending were to grow just 1 per cent per year faster than in the CBO projection, the on-budget surplus would be largely eliminated by 2010. Moreover, if discretionary spending were to grow in line with GDP after 2010, the unified deficit would be approaching 15 per cent of GDP by 2050, according to another CBO scenario, in which the budget (excluding social security) is only kept in balance. In that case, the fiscal gap would rise to 1¼ per cent of GDP.

Improved economic performance

On the other hand, if the improved performance of the US economy in the past four years persists, public finances will benefit, raising the issue of whether this faster growth would be sufficient to eliminate the need for future adjustments to the level of benefits to elderly people. Improved economic performance generates a better result for the Social Security system in two ways. First, pensions, once in payment, are only indexed to prices. Thus, higher growth of labour productivity reduces the average pension relative to average earnings and hence improves the financial position of the fund. However, the extent of the improvement is limited by the fact that pensions on retirement are linked to the growth of real wages, which will be boosted by faster labour productivity growth. Second, if better economic performance is associated with a higher rate of return on capital, and hence a higher real return on government bonds, then the current surplus of the Social Security Trust Fund will produce higher returns and so, at least partially, obviate the need for benefit reductions or increases in contribution rates though, of course, the interest payments of the remainder of the government would be raised by the higher real interest rates. Indeed, in the annual report of the Social Security Trustees issued in March 2000, the point at which the Trust Fund is exhausted has been pushed back to 2037.

Economic performance does appear to be better than assumed in recent official projections. In the past four years, potential growth has been markedly higher than the norm in the post-1973 period, averaging nearly 3½ per cent (see Chapter I). In its January 2000 long-term projections, the CBO assumes productivity growth of 1.9 per cent for the future, slightly above the growth of labour productivity over the past 40 years, while the Administration assumes growth of 1.8 per cent in its FY 2001 budget and the Trustees of the Social Security Trust Fund assume productivity growth of 1.5 per cent in their annual report for 2000. Such assumptions generate potential output growth of around 3 per cent. Moreover, real interest rates appear to have been some 70 basis points higher than the 3 per cent assumed. On the basis of the elasticities in the last report of the Technical Panel on Assumptions and Methods, an annual improvement in the growth of labour productivity amounting to 1.0 percentage points[26] would lower the deficit of the system, when measured over a 75-year period, from its currently estimated 0.77 per cent of GDP to 0.48 per cent of GDP. If real interest rates were to average 3.7 per cent this would further lower the deficit by 0.2 percentage point of GDP. Incorporating both of these changes would eliminate just over 60 per cent of the social security deficit, which would remain at 0.3 per cent of GDP when measured over a 75-year horizon.

Future demographic movements and the path of the Social Security deficit over time provide two further reasons for not concluding that the recent performance of the economy will eliminate the need for changes in the Social Security system. Given the current age distribution of mortality, the movement of life expectancy in the United States is particularly sensitive to the development of longevity for those who have already retired. In many countries mortality rates at higher ages have declining more rapidly than in the past and, in those countries where there are reliable civil statistics dating from the late 1800s, there is little evidence that this decline in mortality stops at 80. The Technical Panel recommended that the rate of decline of mortality should be increased to be in line with its historical average, rather than being held below this average, as assumed in the last report of the Trustees of the Social Security system.[27] Such a change would raise the Social Security deficit by 0.2 percentage point of GDP. Moreover, as explained in the last *Survey*, the current evaluation method does not generate a stable outcome for the system at the end of the evaluation period. Taking these two factors into account suggests that the Social Security system remains under-funded by an amount close to the estimate in the last report of the Trustees of the Social Security Fund.

While the impact of faster productivity growth on Social Security finances may be limited, the impact on the rest of government finances could be more pronounced. Unlike the state pension system, there is no automatic linkage between the growth of labour productivity and most government expenditure, except to the extent that the real pay of federal employees moves in line with that of the private sector. Given that the share of non-social-security taxation less government pay is around 12½ per cent of GDP, an improvement of economic growth of the order of 0.5 per cent annually would generate an improvement in the present value of future net revenues amounting to about 2½ per cent of current GDP. This would be sufficient to transform the fiscal position over the longer term, allowing both a rise in real discretionary spending and the funding of increased pension benefits.

III. Structural policy developments

The longest US economic expansion on record has raised real national income by one-third in the past nine years. One source of concern earlier in the expansion was that the labour market was not functioning in a way that enabled all to benefit from rising incomes. Now it would appear, on the contrary, that the expansion, with the reform of welfare and moderate increases in relative minimum wages, has drawn an increasing number of the less-favoured into employment, even if the widening in the distribution of income has not begun to reverse. At the same time reform of the education system is progressing, with more standards setting and examination-based leaving certificates. The record in the field of heath care is not as good, though the implementation of the State Children's Health Insurance Program (CHIP) is expected to provide health insurance to an increasing number of children in families, who while not poor, have no such coverage. Elsewhere in the economy, the 1996 telecommunications reform is continuing to bear fruit, and recent regulatory decisions should promote further competition in this area. Meanwhile, the United States continues to make full use of the multilateral trade dispute settlement system. The successive changes in financial regulation have reshaped financial markets; these modifications reached their apogee with the recent replacement of the Glass Steagall Act. Nonetheless, there are still some areas where further reform is needed, notably the status of government-sponsored financial enterprises. This chapter deals in more detail with the areas just mentioned; the impact of deregulation on other areas of the economy was recently discussed in another OECD report *Regulatory Reform in the United States.*

The social agenda

The benefits of robust economic growth have been shared widely in this expansion. Employment gains and higher incomes have spread to the less favoured. Real incomes have risen to record levels across the income distribution, and unemployment rates are at record lows for minorities. The long-term trend increase in income inequality has been arrested in recent years, and poverty rates have fallen, but both remain high relative to other OECD countries. Even though incomes and employment have expanded considerably, health care coverage has declined, particularly for poor women and their children. As a result, the government is seeking to expand programmes like CHIP, which were designed to fill this gap, and to ensure Medicaid coverage is made available to those that remain eligible. A significant reduction in income inequality requires improvements in the education system. Progress has been made in recent years in setting standards for schools, but much still needs to be done to meet those standards.

Labour market performance

The booming economy has generated job opportunities for a wide variety of workers. Unemployment rates have dropped considerably since their cyclical peak in 1992 and have fallen significantly below rates achieved in the last expansion (Figure 23). The overall unemployment rate dropped to just over 4 per cent at the end of 1999, a 3¾ percentage point decline from its peak and a percentage point below its low in the previous expansion. The last time the overall rate was this low was 30 years ago. The improvement has been even larger for groups traditionally subject to higher unemployment rates. The unemployment rates for black and Hispanic individuals have fallen about 6 percentage points since 1992 to their lowest rates since 1972 when such records were first kept. Similarly, the decline in the unemployment rate for adults with less than a high school diploma has been substantially greater than that of those with a college degree. The improvement in labour market conditions for the low skilled continued into 1998 and 1999, while rates levelled off for higher skilled workers. Moreover, the implementation of welfare reform since 1996 has boosted the labour force participation rate for female heads of households, with strong labour demand leading to a very large increase in employment for this group of workers over the past three years.

These gains in employment have led to rising household earnings. In 1998, real median household income (1998 dollars) increased for the fourth consecutive year to an all-time high of $38 900, finally surpassing the previous peak reached in 1989, the year before the most recent recession.[28] Furthermore, real household incomes were at record highs for every quintile of the income distribution. Real incomes had dropped in the early 1990s in response to low demand for labour but began to pick up as the expansion gained momentum. The pickup was particularly large for black households and women. Between 1993 and 1998, real incomes rose 10¼ per cent overall but 15 per cent for black households. Among individuals, the income of women increased nearly 16 per cent over the same period, compared with 11¼ per cent for men. In 1999, real median earnings continued to rise briskly, with similar increases reported across the earnings distribution.

Figure 23. **Unemployment outcomes**

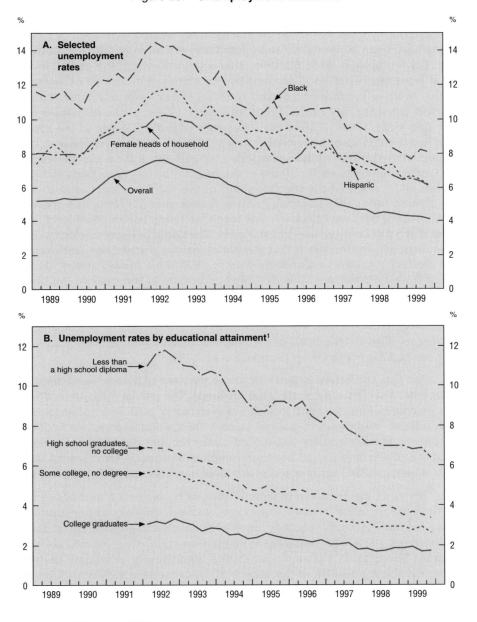

1. Data not available prior to 1992.
Source: Bureau of Labor Statistics.

Distribution of income

Rising real income for a wide range of workers in recent years has damped the long trend increase in income inequality in the United States. Since 1993, real incomes have risen at nearly the same rate for every quintile of the income distribution. For the bottom three quintiles, this is the fastest income growth recorded since at least the 1970s. As illustrated by two standard measures of income inequality – relative income shares and the Gini index – while income inequality increased considerably in the 1980s and early 1990s, it has remained largely unchanged since 1993[29] (Figure 24). The share of income going to the top 5 per cent of households rose dramatically until 1993, while the ratio of median income to income at the bottom quintile was little changed. Since then, the shares of household income going to each quintile of the population has been fairly stable, with only a small increase in the income share of the top 5 per cent of households. While income inequality has stabilised in recent years, it remains very high. In 1998, the top 20 per cent of households received nearly half of household income, and the top 5 per cent received 21 per cent. The Gini coefficient, which summarises the dispersion of income across the entire income distribution (with zero indicating perfect equality) was nearly 0.46 in 1998. This measure was also little changed from 1993 but was considerably higher than at the peak of the previous expansion. Income inequality in most other OECD countries also increased from the mid-1980s to the mid-1990s, and, in many cases, at a faster pace than in the United States. Nonetheless, while differences in measurement make cross-country comparisons difficult, the level of income inequality in the United States is still among the highest in the OECD (Burniaux et al., 1998).

The Gini coefficient is sensitive to the measure of income used, particularly as to whether government transfers are included. The official measure is based on money income before taxes and includes cash transfers, including public assistance, but excludes in-kind transfers, Earned Income Tax Credits and income from capital gains. Income is more equally distributed under broader definitions that take into account the effects of taxes and non-cash benefits. However, alternative measures of income show a similar pattern of inequality over time (Bureau of the Census, 1999).

The long-run increase in income inequality reflects a number of factors other than the increase in wage dispersion. Indeed, only about one-third of the increase in family income inequality since 1979 was due to growing earnings disparities (Burtless, 1999). The shift away from married-couple households toward single-parent households has also contributed significantly to income dispersion (explaining about one-fifth of the increase), because single-parent households typically have lower incomes. In addition, the decline in income inequality between men and women has boosted household income inequality over time by increasing the number of two-earner couples among the affluent (explained about one-eighth of the increase). Finally, there remains a significant unexplained residual.

Figure 24.   **Income distribution**

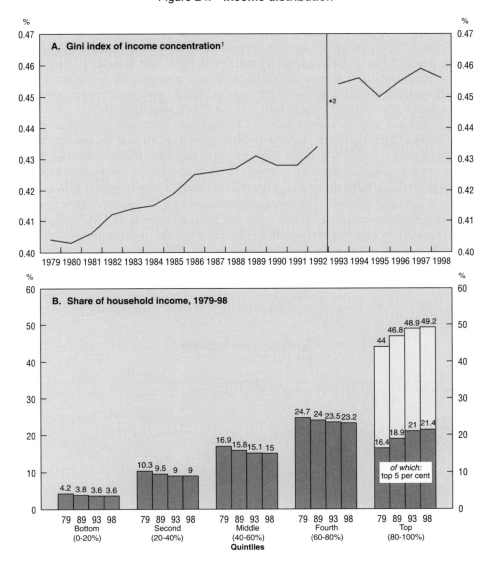

1.   Reported income used in the calculation of the index is truncated above a certain upper limit. This upper limit was raised significantly for the 1993 data (from $300 000 to $1 million), resulting in a much larger increase in reported incomes for wealthy households than in their actual incomes. As a result, this change in methodology overstates the rise in income inequality between 1992 and 1993.
2.   The Gini index would have been 0.447 instead of 0.454 using the upper limits on reported income from 1992.
Source: Bureau of the Census.

Poverty

While the relative income share of the lowest income groups has stabilised, the poverty rate has fallen (Figure 25). The official poverty rate is a subsistence-based measure, which uses an income threshold derived from the share of income needed to purchase an adequate diet in 1955, and is indexed to the Consumer Price Index (CPI). It had risen to over 15 per cent of the population in 1993, but with rising employment and incomes in recent years, it dropped back to 12.7 per cent in 1998, the lowest rate since 1979 (Dalaker, 1999). The decline in poverty for black and for female-headed households has been even more dramatic, reflecting the large drop in unemployment and rapid real income growth for these categories. While still quite high, poverty rates in 1998 for blacks (26.1 per cent) and for families headed by women (33.1 per cent) were the lowest on record, and the poverty rate for children (18.9 per cent) was the lowest since 1980.

A range of alternative estimates of poverty has been produced to reflect different definitions of income. The basic official poverty threshold is compared to an estimate of before-tax income that does not reflect in-kind benefits workers receive from their employers or the government.[30] Given the growth in these omitted sources of income there was a need for an updated measure. In 1995, an official panel recommended changing the definition of income to include in-kind

Figure 25. **Poverty rates**

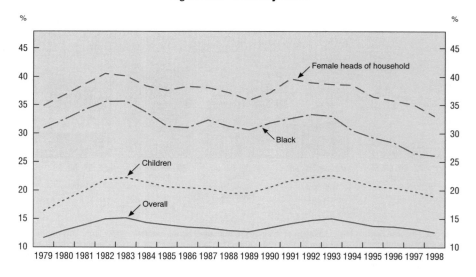

Source: Bureau of the Census.

benefits and the Earned Income Tax Credit (EITC) and to exclude taxes and certain essential expenses, such as medical and child care costs. The panel also recommended revising the poverty thresholds to reflect costs for food, clothing, shelter and other common items. A series of alternative measures, which incorporate the recommended changes, show poverty rates that are higher than the official measure but have declined more since 1993 (Short *et al.*, 1999). The inclusion of the EITC as part of measured income would reduce the overall poverty rate since 1993 by an additional ¾ percentage point, reflecting the expansion of that programme in the 1990s.[31] The measurement of income also affects the ranking of the United States in cross-country comparisons of poverty. Before taxes and transfers are taken into account, poverty rates in the United States appear relatively low, but this position deteriorates once taxes and transfers are included (Oxley *et al.*, 2000).

Welfare reform and the minimum wage

In 1996, the Personal Responsibility and Work Opportunity Reconciliation Act (PRWORA) replaced the old open-ended federal entitlements to welfare assistance with a block grant to states to provide time-limited and work-focused benefits. In general, federally-funded assistance is linked to recipients' efforts to find work within at most two years of receiving aid and has a lifetime limit of five years. Most of the authority to design welfare programs was passed on to the states; some have chosen to set shorter time limits, and a variety of sanctions for non-compliance have been adopted. Welfare caseloads have plummeted, falling in 1999 to half the level of five years earlier and to the lowest share of the population since 1967.[32] Research by the Heritage Foundation looking at cross-state variation in caseload reduction between January 1997 and June 1998 suggests that states with more stringent sanctions or immediate work requirements had larger declines in caseloads than do other states (Rector and Youssef, 1999). They also find that changes in caseloads are not related to variations in the unemployment rate across states. A report by the Council of Economic Advisers (1999*a*) suggests that over a longer period of time (1976 to 1998) the implementation of welfare reform programmes (PRWORA and earlier waiver programmes) has reduced welfare participation, and the more severe the work sanctions the more the reduction in participation. This study, however, finds that other factors have been important as well, including lagged changes in the unemployment rate and changes in the minimum wage (discussed below). It estimates that one-third of the reduction in welfare caseloads between 1996 and 1998 was due to the implementation of PRWORA and another 10 per cent was due to falling unemployment.[33]

Although minimum wage increases generally redistribute income among low-income families, recent minimum wage changes may have boosted labour income in the bottom half of the income distribution given the extraordinary growth in employment.[34] After remaining unchanged for five years, the federal minimum wage was raised in 1996 and 1997 to $5.15 per hour. By the end of 1999, the real value of the minimum wage had fallen back and is now at its 1991 level (Figure 26). President Clinton asked for an additional hike in the minimum wage of $1 per hour over two years in his 1999 State of the Union address, and such an increase was passed by the House this year. In a separate bill, a $1 increase spread over three years was passed by the Senate this year but the bills have not been sent to Conference Committee.[35] The booming economy appears to have mitigated the usual disemployment effects of the recent minimum wage hikes, and both have induced welfare mothers to enter the workforce.[36] The Council of Economic Advisers' study (1999a) estimates that about 10 per cent of the decline in welfare caseloads between 1996 and 1998 was attributable to increases in state and federal minimum wages. Empirical research on the impact of earlier minimum wage changes on welfare caseloads is mixed.[37] Furthermore, research that looked at a wider group of individuals has concluded that changes in minimum wages have generally not reduced the proportion of families that are poor (Neumark and Wascher, 1997).

However, even if raising the minimum wage helps the poor on balance, it is a poorly targeted instrument. The majority of low-wage workers do not live in poor households. In fact, more of the benefits from minimum wage increases go to

Figure 26. **Minimum wages**
$ per hour, 1999 prices

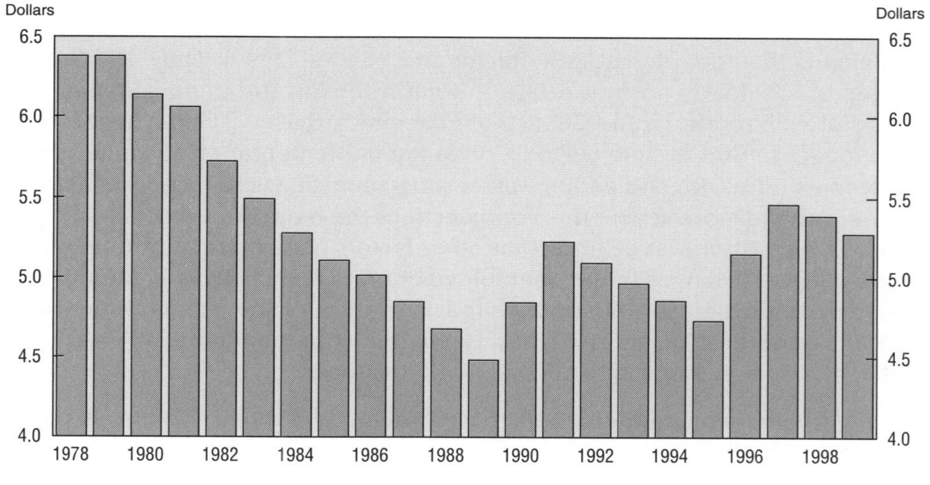

Source: Bureau of Labor Statistics and OECD.

relatively affluent households (those with incomes at least three times the poverty threshold) than go to the poor and near-poor (households with incomes up to 1½ times the poverty threshold) (Burkhauser et al., 1996). Many minimum wage workers live with parents, relatives or a working spouse. Two-thirds of the workers directly affected by the proposed minimum wage changes have no children to support, over half work part-time, and 30 per cent are teenagers. While many people begin their work careers in minimum-wage jobs, the vast majority go on to higher-paying jobs relatively quickly. Ten years after leaving school, less than 4 per cent of all workers have spent more than half their time in minimum-wage jobs (Carrington and Fallick, 1999).

States also set minimum wage requirements, while local authorities are able to specify minimum wage levels to be paid by their private-sector contractors. So-called "living wage" policies have been adopted in about 40 cities and counties since 1994 when Baltimore first implemented its ordinance, and numerous similar proposals are pending, notably in California. Such ordinances generally require companies that hold contracts or receive subsidies from local governments to pay wages that are higher than the state's minimum wage. These wages are typically defined as half average local wages. The highest "living wage" is currently $10.75 per hour (without health insurance) in San Jose, considerably above California's minimum wage of $5.75. These policies have generally not been in place long enough to evaluate their impact on employment, but the impact over time will probably depend on how much of the resulting increase in costs the local governments are willing to absorb.

Rather than raising the minimum wage, the government should consider increasing the EITC. Unlike the minimum wage, the great majority of EITC benefits go directly to poor families (Burkhauser et al., 1996), and the EITC appears to raise labour force participation among single mothers significantly (Meyer and Rosenbaum, 1999; Eissa and Liebman, 1996) and reduce rates of poverty. Between 1993 and 1997, the real value of the EITC payment increased by nearly 40 per cent for single mothers with one child and more than doubled for those with more children (Council of Economic Advisers, 1998). Over this same period, the labour force participation rates for single mothers increased over a percentage point, while the rate remained unchanged for other single women. The Administration has proposed a major expansion of the EITC that would expand the credit for working families with three or more children and for married, two-earner couples and would lower the phase-out rate for benefits, thus reducing work disincentives.

Health care

Although the United States spends far more per capita on health care than other OECD countries, it has one of the highest rates of premature mortality, most of which is not explained by economic or environmental factors (Or, 2000). In light of this, the 1996 review of US implementation of the OECD *Jobs Strategy* expressed concern about declines in health care coverage in the United States.[38] Yet, according to government surveys, the number of uninsured rose somewhat further in 1997 and 1998. Over 44 million people, or about 16 per cent of the population, lacked health insurance at some point in 1998, an increase of 2½ million since 1996 (Campbell, 1999). Private health insurance plans covered 70 per cent of individuals in both 1996 and 1998. Most private plans are based on employment, and the employment-related share of private plans has been rising over the 1990s as employment and hours worked have expanded.[39] As a result, full-time workers are more likely to be insured than either part-time workers or the unemployed. Nonetheless, 17 per cent of full-time workers did not have health insurance in 1998. Some of these workers may have turned down employer-sponsored insurance plans for cost reasons, while others work for small firms that are much less likely to provide such insurance.

Lack of coverage is particularly acute for low-income households. The share of the poor who had no health insurance increased slightly to one-third in 1998, despite a pickup in employer-based insurance for this group. Among the poor who worked full time, coverage expanded considerably over the past two years but still remained below the coverage for poor people who did not work at all (likely reflecting the availability of government-sponsored insurance for single mothers with young children who do not work). The share of uninsured children also edged up over the past two years to 15.4 per cent overall and to 25 per cent of poor children, although this figure is likely to decline as the State Children's Health Insurance Program (CHIP) becomes fully effective. By contrast, amongst the elderly, the availability of Medicare resulted in nearly universal coverage, although some outlays, such as for prescription drugs, are not reimbursed. Medicaid, the other major government insurance programme, covered about 40 per cent of all poor people and nearly 60 per cent of poor children in 1998, somewhat less than in 1996. According to survey data, Medicaid coverage fell by 3.6 million between 1996 and 1998, but official administrative records show a much smaller decline, of about a million, over the same period.

Given the booming economy, these developments are disappointing. Health care continues to be a public concern, and efforts to enact legislation setting new standards for health plans and expanding access to health care continued last year, although no significant progress was made. In 1999, Congress failed to agree on legislation to establish a "patients' bill of rights", restructure Medicare or address the President's proposed expansion of Medicare coverage to prescription drugs. However, an additional $16 billion was allocated over five years primarily to raise reimbursement rates for Medicare providers. In addition, recent efforts to reduce fraud and abuse in the Medicare system have led to a large reduction in error rates, leaving more funds for their intended purposes. CHIP, which was passed in 1997, began to be implemented in late 1998. This program, which will cost $24 billion over five years, is aimed at providing insurance coverage to children whose families have incomes too high to qualify for Medicaid but too low to afford private health insurance. In September 1999, 2 million children were enrolled in CHIP, and the government has implemented an outreach programme to attract all eligible individuals to participate in CHIP and Medicaid. As a result, the number of enrolees is expected to expand further this year. The Administration's budget proposal for FY 2001 includes plans to expand enrolment to the parents of children who are eligible for coverage under CHIP and Medicaid. Among other features, the plan would also help low-income workers buy employer-offered health coverage. In addition, a Congressional plan to provide tax credits for health insurance has been proposed and has sponsors from the two major political parties.

As discussed in the 1999 *Survey* (OECD, 1999c), a Presidential Commission recommended sweeping changes to the health insurance system in 1997. The Administration has implemented most of the recommendations pertaining to public programmes, such as Medicare, Medicaid, and CHIP, but legislation is required for changes to private-sector plans. The Senate and House passed very different "patients' bill of rights" legislation last session, and the bills are currently in Conference committee. Key issues include the number of individuals covered, the ability to sue insurance companies and health maintenance organisations for injury or death resulting from denial of medically necessary treatment, the inclusion of a "prudent person standard" for emergency room visits, and greater access to specialists and drugs. A cornerstone of the House bill is a provision that would expands patients' rights to sue their health plans in coverage disputes, while the Senate measures contain no such liability provision. Some of these changes address concerns outlined in the 1992 *Survey* (OECD, 1992), but both bills still fall short of the called-for comprehensive overhaul of the US insurance system. The Congressional Budget Office estimated that the House bill, which is much more comprehensive, would raise premiums by no more than 5 per cent.

Concerns about increases in health care costs imposed by legislation come at time when the recent decline in health care costs appears to have ended. Over the past two years, insurance costs for firms have begun to creep up somewhat, rising 5¾ per cent in 1999 (Figure 27). Medical prices, especially prices of prescription drugs, have accelerated, and the tight labour market may have prevented employers from continuing to pass a larger share of costs to their workers. Health insurance costs made up 5½ per cent of overall compensation costs in 1999, down from 6¾ per cent in 1994.

Structural change in the medical industry has helped reduce the rate of increase of health insurance premiums, but families have also been bearing a larger share of costs themselves. By the mid-1990s, the level of expenditure on health care benefits per employee paid for by employers had stabilised (Schwenk, 1999). Firms implemented a wide range of changes in order to reduce

Figure 27.   **Health insurance and medical costs**
Twelve-month percentage changes

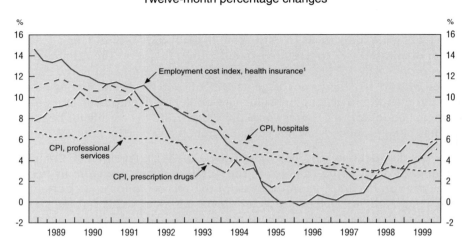

1.   Unpublished estimates.
Source: Bureau of Labor Statistics.

their costs, including requiring greater employee contributions and shifting away from fee-for-service to managed care plans. By 1997, three-quarters of the employees of medium-sized and large private firms receiving medical insurance were enrolled in managed care plans, compared with only one-third in 1991 (Bureau of Labor Statistics, 1999). By 1997, between 70 and 80 per cent of families were required to contribute toward their coverage. As a result, out-of-pocket spending on health insurance and drugs has grown in real terms over the past ten years, by 3¾ per cent and 1½ per cent, respectively, at an average annual rate.

While harder to measure, access to health care is broader than insurance coverage. Safety net institutions, such as public hospitals, still care for the uninsured, but their margins have been squeezed considerably, making such care more difficult. It is also a condition of a hospital's participation in Medicare that it must provide emergency services to all who seek such care. In addition, a variety of federal grant programmes provide support for vulnerable populations. These include subsidies for primary care and reproductive health clinics that serve low-income populations, services for people with HIV infection, and immunisation of low-income children. Recently approved increases in payment rates for Medicare providers may relieve some pressure on safety net institutions and the relevant FY 2000 appropriations bill included a boost in "disproportionate share payments" made to hospitals that treat a large number of uninsured patients. However, these payments are for hospitals only and do not always target well those hospitals that are bearing the largest share of the burden. Finally, in poor urban areas access to care may be limited by the lack of accessible physicians, and given the shortage of health care professionals in remote rural areas, access continues to be limited there, even for those with insurance coverage.

Education policy

A key element in the Administration's approach to improving education has been the Goals 2000 Educate America Act, passed in 1994. These national goals for education emphasised the importance of making young children ready for school and called for an increase in high school completion rates, greater academic achievement, especially in mathematics and science, better qualified teachers, greater adult literacy, safer schools and enhanced parental participation. As of mid-1998, the Goals 2000 programme had allocated $1.7 billion in federal grants to local school districts to develop education reform plans and implement voluntary educational standards. In addition, funds for the Head Start programme were increased by over 50 per cent between FY 1993 and FY 1999 in order to improve pre-school children's readiness for school.

By 1999, nearly all states had adopted standards for English, mathematics, science, and history or social studies, whereas in 1996 only fourteen states had academic standards in place. The majority of states (36) now issue some sort of report card that measures the performance of each school, and a number of states provide assistance to schools identified as low-performing and reward schools that make significant progress. Furthermore, about half the states require pupils to pass examinations for high school graduation, and an increasing number require and fund intervention programmes for students who are struggling to meet the standards. Despite this progress, the process of setting standards and assessing achievement has been highly contentious and will probably require adjustments over time. The National Educational Summit in 1999 questioned the quality of standards and assessments to date and called for more rigorous and uniform standards and a better alignment between standards and assessments (Achieve, 1999).

While progress has been made toward implementing the OECD Jobs Strategy's goal of promoting the adoption of output standards for primary and secondary schools, much still needs to be done to bring students' performance up to the standards that have been agreed upon. According to the National Education Goal Panel, 12 out of 27 statistical indicators used to measure progress between 1990 and 1999 in individual achievement showed improvement, deterioration occurred in five indicators, while there no change for the others.[40] More children were "ready to learn" when they entered kindergarten, and pupils demonstrated an improvement in mathematics proficiency and slight progress in reading proficiency. However, even with some improvement, less than half of students scored at or above "proficient" in reading and less than a quarter of students scored at or above "proficient" in mathematics.[41] By contrast, pupils performed quite well on international science achievement examinations.[42] In other areas, the panel reported that there had been some deterioration in teacher quality, measured by the proportion of teachers holding college degrees in the main subject they teach, and in school safety, where illicit drug sales and use in high schools had risen. Moreover, high school completion rates, nearly the lowest amongst all OECD countries, remained unchanged since 1990.

Public support for standards and accountability in schools has also been reflected in the charter school movement. Charter schools set their own achievement and performance goals for which they are held accountable by their sponsors and the parents and students who choose them. Since the first charter school opened in Minnesota in 1992, their number has grown to over 1 700 across 32 states. Federal funds to support charter schools has increased from $6 million in FY 1995 to $130 million in the current fiscal year. In addition, charter schools are eligible for funding under other federal programmes, including Goals 2000 grants, and 20 states have included funding initiatives for charter schools in their FY 2000 budgets.

Average expenditures per student in the United States are among the highest in the OECD countries, but considerable variation exists across regions. In 1995, less than 10 per cent of funding for primary and secondary education came from the federal government, with the remainder split between state and local government funds. This contrasts considerably with many other OECD countries, where on average over 50 per cent of funds are provided by the central government (OECD, 1998). In 1996, the OECD *Jobs Strategy* called for more equitable financing of schools in the United States; some progress has been made in that area recently. The fiscal 1999 budget bill authorised the expenditure of $1.2 billion as a first instalment on the Administration's proposal to subsidise the hiring of 100 000 new teachers to reduce class sizes over the next seven years. After considerable debate, the Omnibus budget bill for fiscal 2000 provided a one-year extension of funding for the Administration's proposal to hire new teachers, but the future for such funding remains under discussion.

Further action will be required this year as the act governing federal aid to public schools, which provides about $14 billion per year, expires and must be reauthorised. Sizeable differences exist between the two main political parties on key issues dealt with by this bill, including the Administration's request for additional funds for school renovation and construction and class-size reduction and the House Republicans' support for converting a wide range of existing education programmes into broad block grants. The House opposes any further funding for new teachers, while a Senate plan would provide most of the funding for new teachers that the Administration requested. The House plan would give states considerably more control over education funds, while the Administration wants to continue to direct their allocation.

There have been a few initiatives at the State level to implement voucher programmes that allow parents to manage education funds. The constitutional status of taxpayer-funded voucher programmes that extend to religious schools is still uncertain. State court rulings have been divided on this issue. The Supreme Court has refused to hear appeals in three voucher cases since late 1998, letting stand rulings that both allow and prohibit taxpayer-funded vouchers for private and religious schools.[43] Florida implemented a new voucher programme last year that provides tuition assistance to students of poorly performing schools, but in March, a state judge ruled that this programme is unconstitutional. According to the court ruling, under Florida law, public funds may not be used to send children to any private schools. At a national level, proposals to set up pilot programmes to test private school vouchers were defeated in the House in 1999 and were in any case unlikely to have gained majority support in the Senate.

Scope for further action

Better long-term prospects for growth could be achieved through government policies aimed at improving health and education. The government should consider expanding state and federal initiatives to make financing of education more equitable. Further efforts to expand educational achievement to meet academic standards in place are needed. For those who have not succeeded academically, expanding the earned income tax credit would better target their needs than another increase in the minimum wage. Despite large per-capita expenditures, health outcomes are poor and are not likely to improve while insurance coverage is declining. Access to health insurance and to health-care providers needs to be expanded for the poor. Recent government initiatives in this area should improve coverage for poor children, but coverage and, more importantly, access is likely to remain inadequate for poor adults.

Product market efficiency

Product market regulation in the United States is market oriented with competition principles underlying the legal framework for regulation (OECD, 1999b). In telecommunications, regulatory reforms and strong competition policies combined with the rapid evolution of technology has opened up long-distance markets to competition, and while extending competition into local markets has proven more difficult, there has been some recent progress in this area. Concerns about competition in other markets prompted the government's antitrust suit against Microsoft and the recent announcement that it plans to block the merger of two large oil companies. In the international arena, the United States has been an active participant in multilateral dispute settlement mechanisms and has stepped up its use of anti-dumping and countervailing duty investigations, particularly in steel.

Telecommunication

The telecommunications industry has been extraordinarily dynamic. Regulatory reforms and rapid technological advances in the production of communications equipment have encouraged considerable capital investment, brisk labour productivity growth in telephone communications services, and a pickup in the sector's employment. These investments have provided the backbone for data and information services, where demand continues to expand rapidly. The number of hosts for Internet sites has exploded in recent years, and availability of high-speed data transmission services is expanding rapidly. About 30 per cent of households had access to the Internet in 1999, compared with roughly 10 per cent in 1995, and the share using high-speed, broadband connections doubled. Demand for more traditional telecommunications services has also expanded. In particular, long-distance volumes increased 40 per cent between 1993 and 1998.

Competition in the long-distance telephone market has expanded further in recent years. Prices for interstate calls have dropped almost continuously for three years, and in-state long-distance rates began to fall last year (Figure 28). At

Figure 28. **Telephone prices**
3-month moving average, 12-month percentage changes

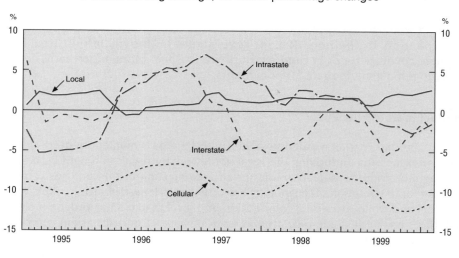

Source: Bureau of Labor Statistics and Federal Communications Commission.

the same time, long-distance usage has surged. AT&T's share of long-distance service in the United States has continued to decline.[44] Market shares for other large providers – MCI WorldCom and Sprint – have remained fairly stable, while the market share for smaller providers has expanded rapidly. There has also been a shift toward using Internet backbone infrastructures for data and voice traffic. Some of the smaller providers entering the long-distance market have been incumbent local exchange carriers (ILECs). While until quite recently no Bell operating company had received the Federal Communications Commission's (FCC) approval to provide long-distance services, other local telephone companies have not faced the same restrictions on providing such services to their local customers.[45] In 1996, 66 local telephone companies offered long-distance service, up from seven in 1989. Their share of customers was 13 per cent in the markets they served and 2½ per cent nationwide.[46] In December 1999, the FCC announced its approval of Bell Atlantic's application to provide long-distance service to its customers in New York State, making it the first local Bell telephone company to win such authority. In other developments, MCI WorldCom, the second largest long-distance company, and Sprint, the third largest, have announced their intention to merge. The combined company would be able to offer broadband access and digital wireless voice and data services in addition to long-distance services. Approval is likely to be difficult. The FCC has signalled that a strong case will have to be made that the merger will benefit consumers.

Competition in the local telephone market has expanded since the Telecommunications Act of 1996 made sweeping changes aimed at encouraging local service competition.[47] Local service revenues of competitive local exchange carriers have increased 5½ times between 1995 and 1998. However, even under a broad definition of local service competition, incumbent local exchange carriers retained 96 per cent of local service revenues in 1998, compared with over 99 per cent in 1995. Competition is largely limited to the provision of services to large business customers, the most profitable part of the market. In most areas, regulation keeps rates for residential local telephone service low, and revenues received from access charges that long-distance carriers pay to local networks are generally lower for residential customers than for business (Council of Economic Advisers, 1999b). Furthermore, geographic rate averaging requirements force urban customers to subsidise rural rates. As a result, there has been slow entry into residential markets, especially outside of urban areas, while there has been growing business telephone competition. Converting implicit subsidies to explicit charges to pay for universal telephone access and re-balancing local telephone rates between residential and business customers to reflect cost differentials could help spur entry into local markets.

Despite the lack of significant progress in boosting competition for local telephone services, the rapid growth of cellular phones is, in some cases, providing alternative suppliers of some local services. There is significant competition in the cellular phone market in the United States, with consumers having several operators to pick from in most markets. Some areas have seven networks in direct competition, and three-quarters of the population have access to at least five mobile operators. Cellular phone service has grown dramatically as prices have dropped. Between 1995 and mid-1999, average monthly charges fell nearly 30 per cent (Federal Communications Commission, 2000) and have continued to drop since then. Over the same period, the number of cellular telephone subscribers tripled to 76 million, equal to about 30 per cent of the population. Despite this rapid growth in subscribers, mobile phone penetration has increased less rapidly than in other OECD countries. In 1995, the United States ranked fifth among OECD countries in cellular penetration, but its ranking fell to sixteenth in 1999 (OECD, 2000c). This development does not reflect price differentials in the United States. US prices for cellular service are well below the OECD average and about in line with the countries with the highest market penetration. The elimination of monopolies and duopolies in a number of countries contributed to the rapid growth of their markets. In addition, the advent of pre-paid cards in calling-party-pay systems – such as the Netherlands, Italy and Portugal – seems to have been the most important factor in boosting the growth of these markets relative to the US (OECD, 2000c).[48] In a move that may also boost cellular penetration, the FCC is seeking to remove regulatory obstacles to the offering of calling-party-pays services by mobile operators. While price differentials still make it difficult for mobile service to compete on price with primary fixed connections that offer unmeasured local calls, they are more price competitive with second telephone lines, primary lines in areas with local toll charges, and payphones. Nevertheless, at this point, only 1 per cent of all telephone customers use a cellular unit as their only telephone.

In addition to mobile services, a variety of other alternative systems are likely to provide competition in the local market in the next few years. Cable companies are strong potential competitors as they develop the ability to promote high-speed Internet access along with voice telephone service on a widespread commercial basis.[49] Wireless local loop technology is being developed that can provide broadband data and voice services similar in quality to cable. Early in 1999, the FCC announced it will auction most of the electromagnetic spectrum that can be used for high-speed Internet access and next-generation wireless telephones.

As new technologies have spread, policy-makers have become concerned that some sectors of the economy have been left behind, creating the so-called "digital divide". Over 40 per cent of households owned computers and a quarter had Internet access at the end of 1998, but households with low incomes and those in rural areas were much less likely to have such access (National Telecommunications and Information Administration, 1999). Even holding income constant, black and Hispanic households are far less likely to have Internet access, and these gaps have generally widened over the past five years. In response, the government has broadened its goal for universal service in telecommunications to include access to information services, including the extension of broadband networks to rural areas. The FCC recently directed local telephone companies to share their telephone lines with providers of high-speed Internet access and other data services.[50] This change enables competitors to provide high-speed digital services to customers who currently receive voice service from the incumbent phone company and is intended to encourage the rapid deployment of broadband and other advanced services to households and small businesses. While the FCC has not required cable companies to provide competitors access to their high-speed cable lines, legislation has been proposed that would also require open access by cable providers of Internet services (Ota, 1999). However, the recent proposed merger of a large Internet service provider (AOL) and a large cable company (Time Warner) has lessened the lobbying for such a change. Other legislation aimed at closing the "digital divide" would allow the Bell operating companies into the long-distance data transmission market if they build the capacity to bring high-speed Internet access to rural areas (Bettelheim and Ota, 2000).

Other product market developments

Government agencies have also made efforts to ensure that product markets remain as competitive as possible. In that respect legal actions have been undertaken with the objective of preventing anti-competitive behaviour in certain parts of the private sector. In May 1998, the Department of Justice (DoJ) and a number of states filed an antitrust suit against Microsoft in US District Court, alleging the firm engaged in anti-competitive practices in an effort to maintain its dominant position in operating systems for personal computers. After a year-long trial, the judge in the case issued findings of fact in November 1999 that suggested he would almost certainly find Microsoft guilty of maintaining its Windows monopoly through unlawful means when he later ruled on the law in the case and the court appointed a well-known judge from the US Court of Appeals in Chicago to try to mediate a settlement in the case.

After mediation talks failed to produce a settlement, the judge ruled in April 2000 that Microsoft violated the antitrust laws. He found that Microsoft maintained its monopoly in operating-systems software by anti-competitive means and attempted to monopolise the Internet browser market by illegally integrating its Internet browser with Windows. Hearings on proposed remedies are scheduled for late May. Possible court-imposed remedies range from restrictions on certain behaviours to wide-ranging structural changes. Structural remedies could involve a break-up of the firm – either horizontally along business units or into identical pieces – or the auctioning or open licensing of Windows' source code. A horizontal break-up would prevent Microsoft from using its Windows monopoly to apply pressure in its application software and Internet businesses, but it would still leave a monopoly in the market for operating systems. An approach of restraining conduct could involve intensive court supervision of Microsoft's contracts, pricing procedures and other business decisions. Other remedies include disclosing the code for Windows and/or Internet Explorer, publishing a fixed price list for operating systems that is the same for all computer makers, and letting customers select the Internet browser shown on the desktop screen. It will be a challenge to develop remedies that both encourage competition and promote innovation in the information-technology market overall.

In other antitrust decisions, in December 1999 the Federal Trade Commission (FTC) approved Exxon's acquisition of Mobil for over $81 billion on the condition that the companies divest themselves of nearly 2 500 US gas stations, a major refinery and other assets. At the same time, the FTC warned that in the future big oil mergers might be blocked, and in February, the Commission announced it would seek an injunction in federal court to prevent the merger of BP Amoco and the Atlantic Richfield Company, which would create the largest US oil producer and refiner and third-largest private petroleum company in the world. The Commission argued that the deal would violate antitrust laws by allowing one firm to control 75 per cent of Alaska North Slope crude oil[51] and more than 40 per cent of the pipeline and storage facilities serving Cushing, Oklahoma.[52] However, many observers point to the global nature of the oil market as an argument rendering these market shares of only marginal economic significance. The merger was allowed after BP Amoco agreed to sell Atlantic Richfield's holdings of oil properties in Alaska and to sell facilities in Cushing.Finally, the US authorities have engaged in a surge in competition enforcement activity aimed at international price-fixing rings for some major traded goods, such as vitamins and lysine (a feed additive).

Commercial and external relations

During the past year or two the US economy has participated increasingly in world trade. Imports as a share of GDP rose from 12½ per cent of GDP at the beginning of 1997 to nearly 14 per cent at the end of 1999 (Figure 29). As well as reflecting the strength of demand, this is also the result of the falling level of tariffs imposed by the United States. Nearly one-third of all national tariff lines are now zero, while the average Most-Favoured-Nation rate has declined from 6.4 per cent in 1996 to 5.7 per cent in 1999. This rate can be expected to drop to 4.6 per cent once the implementation of the Uruguay Round and Information Technology Agreements are completed. In 1998, almost 60 per cent of all US imports entered the country tariff free, and, according to World Bank estimates, the average tariff rate was about 2.8 per cent. However, a number of tariff rates are at least three times the average in the areas of textiles, clothing and footwear and also on certain agricultural and food products. In the latter area, there are also a number of export and production subsidies. Recently, a new $100 million assistance plan was intro-

Figure 29. **Import penetration in the US market**
Imports of goods and services as per cent of GDP

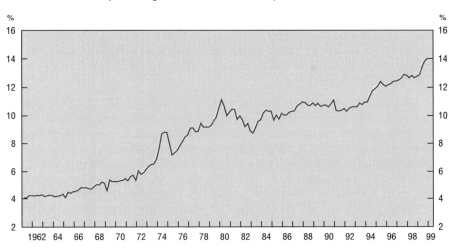

Source: Bureau of Economic Analysis.

duced for lamb; this has been the cause of some displeasure expressed by the Australian and New Zealand authorities. The principal elements of the programme were a three-year $30 million payment to improve quality through genetic selection and feedlot improvement; $15 million to help eradicate scrapie and $15 million of direct purchases of lamb by the Department of Agriculture.

The United States has been an active participant in multilateral dispute settlement mechanisms. In the period 1996 to March 1999, it was a party to 78 disputes brought to the World Trade Organisation (WTO), 48 as a plaintiff and 30 as a defendant. The past year was notable for several WTO rulings in favour of the United States. The WTO found that the European Union (EU) beef import ban generated unjustified economic loss to the United States. This followed a similar ruling in the area of bananas. In both cases, the United States was allowed to raise tariffs on a number of EU exports to the United States to compensate for the loss incurred following EU non-compliance with the ruling. The United States also won a case against Australia, following which the government of that country re-claimed part of the initial grant paid to the leading leather exporter but offered a further interest-free loan to the company. The WTO has ruled against this action, and the case is not yet finally resolved. It also won two cases against Canada. In the first, the United States had argued that the pervasive involvement of the government in a system that provides low-cost milk for export constituted an illegal subsidy. Canada is appealing the case. In the second case, the two governments settled a dispute over magazines. The agreement allows US magazines exported to Canada to carry 12 per cent of advertisements directed solely to the Canadian market. On the other hand, the United States lost the case that dealt with whether the partial US exemption of company taxation on certain export sales, through the use of export corporations, represented a subsidy. The United States has given notice that it will appeal that decision.

Multilateral discussions, under the aegis of the WTO, to initiate another round of trade talks have not yet resulted in a mandate for negotiations. Considerable differences existed between the United States and its partners in areas such as agriculture and labour standards at the December 1999 meeting in Seattle. Another set of multilateral talks, on trade in living modified organisms (LMOs), ended more successfully in January 2000. The talks were held under the auspices of the Convention on Biodiversity that was agreed at the 1992 Rio de Janeiro summit. The United States, which is not Party to the Convention, had expressed concerns that the Biosafety Protocol would impede trade in genetically modified food. This was of particular concern as last year more than a third of the planted area of corn, soyabeans and cotton in the United States used genetically-altered seeds.[53] The agreed text requires exporting countries to inform importing countries, and obtain their consent, before shipping any LMOs that may have adverse effects on conservation and the sustainability of biological diversity, although this obligation does not apply to genetically modified food, which only needs to be labelled as such. While the absence of scientific certainty cannot impede Parties from taking whatever risk management decision they see fit, they still have to respect their WTO obligation to provide scientific evidence for any trade-restrictive decisions they take.

Bilateral trade relations focused on Asia in 1999. On 15 November a bilateral agreement on WTO accession was concluded with China. Assuming other WTO members conclude their arguments and a multilateral agreement is reached on the application of WTO rules, the way will be open for China to join the WTO. The agreement provides for a significant cut in China's average tariff, with greater reductions in agricultural items of particular interest to the United States. Large and increasing tariff-rate quotas will be established for trade in certain bulk agricultural commodities such as grain, cotton and vegetable oil, with transactions moving progressively to the private sector. China promised to phase out agricultural export subsidies while agreeing to special safeguard rules. Outside the WTO, but on an enlarged bilateral basis and respecting WTO obligations, the United States and the European Union came to an agreement with Japan, Korea and later Taiwan concerning semiconductor trade practices. This accord replaces the 1994 US-Japan version that expired in July 1999. It provides that the chairmen of industry companies will meet, under the auspices of the World Semiconductor Council

(WSC), to discuss standardisation and market developments. The agreement provides that the competitiveness of companies and products should be the determinant of industrial success, not government intervention. Other countries can become party to it if their national industrial associations join the WSC. Elsewhere, the United States and Canada settled a dispute about the pricing of timber in British Columbia. They also resolved a dispute about regulations concerning sport fishing and tourism services in Ontario. In addition, the United States urged Japan to deregulate certain key sectors of its economy, for example, electricity transmission, telephone interconnection rates and policies in the area of housing. The United States also received a number of submissions from Japan dealing with certain preferential treatments for US products and services and various trade-related measures in distribution and telecommunications.

Issues involving anti-dumping and countervailing duty impositions

One of the areas that has elicited the most frequent and severe tensions between the United States and its trading partners continues to be US recourse to anti-dumping and countervailing duties. These remedies are allowed by the provisions of the Uruguay Round Agreements Act in 1994 that ensures compliance with the WTO Anti-Dumping Agreement. They are also theoretically justified as an attempt to offset international price discrimination[54] and unfair provision of public subsidies. However, some allege that many cases are launched by the producers in an attempt to discourage foreign competitors,[55] whether or not there is a clear case of pricing that violates WTO provisions. Once they become adept at filing such petitions the incentives for them to file further petitions in the future may be enhanced. Furthermore, other countries may, in turn, increasingly rely on such instruments of their own.[56] For many reasons governments have restrained their use of overt subsidies in recent years, and the number of US countervailing duty cases has trended down steadily since the mid-1980s (Figure 30). Accordingly, focus has been increasingly concentrated on alleged cases of dumping and the resulting question of protective duties. US anti-dumping case initiations also fell off in the late 1980s, in line with improved economic conditions[57] in the tradable-goods sectors that resulted from the dollar's depreciation and the business cycle expansion phase. But such pressures for protection rebounded once the economy weakened in the early 1990s, before receding once again in the current upswing. However, it is noteworthy that the year 1998 saw a resurgence in case activity despite the strength of the ongoing expansion, largely because of the Asian crisis.

It is in the steel sector, a long-time *habitué* of such instruments,[58] that there have been the greatest tensions in the past couple of years, as a number of anti-dumping and countervailing duty cases have been instigated and duties implemented, no doubt resulting from record post-war price declines in the wake of the 1997-98 Asia crisis and the increase in imports' US market share. Most recently, in

Figure 30. **Anti-dumping and countervailing duty investigations**

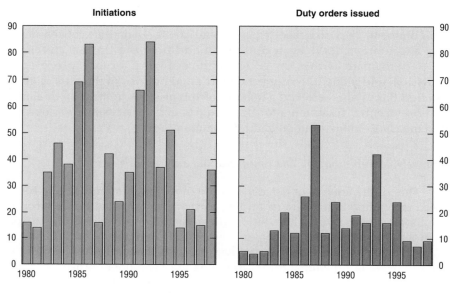

A. Anti-dumping case activity

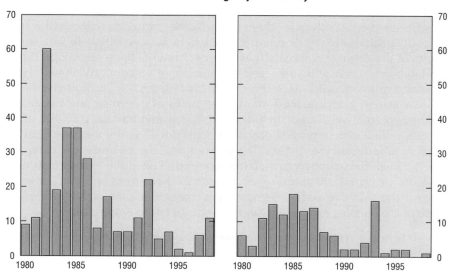

B. Countervailing duty case activity

Source: Department of Commerce, International Trade Administration.

January 2000, the US Commerce Department proposed anti-dumping duties of up to 80 per cent on imports of cold-rolled steel sheet from six countries. At the same time, following a favourable finding by the US International Trade Commission, duties were imposed of up to 59 per cent on Japanese heavy steel plate exports to the United States. Both decisions have elicited strong reaction by Japanese producers and the Government of Japan. By 1999 about 80 per cent of Japan's steel exports to the United States were covered by anti-dumping duties. Despite the establishment of a "US-Japan Steel Dialogue" in September 1999 to discuss sectoral trade issues, the Japanese authorities decided to request bilateral consultations with the United States in accordance with WTO rules regarding a number of issues related to the US anti-dumping finding on hot-rolled steel. Japan has now requested the establishment of a WTO settlement panel to examine the matter. Also, the European Communities and Japan, complained to the WTO that the 1916 US Anti-Dumping Act, which was being cited by US steel producers in cases against German and Japanese steel producers, was not in conformity with the WTO trade rules nor with the Anti-Dumping Agreement. The WTO panel recommended that the Act should be repealed, since it is the Wilson Tariff Act of 1930, as amended, that is the implementing legislation for multilateral anti-dumping provisions. The United States is to appeal this decision.

Agriculture

In the past two years, government support to agriculture has soared. The producer support estimate has risen to 24 per cent in 1999 from just 14 per cent in 1997. This reversal in the longer-term trend to lower aid came despite the Federal Agriculture Improvement Reform Act of 1996 that specifies a progressive reduction in payments for certain crops in the period to 2002. In the last two years, exceptional payments, totalling $5.5 billion in 1999, were made to producers through the market loss assistance programme, in order to compensate them for low prices and falling income, and natural disaster relief payments of $1.2 billion were made. Moreover, loan-related deficiency payments to crops increased from $250 million in 1997 to $4 billion in 1998 and $10 billion in 1999. The scheduled end of the Dairy Support Purchase Programme was postponed until 2000, and the average export subsidy for milk rose by 13 per cent, bringing the producer support estimate for milk to 57 per cent, the second highest for any product. In addition, an import quota was introduced on sheep meat imports, lessening the linkage of this sector with world markets. However, aid to farmers has been concentrated on measures that do not directly affect domestic prices except in the dairy and sugar sectors. As a result, domestic agricultural prices are closely aligned with those seen in external trade, and consumers only paid an implicit tax of 2 per cent over world prices, net of the subsidies paid through the Food Stamp programme. Overall, the significant increase in payments based on crop output indirectly depressed both domestic and world market prices and helped isolate producers from market signals.

Scope for further action

While competition in local telephone service has been relatively slow to emerge there is considerable promise for local competition to develop due to technological advances in alternative delivery systems. However, the speed at which these systems develop depends in part on regulatory developments aimed at implementing existing unbundling policies for the local loop and ensuring access to high speed local infrastructures by new market entrants. In this context, the recent action by the FCC that directed local telephone companies to share their lines with providers of high speed Internet access and other data services is an important step. The universal service funding mechanism should be reviewed to minimise the economic distortion in the telecommunications market. While the regulatory structure remains complex, with overlapping jurisdiction between state and federal regulators, the 1996 Telecommunications Act, which provides for the pre-emption of state legislation that raises barriers to entry, was a step i n the right direction. The United States has become even more open in recent years with the import share rising and tariff rates falling. The government has been heavily involved in the international trade area. The United States has been a party to a large number of multilateral trade disputes in the WTO in the past few years and last year negotiated a bilateral trade agreement with China and a multilateral agreement on semiconductor trade practices. Nonetheless, protectionist pressures in certain industries, particularly steel, have grown. Anti-dumping and countervailing duty investigations have picked up in this area. To the extent that discretion is involved, it is important that the use of these mechanisms be kept to a minimum.

Financial modernisation

Gradual deregulation over more than a decade

The strict regulation imposed on the association of banks, other financial enterprises by the Glass Steagall Act and the Bank Holding Company Act has been gradually eroded. The exposure of commercial banks to the remainder of the financial sector was, in theory, strictly limited. In practise, the pressure from the convergence of banking and capital markets and new technological developments has meant that for more than a decade there has been a progressive movement to eliminate these barriers. In particular, bank holding companies have been allowed to move steadily into the provision of other financial services. As long ago as 1987, the Federal Reserve Board allowed bank holding companies to establish so-called section 20 affiliates that could engage in certain activities linked to the trading or underwriting of commercial paper and mortgage-backed securities. In 1989, this provision was broadened to allow trading and underwriting of corporate debt and equity, provided that the revenue from all of these types of activity did not exceed

5 and then 10 per cent of the revenue of the section 20 affiliate; this proportion was raised to 25 per cent in 1996. By December 1999, there were 23 domestic bank holding companies engaged in corporate bond or equity dealing or underwriting in the United States, and their commercial bank affiliates accounted for almost 50 per cent of the total domestic assets of the US banking system. All of the 20 largest commercial banks had holding company affiliates that were engaged in this type of activity. In addition, there were 17 foreign bank holding companies engaged in this sector.

Other fields have also been opened to deposit-taking institutions. Since 1913, national banks could sell insurance in towns of less than 5 000 inhabitants. A 1996 court decision clarified that states were not able to prohibit this activity. This court ruling allowed banks to sell insurance, provided that the insurance subsidiary was physically located in a town with less than 5 000 habitants. Finally, the linkage between commercial activities and deposit-taking was blurred by the spread of thrift holding companies that owned only one savings and loan institution – a so-called unitary thrift – and which were able to have commercial subordinates. By the beginning of 1998, one-quarter of all thrift deposits were held by unitary thrifts also engaged in non-banking activities, while over two-thirds of total thrift assets were held by unitary thrifts. The pace of change appeared to be accelerating in 1998-99 when both financial and non-financial companies applied for unitary thrift charters.

At the same time as this liberalisation was underway, the last elements of protection for small banks were being removed with the passage of the Riegle-Neal Interstate Banking and Branching Efficiency Act in 1994. This change was the culmination of a trend towards greater freedom of establishment for banking institutions. It had started in the late 1980s with the abolition of intra- and inter-state restrictions on branching and was followed by many states, allowing out-of-state bank holding companies to establish or buy separately chartered banks in the state. The 1994 Act allowed out-of-state banks to avoid the need to establish new banks to cross state borders and permitted interstate branch banking. States had until mid-1997 to opt out of the provisions of the 1994 Act. The net result of this liberalisation has been a marked consolidation of the banking system, with the number of banks falling by 20 per cent between 1993 and 1998. Since 1997, there has been a move to mergers amongst major institutions that has created several banks with national reach. Indeed, over the 1990s the share of national bank deposits held by the major ten banks almost doubled. Concentration in major metropolitan areas did not, however, increase.

The Gramm-Leach-Bliley Act

With many of previous barriers to entry in the banking and finance sector having been reduced, either through legislation, regulatory action or judicial review, in 1999 Congress finally passed a replacement for the 1933 Glass Steagall Act and authorised a general broadening of the financial operations allowed for organisations that owned a bank. This bill, the Gramm-Leach-Bliley Financial Modernization Act, provides for a considerable widening of the activities that both bank holding companies and banks can undertake. Their range of activities is extended to cover a long list of existing financial activities. In addition, any other activity that is not included in the list can be added, provided that the Federal Reserve and the Treasury consider that the activity is financial or incidental to financial activities. Moreover, any activity that the Federal Reserve considers to be complimentary to a financial activity and which does not pose a substantial safety and soundness risk to the bank or bank affiliate can also be added to the approved list of activities. The legislation explicitly prevents state laws from overriding its provisions.

Banking organisations that are well capitalised and well managed are now, in principle, allowed to enter fully three fields where their scope was previously restricted. Once detailed regulations are set, they will be able to own and operate insurance companies without any geographic limitation and will be able to underwrite insurance for the first time. In addition, all banks will be able to undertake title insurance, an area that was previously open only to state-chartered banks. The qualified holding companies will also be able to undertake merchant banking activities, which are generally defined as the purchase and holding for resale of equity and business assets.[59] In addition, there will no longer be a restriction on the proportion of income that a bank holding company affiliate can derive from underwriting or dealing in corporate debt or equities.

Financial institutions are faced with a choice as to the structure that is used to deliver this wider range of subsidiaries. Well capitalised, well managed nationally chartered banks, whose debt has an A rating, can create financial subsidiaries to undertake the sale of insurance or underwriting and dealing of securities, but the equity investment in the subsidiary cannot be counted towards fulfilment of the bank's equity-capital ratio. Financial subsidiaries, however, will not be able to undertake merchant banking activities for at least a further five years, nor will they be able to undertake insurance underwriting or real estate development. Moreover, financial subsidiaries cannot exceed 45 per cent of the bank's total assets, with a ceiling of $50 billion, and the 50 largest nationally chartered banks will have to issue debt that obtains a high rating from private credit agencies before they can establish such subsidiaries. Bank holding companies that are well capitalised and well managed can be transformed into Financial Holding Companies whose subsidiaries can then undertake all allowed financial activities. Both they and national banks, however, will have to obtain satisfactory ratings under the Community Re-Investment Act[60] (CRA) in order to create subsidiaries conducting the wider business lines that are now permitted. Financial holding companies created by insurance and securities firms that purchase a bank will be allowed to continue with any non-conforming non-financial activities for only ten years, with a possible further five-year extension.

In contrast to the widening of the scope of banks in the financial sector, the new Act reduces the extent to which deposit-taking institutions can be linked to commercial enterprises. Banking organisations have always faced that prohibition, and continue to do so, but the Act ends the authority for unitary thrift holding companies to acquire a non-financial firm. However, existing unitary thrift holding companies can continue to operate and will not have to divest any commercial activities but can make no additional non-financial acquisitions. On the other hand, existing unitary thrift holding companies cannot be sold to commercial companies. Legislators appear to have been concerned about the linkage of "commerce and banking" and thus eliminated the one exception to the general prohibition of such linkages. An early proposal to create a new form of uninsured wholesale bank, that would be subject to only modest regulation and would only take deposits above the limit for federal deposit insurance ($100 000), was not included in the final legislation. It became clear that there was no support for allowing financial holding companies that had a bank affiliate to create such a new bank because it would not be subject to the lending restrictions of the CRA.

Regulation of the new financial conglomerates

Many industry sources expect that most links between banks and other financial enterprises will be created through financial holding companies rather than through subsidiaries of national banks. In this case, the Federal Reserve would become the overall supervisor of the institution. Nonetheless, the individual non-bank affiliate will continue to be supervised by the appropriate industry regulator, either the Securities and Exchange Commission or state insurance agencies. The Federal Reserve will not directly regulate the non-bank affiliates, as to do so might have generated the expectation that the federal government was implicitly guaranteeing the safety and soundness of these companies, thereby widening the federal safety net. Rather the Federal Reserve will act as an "umbrella" supervisor. It will be particularly concerned with developments in the affiliates that could create risks for the bank and undermine its safety and soundness. In this regard it will pay particular attention to cross-lending between banks, affiliates and their customers, unusual risk exposures in affiliates and to the consolidated position of the financial holding company and the adequacy of its centralised risk management.

The role of government supervisors could be augmented by greater reliance on information from the market on the health of financial enterprises. There have been a series of proposals for the greater compulsory use of non-insured liabilities by banks. Most recently Calomiris (1997) and Litan and Rauch (1997) have suggested that banks should have to issue such liabilities regularly, with a compulsory issuance schedule. Such securities would provide direct information from the primary market, and further indirect information would come from their subsequent pricing in the secondary market. In theory, the market information provided by the scale of issuance and prices could be used to trigger bank examinations or even to result in a forced contraction of bank balance sheets (Calomiris, 1999). Indeed, the recent Gramm-Leach-Bliley Act requires supervisors to study the use of subordinated debentures by banking organisations.

There is already a substantial market in the subordinated debt of financial institutions. By end-1998 bank holding companies had issued $102.8 billion of such debt, more than four times end-1991 figures in real terms, representing an average annual growth of 23 per cent. This debt is however almost exclusively issued by the 50 largest bank holding companies. It represents about 2.9 per cent of their total assets. Smaller banks find the issuance costs of subordinated debt too large, though some scholars suggest that this may change if pools of small bank liabilities are eventually securitised. Market terms for large organisations' subordinated debt have become standardised, facilitating comparisons across companies, with the initial term typically being ten years, and there being no embedded call or put options. The banks generally sell the interest coupons on their debt for floating rate coupons in the swaps market.

There is evidence from the market that spreads over Treasuries for a given bank or holding company are correlated with accounting measures of risk. This is even the case for banks that are generally classed as too big to fail (Federal Reserve System Study Group, 1999), though the premium demanded from them is generally less than for smaller banks, other things being equal. Further research suggests that the information provided by the market and supervisors is complementary. However, there is evidence that the market underprices risk, in that issuance activity appears to increase as accounting measures of risk rise.

Overall, the evidence suggests that official regulators would gain considerable insight into the riskiness of banks through requiring them to regularly issue subordinated debt. Market practices would have to change though. Such a provision for regular issuance of debt could, however, apply only to large banks. Issuance costs are prohibitive for smaller banks, and small issues quickly become illiquid in the secondary market. According to the Federal Reserve System Study Group (1999), it is difficult to determine the optimum amount of debt that should be issued and the regularity with which it should be marketed. However, these parameters would need to set by the supervisors, taking into account issuance costs and the size of the bank's balance sheet.

Government-sponsored enterprises

At about the same time as the now-abandoned Glass-Steagall Act was introduced in the 1930s, a number of government-sponsored agencies, later to become enterprises, were created (for a more detailed discussion of these enter-prises see Annex I). These institutions were developed in order to overcome per-ceived problems of the financial system as it was then. In particular, the institutions were charged with developing the market for housing and agricultural finance. In exchange for agreeing to specific limits on their activities, these now privately-owned institutions enjoy some privileges denied to other private firms. Even though no explicit guarantee exits, the market appears to believe that the federal government will not allow these institutions to default on their debt. In addition, they enjoy a line of credit with the Treasury and a number of other advantages (see Annex I). Recently Administration officials have suggested that this line of credit should be abolished, sparking a widening in the spread of GSE notes over Treasuries. These institutions are now major players in the financial markets, and, in 1998 issued net new debt of $278 billion (3.4 per cent of GDP), in addition to their role in marketing a further $181 billion (2.1 per cent of GDP) of federally-guaranteed pooled-mortgage debt.

One of these institutions has developed in way that was scarcely foreseen by Congress. The Federal Home Loan Bank System was initially created to provide long-term finance for savings and loan associations, with the objective of helping capital to flow to those regions that were short of deposits. In practice, the System functions as provider of finance for any bank that cares to join, as the rules that res-tricted membership to banks with more than 10 per cent of their assets in mortgages have become easy to fulfil through the purchase of mortgage-backed-securities. The System had assets of $531 billion by end-September 1999, making it bigger than all but one bank and all but two bank holding companies. Indeed, it was the largest issuer of securities in the world in 1998, though much of this reflected re-financing of short-term bills. While the System was designed to aid local thrift institutions, over 31 per cent of its advances went to ten large borrowers in September 1999. In addi-tion, the System uses its funding advantage to invest in market securities. The Sys-tem appears to be well-capitalised, but in reality government-insured deposits fund most of its capital stock. Banks only have to put up 1.6 per cent of their own equity for each dollar of stock that they own in the System.

The newly enacted Gramm-Leach-Bliley Act widened the activities of the Federal Home Loan Bank System. Notably, it has been given the right to make advances to smaller depository institutions in support of non-housing assets. The capital structure of the System has also been altered in a way that appears to per-mit the System to operate with less capital (see Annex I). Finally, the fixed pay-ment that the System was obliged to pay to help finance the clean-up of the savings and loans crisis has been converted to a payment based on a percentage of System earnings. This gives Congress an incentive to allow even further expan-sion of the system as higher payments to the government coffers would allow grea-ter expenditure under current pay-as-you-go budgetary rules.

As far as the other institutions are concerned, the major policy issue continues to be the extent to which they are subsidised. Various government studies in
the early 1990s concluded that the institutions were indeed able to raise money at
lower rates than comparable private-sector institutions. Moreover, a significant
part of the lower margin was not passed on to mortgage borrowers but captured by
the shareholders of these enterprises. More generally, however, there must be
doubt about the need to favour the financing of house purchases when the return
on such investment is low relative to that on other forms of capital.

Highly leveraged institutions and derivatives

The President's Working Group for Financial Markets established after the
near failure of Long Term Capital Management (LTCM) found that as a group hedge
funds do not pose any particular risk to the financial system. Their total capital is
relatively small (between $200 and $300 billion), although they held about
$1 trillion of assets, which is considerably less than the almost $7 trillion held by
pension funds, $5 trillion by mutual funds and $4 trillion by commercial banks.
Moreover, their capital is spread between some 3 000 different funds. In any event,
LTCM had managed to accumulate a very highly levered portfolio, but not one that
was unusually large by the standards of those held by a number of banking institutions. For instance, at end-1998, the nominal values of outstanding derivatives
held by five bank holding companies and two investment banks were each greater
than $1 trillion – about the amount held by LTCM, while the leverage of the five
largest investment banks was similar to that of LTCM. Seen from a systemic point
of view, then, the LTCM was more an example of the risk that a highly leveraged
institution can generate than of the risk posed by hedge funds themselves.

The proposals of the Administration thus focussed on reducing the risk
flowing from excessive credit extension, rather than proposing new regulations
concerning hedge funds. Two legislative proposals were made both to amend bankruptcy legislation. One would improve the ability of counter-parties to net out
transactions across financial products, and the other would ensure that a foreign
receiver did not have priority over US laws when the principal business activity of
a foreign enterprise (such as LTCM)[61] was mainly in the United States. Managing
lending, though, was seen as an essentially private-sector activity that could be
enhanced by greater disclosure by hedge funds and by banks with credit exposure
to highly levered institutions. However, it is often not the size of the exposure but
the riskiness of the counter-parties' portfolio that is the problem. Here, banking
and securities supervisors have to ensure that lending institutions have appropriate risk management systems in place. In this context, in 1999 twelve major
financial institutions formed a Counter Party Risk Management Group that developed a number of concrete proposals for dealing with the management of risk for
those who provide credit-based services to major counter parties.

The last *Survey* also concluded that a number of changes to the Commodity Exchange Act (CEA) would have improved the transparency of a number of financial derivatives markets. Notably the report argued that there should be no regulatory impediment to the development of clearing houses in derivative markets or to hinder the growth of new computerised markets in this area. Finally, it was argued that the legal position of swap contracts should be clarified. In 1999, the President's Working Group proposed changes to the CEA that went along the same lines as these recommendations. They would allow the development of computerised trading of standardised derivatives and of clearing houses, as well as clarifying the position of swaps and a number of hybrid financial instruments so that they can develop outside the remit of the CEA.

Evaluation and scope for further action

Financial deregulation has been pursued in order to improve the economic welfare of the public through efficiencies, increased competition, convenience, lower prices and new products. The hope behind the latest legislation is that by allowing the combination of financial intermediaries costs can be reduced more competitive pressures can be unleashed and the public will receive improved financial services. The experience of the 1990s suggests that gains can be expected both from the new Act and from the earlier 1994 branch banking act. There has been some controversy as to whether bank consolidation has resulted in efficiencies. Banking industry consultants and analysts have pointed to significant savings, but most economic analyses have been sceptical about the extent of cost savings. Recently, however, more evidence has emerged that suggests mergers have effectively reduced costs. Kwan and Wilcox (1999) suggests that the reason that earlier studies have failed to find cost savings is that they have failed to distinguish between economic and accounting costs.[62] Notably, mergers can result in a significant increase in depreciation charges that do not represent an economic cost. Excluding such charges, bank mergers have resulted in significant reductions in labour costs and, in the period 1993 to 1995, reduced total non-interest costs by 0.1 per cent of total assets, with cost savings maintained as the size of the merger increased. Indeed, a growing number of mergers have been amongst major banks, reflecting a desire to increase geographical scope after the deregulation of interstate banking. The experience of earlier deregulation of branch banking appears to have been positive as well. Jayaratne and Strahan (1997) found that the most profitable banks expanded after deregulation and that states that deregulated subsequently experienced increases in the growth of real disposable income and state product.

As to the use of section 20 affiliates by bank holding companies, this too appears to have improved banks' financial position. Kwan (1998) found that while earnings from some activities, notably securities trading, did exhibit greater volatility than traditional banking activity, the fact that there was little correlation between the average returns in banking and the new operations brought an improvement to the overall return of the bank holding companies' portfolios.

While the continued modernisation of the financial system has been achieved in a way that should minimise any extension of the federal safety net, it has not resulted in any roll-back of implicit federal subsidies to insured depository institutions or government-sponsored enterprises and their clients. Nor has it lowered the extent to which they are captured by the private sector. If anything, the Gramm-Leach-Bliley Act has increased the scope of one of these institutions – the FHLB system. It appears to lower the capital ratio for the FHLB System; to reduce the power of the regulator to appoint key managers; to increase the scope of its activities outside the housing sector; and, by taking no action to reduce the arbitrage portfolios held by the System, to accept activities that appear outside the System's public policy remit. In a modern, technologically advanced financial system in which large thrifts can obtain market financing, there appears little purpose for the FHLB System.

The other parts of the GSE network should also be reformed. The implicit subsidy to these enterprises appears to be captured mainly by their shareholders, suggesting breaking any possible linkage with the Federal government, or if this is not possible, charging for the implicit subsidy and remove special exemptions on securities registration. Indeed, the CBO (1999a) estimates that charging for registration on GSE debt would raise some $2 billion of revenue over the period 2000-09, lowering the high rate of return of equity for GSEs by 1 percentage point. However, there is a larger question as to whether even that part of the subsidy that is passed on to people who hold mortgages represents an effective use of public funds. The social rate of return on housing in the United States is well below that on either education or other physical capital, even when account is taken of the lower risk of real-estate investment (Taylor, 1998). Moreover, a residential mortgage is not necessarily used for real-estate investment but can be used to fund consumption or to refinance non-housing debt.

Finally, no progress was made in rationalising the regulation of deposit-taking institutions. As the 1999 *Survey* pointed out, there are five different types of institutions that are regulated by four different federal agencies and at least 50 state agencies. With thrifts becoming more bank-like and less specialised in mortgage lending there is the question as to whether the Office of Thrift Supervision should not be merged into an expanded Office of the Comptroller of the Currency. This agency could also take over the role of the FDIC in regulating state-chartered banks that are not members of the Federal Reserve system. More fundamentally, there is a case for giving a greater role to the market as provider of early warning signals on the health of banks. Such an approach would require the regular issuance of subordinated debt by the largest banks.

Summary

The strength and flexibility of the US economy has been amply illustrated in the past few years. The ease with which financial markets can direct capital to new and emerging industries has been well illustrated, while the ability of the labour market to redirect workers and deliver low nominal wages has also been clearly demonstrated. Nonetheless, there are areas where structural reforms could still be made, especially in fields that are sometimes removed from economic considerations. This is noticeably the case in education, health and agriculture. All the new recommendations that have been made in this Chapter are summarised in Box 6. A considerable number of structural policy recommendations have been made in previous surveys (Box 7), but many remain unheeded.

Box 6. Structural recommendations in this Survey

Social markets

- Improve health care coverage for poor adults;
- Focus aid on those working on raising the Earned Income Tax Credit, rather than boosting the minimum wage;
- Expand funding for charter schools;
- Improve resources available to under-funded school districts;
- Bring more schools up to the standards that are in place.

Product markets

- Roll back the extra support given to farmers in the past two years;
- Remove regulatory barriers to the introduction of calling-party-pays cellular telephone service;
- Review the universal service funding mechanism to minimise economic distortion;
- Keep the use of anti-dumping and countervailing duty orders to a minimum.

Financial markets

- Reduce the number of bank regulators.
- Require major banks to issue subordinated debt regularly.
- Implement recommendations of President's Working Party to lessen controls over the development of OTC markets.
- Implement new netting arrangements for financial products in bankruptcy procedures.
- Break links of government-sponsored-enterprises with the federal government.

Box 7. Summary of previous structural recommendations

Year	Recommendation	Action
Labour markets		
1996	Avoid increasing the federal minimum wage any further	Real minimum wage increased somewhat
1996	Expand Earned Income Tax Credit	Proposal in 2001 Budget
1996	Improve support for training and child care under welfare reform	The combination of a fixed block grant and falling welfare rolls has allowed increased state-level spending in this area
1996	Identify strategies to increase employment of disabled	None
1997	Boost training and education for the low-skilled in areas with high low-skill immigration	None
1997	Adopt a more skilled labour focus to immigration policy	Number of visas for employment in high-tech industries increased
1997	Reduce maximum duration of visas	None
1997	Increase number of wage-and-hours inspectors to reduce exploitation of immigrants	None
1997	Penalise employers of illegal immigrants	None
Education		
1996	Develop national standards for educational subjects	Voluntary standards introduced
1996	Experiment with non-traditional schools	Charter schools expanded, voucher systems started in some States
1996	Reduce funding disparities across school districts	None
1997	Improve public efforts to offer English language training to immigrants	None
Ageing and health care		
1996	Improve access to health insurance for working poor	Child Health Insurance Program introduced
1999	Take appropriate steps to secure the future of the Social Security System	No reforms, but non-Social Security budget balanced
1999	Make proposed voluntary savings accounts mandatory in order to complement Social Security	Initial proposal not passed, new proposal in 2000 Budget
1999	Curb Medicare spending	1998 Budget curbed spending but 1999 Budget reversed some changes
1999	Introduce more effective gate-keeping for long-term care	None
1999	Develop proposals for greater use of managed care in government health programmes	Proposal to increase price competition through competitive defined benefit schemes
Product markets		
1996	Reduce spending under new farm legislation	Spending has increased and there are new proposals for further spending in 2001 Budget
1996	Reform environmental legislation and regulations	Trading in nitrous oxide emissions introduced
1999	Improve competition in telephone and electricity industries	New proposals on the wholesale transmission of electricity
Financial markets		
1996	Pass legislation to decompartmentalise the financial industry	Gramm-Leach-Bliley Act passed
1996	Allow banks to hold equity stakes in companies	Possible under Gramm-Leach-Bliley Act
1997	Reassess bankruptcy and patent laws with aim of curbing abuses	Proposed legislation failed to pass yet
1999	Allow organised markets for OTC derivatives with less regulation than in retail markets	Proposals made for reform
1999	Quickly resolve issues of competence over supervisors for proposed financial conglomerates	Federal Reserve becomes the umbrella supervisor for the new category of financial holding company

IV. Encouraging environmentally sustainable growth

The extent to which the world's advanced and developing economies alike have been progressing in a narrow material fashion at the cost of drawing on finite natural assets and damaging their ecologies is a subject of both popular and professional debate. The question of whether expectations of ever-increasing affluence can be met without irreversible environmental deterioration can be set against a belief that increasing incomes and wealth provide the wherewithal to pay for better environmental outcomes. Whether economic development is sustainable in both environmental and other social dimensions has become a focus of increasing attention in recent years, both in the United States and in the OECD more generally.[63] In the United States a "President's Council on Sustainable Development" was set up in 1993; its recommendations were published in 1996 and were further developed in its report in 1999 (President's Council for Sustainable Development, 1999).

Sustainable development covers a very wide range of issues that cannot all be dealt with here. This chapter limits discussion to a number of environmental and natural resource issues, highlighting their links with economic activity and economic policies, in particular investigating how well the implementation of environmental and economic policies are integrated so as to take account of externalities and spillovers between them. After presenting some background to the evolution of US environmental policy and the institutions charged with developing and implementing it, the chapter outlines some of the most important current policy problems. Looking at how they are being tackled, the analysis will focus first on certain particular environmental or natural resource issues, then on the use of certain types of policy instruments, and finally on some specific economic sectors. A separate section discusses the role of cost-benefit analysis in the design and operation of environmental policy.

Environmental policy in historical perspective

A number of spectacular incidents in the late 1960s brought environmental problems to the attention of both policymakers and a much wider public than previously.[64] The creation of the President's Council for Environmental Quality (CEQ) in 1969 and of the Environmental Protection Agency (EPA) in 1970 followed on from this. The Clean Air Act (1970) and the Clean Water Act (1972) were the first major pieces of comprehensive federal environmental legislation.[65] The 1969 National Environmental Policy Act brought in a requirement for federal agencies to prepare an Environmental Impact Statement for any major federal action likely to have a significant impact on the environment; this did not, however, require an assessment of the costs of this impact.

The consideration of cost has been the source of some tension throughout the subsequent period. The legislation of the 1970s did not generally require proposed environmental regulations or action to pass any cost-benefit test although some legislation did specify cost, feasibility and cost-effectiveness in setting standards.[66] According to Portney (1998), while legislation did not explicitly rule out the use of cost considerations, court cases have established the principle that unless such considerations are explicitly required, they are not allowed. Also, as in all other countries, the instruments used to implement policies were of the "command and control" type, where standards were set and "best available" technologies mandated without formal analysis of whether they entailed the most efficient use of resources.

Although concern with the costs of environmental policy was never completely absent, the environmental improvements that resulted from this wave of legislation were generally felt to be so substantial that their benefits exceeded the costs by a wide margin, even if the costs of the gains achieved could nevertheless have been lower. During the 1980s, concern with the possible costs of regulation (not only in the environmental arena) grew; the implementation of Regulatory Impact Assessments[67] – under which the costs and benefits of major proposed regulations must be assessed before they are introduced – is a response to this.

The setting-up of the Environmental Protection Agency (EPA) might have been expected to lead to a concentration of responsibility for all, or at least most, environmental issues in that agency. This did not occur, however, although the EPA does have responsibility for the major clean air, clean water and toxic waste programmes. Some sectoral agencies have responsibility for environmental issues relating to that sector or their own facilities, notably the Departments of Agriculture, Energy and Transportation. The Interior Department is charged with handling most conservation and natural resource management issues; it contains, for example, the Fish and Wildlife Service, although the National Oceanic and Atmospheric Administration of the Department of Commerce covers maritime fisheries.[68]

In addition to federal legislation and agencies, individual States can set their own standards for many media. They are responsible for ensuring compliance with federal or local air quality standards, for example, following a State Implementation Plan that must be approved by the EPA. The enthusiasm with which compliance is enforced varies from state to state.

Although the CEQ exists to give the President advice on the general direction of environmental policy and often has a co-ordinating role in policy development, it is not an agency for co-ordinating the implementation of environmental policy with that of other programmes. This role falls to the Office of Management and Budget (OMB).[69] A pilot programme of risk management budgeting (planned under the Bush administration for the 1992 budget) intended to direct resources to lower cost rather than high cost programmes was not implemented in subsequent years by the succeeding Clinton administration.

Quite apart from these government agencies in the executive branch, non-governmental organisations also play an important role. On the one hand, a variety of non-profit organisations engage in activities ranging from pressing for particular policies to disseminating information and undertaking research. On the other hand, the courts are involved in a large part of the policy implementation process on both sides: there are challenges to government environmental standards or actions that must be adjudicated, at the same time as environmental groups take legal action to force government agencies to take more vigorous regulatory and enforcement measures. In practice, the courts often play an important role, setting constraints on the EPA's interpretation of the Clean Air Act, for example, as well as having an important influence on its regulatory and enforcement priorities. The potential influence of the courts can be important also in the interpretation of legislation[70] and may also affect the design of regulations – the need to reduce the possibility of ambiguity that court actions could expose may lead regulatory agencies to favour simple schemes over potentially more cost-effective schemes to reduce the possibility of disruptive litigation.[71]

A brief overview of some major current environmental issues

The United States has examples of most kinds of environmental and natural resource problems. The OECD *Environmental Performance Review* of the United States (OECD, 1996) provided a comprehensive overview of most such problems, which vary enormously by region. The present chapter focuses on:

- the economic and policy issues arising from particular environmental issues, specifically air and water pollution and global warming;[72]
- certain specific industries, agriculture and road transport; and
- certain issues common to all environmental policies, in particular the role of the courts and of cost-benefit calculations.

As in most OECD countries, levels of air and water pollution have generally been much reduced since the 1970s and are continuing to decline as revisions to the Clean Air and Clean Water Acts or periodic re-evaluation of regulations have progressively tightened standards. Nevertheless, air quality is still a major issue, with relatively more attention now being paid to ozone concentrations and fine particulate matter.

Global warming is a related issue, since the same emission sources are generally responsible for greenhouse gases (GHGs) and air pollution. The United States, along with most other countries, will not meet the commitment made in 1992 (when the UN Framework Convention on Climate Change (UNFCCC) was established at Rio de Janeiro) that GHG emissions be no higher in the year 2000 than in 1990; however, it is a signatory to the Kyoto Protocol to the UNFCCC (though it has not ratified it), which would commit it to quite substantial reductions in emissions by 2008-12, compared with those projected in the absence of policy changes. The United States, with much higher emissions, both per capita and in absolute terms, than other countries, is a major contributor to increases in global concentrations of GHGs. It is also potentially quite sensitive to damaging effects of climate change on agriculture and on the sea level, for example. These impacts are rather uncertain and are the subject of ongoing research in the United States; some recent work suggests that the economy could adjust so that the economic costs of such changes in the United States might be lower than early estimates suggested (see Mendelsohn *et al.*, 1994 and Mendelsohn, 1999).

Given low population density, the disposal of non-hazardous waste appears to be less of a problem generally in the United States than in many other OECD countries (at least as far as the federal authorities are concerned), even though per capita municipal waste generation is the highest the world, and the waste recycling rate, especially for glass, is relatively low.[73] Toxic waste, with its more obvious impact on health and well -being, has a higher profile. Dealing with existing contaminated sites raises somewhat different problems from preventing or cleaning up after new releases of toxic substances, even if the environmental impacts are similar. In both cases the United States is becoming "cleaner" after two decades of action under "Superfund" and other legislation.

Water supply (as distinct from its quality) poses a number of interesting questions throughout the western United States. The geographical distribution of rainfall, the structure of property rights governing water and changing population and industrial structures have made it hard for the competing needs of households, agriculture, industry and wildlife to be reconciled.

Environmental policy in practice

By selecting the relatively narrow range of issues outlined in the previous section, the coverage of US policy presented here is necessarily incomplete. The aim of this section is to use these examples of US policy and the policy formation process to illustrate some of the strengths and weaknesses that have relevance beyond this immediate focus.

Air quality standards

The Clean Air Act (CAA) was originally passed in 1970. The legislation itself does not define what is "clean" air but requires the EPA to identify air pollutants that are harmful to human health and welfare and promulgate National Ambient Air Quality Standards (NAAQS) that protect human health with "an adequate margin of safety" – the primary standard.[74] The EPA thus establishes air quality standards in the form of limits on concentrations of sulphur dioxide, nitrogen dioxide, lead, particulate matter, ozone, and carbon monoxide (CO)[75] in the light of its own views on what is feasible and desirable. The NAAQS are indeed revised from time to time: those currently in force date from revisions promulgated in 1987. In 1997 the EPA promulgated tighter standards for two pollutants: ozone and particulate matter.[76]

A number of industry associations and two states appealed against these tightened standards, and in May 1999 the Washington DC circuit appeals court upheld the appeal, effectively preventing implementation of the new standards, pending action by the EPA to meet certain conditions or a successful appeal by the EPA to a higher court. Although this case may be rather special, it and its context reveal a number of important points about US environmental policy-making.

One is that air quality standards are being tightened while many states are not in compliance with the existing ones and while air quality is still generally improving as measures taken to meet existing standards take effect (Figure 31). The EPA appears to be aiming for a continuous improvement in air quality, while accepting that different states are more or less compliant with existing standards. It has in any case only limited, often indirect, means with which to enforce compliance by states – for example, making states ineligible for certain kinds of federal funding, such as for public transport infrastructure projects, unless they meet the NAAQS. It implicitly recognises that fully uniform standards cannot be achieved across all states.

Two further related points can be found in the written judgement of the Washington D.C. appeals court.[77] The grounds on which the court upheld the appeal had practically nothing to do with the environmental issues; the court agreed only with the claim that the manner in which the EPA issued the new standards was unconstitutional, because it appeared to be following no clearly identifiable principle in setting the standards.[78] The written decision notes that a candidate for such a principle would be the application of cost-benefit analysis; but the judgement further notes that – following earlier opinions of the same

Figure 31. **Air pollutant concentrations**

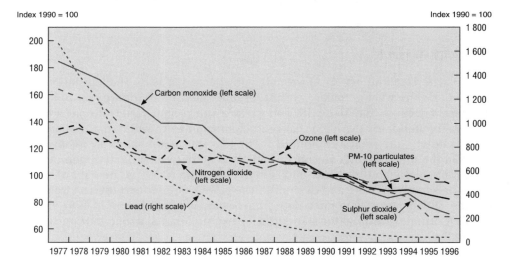

Source: Council on Environmental Quality (1997).

court – the application of cost-benefit analysis to setting standards is not allowed under the Clean Air Act.

This linking of the constitutional issue with the use of cost-benefit analysis is ironic, because a considerable amount of cost-benefit analysis was in fact carried out in support of the new standards – as indeed is *mandated* by Executive Order 12866[79] – and was discussed between the EPA and other relevant agencies before they were issued.[80] The constraint on the use of cost-benefit analysis to help take decisions on environmental policy issues leads to somewhat bizarre results, where EPA departments sometimes carry out, or are aware of, cost-benefit analyses justifying their actions, but avoid making this known to the EPA Administrator,[81] because the statute prohibits consideration of cost.

Emissions trading

A particularly innovative approach to pollution control – emissions trading – has been introduced in two programmes under the Clean Air Act. The SO_2 trading system, embodied in the Acid Rain programme, has been in operation since 1992. The year 1999 saw the start of full trading of NO_x emission permits in twelve eastern states; this is a seasonal programme, with trading in permits issued for emissions in May to September, when the incidence of smog and atmospheric pollution is at its greatest. Both programmes are restricted, so far, to emissions from power generation.

The SO_2 trading scheme was provided for in the 1990 amendments to the Clean Air Act. Although this was not the first time that permit trading had been used in the United States,[82] it was the first time that unrestricted trading within an overall cap was made the sole means of meeting particular emissions targets.[83] A number of aspects of these trading schemes are noteworthy, particularly in view of current interest in such schemes at the international level, in the context of attempts to limit global greenhouse gas emissions (Box 8).

The SO_2 scheme is generally regarded as highly successful. The market for permits has been deep and liquid, with prices not showing excessive fluctuation and generally below earlier estimates of what abatement costs would be (Figure 32).[84] At the same time, emissions have fallen rapidly, resulting in reduced atmospheric SO_2 concentrations.[85] This is to some extent due to fortuitous circumstances: rail deregulation facilitated more rapid substitution of low-sulphur coal for its higher-sulphur counterpart than had appeared likely; and many facilities, worrying that they might not be able to trade if the planned market failed to materialise, over-invested in emission reduction equipment. Consistent with this, although permit prices are below earlier estimates of costs, estimates of actual abatement costs *ex post* appear to be within the range of *ex ante* cost estimates (Smith *et al.*, 1998). Nevertheless, although the low permit price cannot be taken to indicate that either marginal or average abatement costs are equally low, reasonable estimates are that considerable savings have been made compared with the previous command-and-control approach. The future may see a more severe test of the system, as smaller emitters are brought into the scheme and as the overall emission limit begins to bite more severely. The fact that emissions have actually been below the allowed limit is not so much a surprise as a logical consequence of the system: unused permits can be saved ("banked") for future use and, since the overall emissions constraint will be tightened considerably in the year 2000, many permits have therefore been "banked" to cover future emissions.

The NO_x trading scheme has only just been brought into operation. Although both sets of gases were covered in the 1990 amendments to the Clean Air Act, only for SO_2 was a federal trading scheme mandated. The SO_2 scheme, developed and run by the EPA, covers the eastern half of the United States; but the current NO_x scheme covers only twelve states, which formed a "bottom-up" agreement on trading amongst themselves. A number of states that are home to heavy NO_x emitters border on the participants (they are generally upwind of them, in relation to "average" prevailing winds) but are not currently participating in the trading scheme.

Box 8.   Cap-and-trade or tax?

When an activity is known to cause damage through pollution externalities, the damage will be reduced if polluters are given an incentive to reduce emissions. Economic incentives seek to do this in an efficient manner by trying to align the costs faced by individual polluters with the damage they cause. The latter may not be known with certainty, in which case economic incentives can at least ensure that all polluters face the same marginal cost for equivalent emissions, which should minimise the cost of achieving any particular amount of pollution abatement.

A simple way to achieve this, where emissions are relatively easily measured, is to impose an emissions tax. Simple though this may be, it is not without its complications: at what level should the tax be set? Who should pay the tax? Who should receive the revenue? How should the revenue be used?

Partly because of an inherent dislike of taxes in the United States, and partly because of uncertainty as to what level to set them at, two recent US pollution control measures under the acid rain programme have used a cap-and-trade approach, where instead of setting the cost faced by polluters, the government sets the total quantity of pollution to be allowed by issuing a fixed quantity of permits. This method has its own set of complications: how many permits? Who is required to have them? To whom are they issued? At what price should they be issued?

In the SO_2 trading scheme Congress decided to reduce emissions from power generation by half from the 1985 level, but to phase this in over the period to 2010; a tax could also be introduced with such a phase-in. Initially (as from 1995) only "large" emitters were required to hold permits to cover their emissions, with the scheme extended to all emitters as from 2000; again, a tax-based scheme could use the same approach.

Permits are allocated annually free (with minor exceptions) to existing emitters. This is not full "grandfathering" (where permits would be allocated in strict proportion to past emissions), however; permits are issued in proportion to what emissions would be if emitters had achieved a certain technological standard of emissions control (so that owners of facilities who had acted early to reduce emissions benefited from this action, thus reducing moral hazard). A tax-based scheme could allocate tax credits in proportion to the same hypothetical emission levels to achieve the same effect.

It seems that a cap-and-trade approach avoids the issue of who receives the tax revenue and what to do with it. In fact, this is the case only if permits are issued free: it would be perfectly feasible to auction the permits, treating the proceeds as general government revenue; equally, a tax-based system could refund aggregate tax revenues to the emitting facilities – provided this were done in a way unrelated to actual emissions. In both cases there is necessarily a transfer of resources among emitters, which may be large if abatement costs vary greatly.

Even the crucial difference between a tax-based approach and cap-and-trade – that with the former the marginal cost to emitters is known but total emissions are not, and vice-versa for cap-and-trade – is less clear once a medium-term view

---

Box 8.   Cap-and-trade or tax? (*cont.*)

is taken. Over time, the emission limits of a cap-and-trade system will surely be re-evaluated in the light of the cost of meeting them (*i.e.* the market price of permits) and on-going assessments of environmental damage. Equally, a tax rate would be re-evaluated in the light of resulting emission levels. On economic grounds, and without external constraints, the choice may depend on how much is known about the environmental mechanisms involved. Where there is reasonable information on the marginal damage caused by emissions, a tax might be preferred; where this is not the case but health effects, for example, are known to become severe above a certain concentration level, cap-and-trade may be better.

In the case of the US commitment to reduce emissions of greenhouse gases under the Kyoto Protocol, the existence of an external constraint may favour the adoption of a cap-and-trade approach domestically (though it does not *impose* this choice, since international trading by the government is feasible regardless of the domestic instrument employed). OECD estimates suggest that a tax-based solution would require a carbon tax of somewhere between $10 and $250 per tonne (1995 prices), depending on the degree of international trading (the lower figure for full worldwide trading, the latter with no trading at all), corresponding to between about 3 and 70 cents on a gallon of gasoline and between $8 and $210 on a tonne of oil delivered to power stations (whose average prices in 1999 were around $1.20 per gallon – 32 cents per litre – and $90 per tonne respectively). A more plausible figure than either of these extremes is a price of about $90 per tonne of carbon, with full trading among Annex B countries.*

One difficult question raised by a cap-and-trade system is the question of at what point in the production chain to impose the requirement for permits. In the case of oil, for example, one possibility would be importers and domestic producers of crude oil, a second would be refiners and importers of refined products, a third would be on final sales. Each of these, while in principle and with efficient trading having the same effect on the price to the consumer, would have a different and substantial distributive effect: the market value of the US allocation ("assigned amount") of permits, at $90 per tonne of carbon, would be of the order of $150 billion; if permit allocations were grandfathered, recipients with low abatement costs would be substantial beneficiaries, in effect receiving some of the "tax" that would be paid by consumers.

---

*   This figure is roughly in the middle of the range spanned by results obtained from the main models. See OECD (1999 *c*, Table 7).

The EPA suggested that the environmental effectiveness of the trading would be increased if these bordering states participated in it. Although this was initially challenged in the courts, the scheme is now to be extended to include a total of 22 states and Washington D.C. as from 2004.

Figure 32. **SO$_2$ allowance transfers**

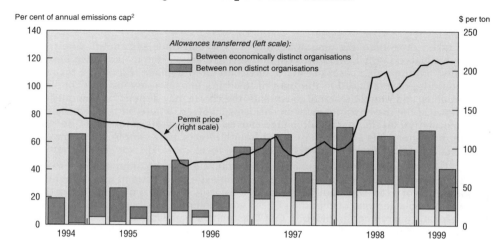

Per cent of annual emissions cap[2]

$ per ton

Allowances transferred (left scale):
☐ Between economically distinct organisations
◼ Between non distinct organisations

Permit price[1]
(right scale)

1. Average of Cantor Fitzgerald EBS and Fieldstone Publications.
2. Annual emissions, from 1995-1999, must not exceed 8.95 million tons.
Source: Environmental Protection Agency.

Water quality

There are two main pieces of legislation covering water quality, the Clean Water Act, covering lakes and rivers, and the Safe Drinking Water Act. The range of activities that can create water quality problems is huge, and therefore only a certain number of issues can be dealt with here.

As far as surface water is concerned, the starting point for quality control is the designation of standards that particular bodies of water should meet. States are responsible for such designation, subject to approval by the EPA, and it is procedurally straightforward. As with air pollution, states are also primarily responsible for enforcing the standards, with the EPA monitoring states' performance with the responsibility to step in where it is inadequate. Once a body of water has received its designation, however, it is procedurally extremely difficult to change.

This asymmetry may lead to cost inefficiencies. The legislation allows the costs and benefits of maintaining water quality to be taken into account when considering designation, but not subsequently when considering appropriate measures to achieve the required standard. In some cases designation took place in the 1960s before the introduction of CWA (see ANNON). In principle this makes sense, since it potentially cuts down the number of times court challenges of anti-pollution measures can be made – once the federal government has decided that the benefits of achieving a certain level of water quality in a particular area exceed the costs (during the designation process), it should logically follow that the benefits of actions taken to achieve those standards exceed the costs. (This conclusion depends on the assumption that they are least-cost measures.[86]) This does not allow for the possibility of mistakes being made in the initial cost-benefit assessment, which might have changed the designation if they had been known at the time.

In 1996, between one-third and one-half of surveyed bodies of water[87] did not meet their designated standards (OECD, 1996, p.75). There are a number of explanations for this quite widespread non-compliance, some of which amount to the EPA in practice taking the costs of compliance into account in an informal discretionary manner, avoiding or delaying enforcement proceedings where compliance costs are clearly high. Others are due to the nature of the water systems being dealt with or to the restricted instruments available. For example, the delay between a polluter making a decision to take effective steps to reduce its discharges, its implementing the decision and then having its full effect on the water body can obviously be significant: indeed, despite the "poor" performance in terms of meeting water standards, overall water quality has been increasing steadily. Instruments are restricted in particular because of the difficulty of dealing with non-point sources of pollution; while point sources are dealt with through a system of permits (discussed further below), non-point sources, which are mainly in agriculture (though also through deposition from air pollution), are subject to very little restriction.[88] The two main such non-point sources are silting due to soil erosion and leaching of nitrates and phosphates (related to fertiliser use), as well as herbicides and other chemical products. An obvious candidate for beginning to tackle some of these problems would be a fertiliser tax – a conclusion drawn, for example, in OECD (1996) – or, better, an excess nutrient tax,[89] but this has never been implemented, perhaps unsurprisingly given the strength of the farm and chemical lobbies. This is not to say that agricultural policy is designed without regard to environmental consequences. Indeed some programmes (discussed in Box 9) show that the Department of Agriculture is well aware of the environmental problems that agriculture can cause, but it prefers to tackle them only through conditional access to subsidies, rather than applying the "polluter pays principle".

Tentative moves towards a more cost-effective approach are being made under the Total Maximum Daily Load (TMDL) programme. A TMDL for different pollutants of a particular body of water is calculated, given its designated use (and including a margin for error). Permits for discharges are then issued by the relevant State or local agency. In some states, non-point discharges (from agriculture) are brought into TMDL programmes. Currently the discharge permits are not auctioned, nor are penalties for violations necessary closely related to damage caused.

Box 9.   Environmental programmes in agriculture

The Department of Agriculture runs a number of programmes that provide incentives to improve the environment or to reduce environmental damage caused by agriculture.[1] A number of them provide technical assistance or information services, though many use methods which give farmers economic incentives to improve the environment. However, despite the considerable use of economic instruments, it is notable that taxes, fees or charges are not used at all; incentives are given either by direct subsidies for particular measures, or by subsidies under some other federal programme (loans or insurance, for example) being conditional on respecting some environmental constraints.

Since agriculture is a recipient of large amounts of federal subsidies, incentives using the conditionality of such subsidies can be quite strong. A number of programmes use these methods so that cost-effectiveness of environmental policy within the agriculture sector is improving; the Conservation Reserve Program is a good example of this. However, the overall level of subsidy to agriculture seems to be determined largely without regard to environmental considerations, and the main subsidies are still tied to production; hence, a sector which is a major source of water pollution, and which is not covered by the main water quality legislation, operates under an incentive scheme that fails to discourage it from polluting.

The Conservation Reserve Program: cost-effectiveness without cost-efficiency

Recent developments in the administration of the Conservation Reserve Program (CRP) provide an interesting example of how cost-effectiveness can be achieved, or at least significantly improved, within a given programme by judicious use of economic incentives. At the same time they also illustrate the difficulties of working towards overall cost-effectiveness across sectors.

The CRP was set up in 1985, allocating subsidies – in the form of a rental payment – to farmers for taking land out of production with the aim of supporting farm incomes while improving the environment.[2] In the 1980s the only environmental criterion used in the selection of land to qualify for the CRP was the degree of erodibility of the land, on the assumption that relevant environmental benefits were highly correlated with soil erosion. Subsequently, a more sophisticated set of indicators was introduced, assessing points to potential programme acres according to a number of different attributes, combined in an "environmental benefits index" (EBI). This has been in use since 1991, though the weights have evolved. A cost factor – the rental rate the landowner bids (in the competition to qualify for the CRP) – is also part of the EBI (with a negative weight) in order to increase the environmental benefits per unit of outlay.

Since CRP acreage is "signed up" under contracts that last ten or fifteen years, it will be some time before the more sophisticated EBI approach is reflected in the actual distribution of CRP land. Feather *et al.* (1999) conduct a simulation of the environmental benefits to be expected if the current CRP acreage (34 million acres, about 10 per cent of total US cropland) were replaced with land selected using the most recent EBI, using a variety of valuation techniques to measure the

---

Box 9.   **Environmental programmes in agriculture** (*cont.*)

monetary value of non-market benefits[3] (the EBI itself is not yet explicitly based on such techniques). The results show that use of the EBI doubles the value (consumer surplus) of some environmental benefits, such as wildlife viewing, with very slight diminution in others. The study also estimates the overall costs and benefits of the CRP: of total benefits of $46-58 billion over a ten-year period, $31-43 billion is accounted for either by increased farm incomes (including increased timber growth) or reduced costs of other farm subsidy programmes and $12-15 billion of strictly environmental benefits; total costs of $44 billion are almost entirely attributable to budgetary costs or higher food prices (see Feather *et al.*, Table 2, p.6). OMB (2000), however, attributes net present values of $30 billion and $13 billion for CRP benefits and costs respectively.

Since not all the environmental benefits included in the EBI are valued in this study, the overall improvement in environmental effectiveness of its use cannot be assessed. However, if the magnitudes in Feather *et al.* (1999) are reasonable, it is clear *a*) that the use of the EBI does improve the cost-effectiveness of the CRP programme substantially, providing a good example of the usefulness of cost-benefit analysis; and *b*) that even when environmental benefits are optimised, the environmental benefits are a rather small proportion of the gross costs.

---

1. In addition to the Conservation Reserve Program, Feather *et al.* (1999) list seven: the Environmental Quality Incentives Program; the Wildlife Habitat Incentives Program; Conservation Technical Assistance; Extension Education; Wetland Compliance; Conservation Compliance; and the Wetland Reserve Program.
2. The seven goals of the CRP are listed as: reducing soil erosion; protecting soil productivity; reducing sedimentation; improving water quality; improving fish and wildlife habitats; curbing production of surplus commodities; and providing income support to farmers. But a table of costs and benefits expected at the time of the programme's introduction, Feather *et al.* (1999) show income gains (including savings to federal farm income support programmes) representing more than two-thirds of the total value of the expected benefits.
3. These include wildlife viewing and hunting and freshwater recreation.

When violations do occur, enforcement action includes taking into account, in addition to the seriousness of the violation, whether it is deliberate or not, as well as the previous compliance record of the violator. This allows local cost conditions to be considered, though the procedures may not be fully transparent. Not all violations are prosecuted: enforcement action frequently occurs when local or national environmental groups take legal action to require the EPA to intervene. Current proposals for changes to the TMDL system do not include allocating permits by auction, but they do suggest development of an "offset" programme under which increases in discharges in one area could be "paid for" by reductions elsewhere – a form of effluent trading. Eventually this might lead to prices being

---

established for at least some permits, allowing some assessment of cost-effectiveness to be made.

Another important cause of water pollution, often by hazardous chemicals, and where the precise source can often be hard to identify, is seepage from waste dumps or from sites such as gas stations. Despite the Resource Conservation and Recovery Act (1976) and the Comprehensive Environmental Response, Compensation and Liability Act (1980) (see below), such discharges, along with those from agriculture, remain among the major sources of water quality problems. Another important source of water pollution is intensive livestock operations, particularly pig farms. This problem is particularly severe in North Carolina where hogs, outnumbering humans, produce some 19 million tons of waste per year, leading to nitrogen pollution, groundwater contamination, and threats to human health, other than the obvious odours – see Environmental Defense Fund (2000).

Water supply

Overall, the United States has abundant water resources, and, despite very high per capita consumption,[90] its intensity of use is similar to that in other major OECD countries.[91] Nevertheless, in some parts of the country water resources are over-stretched, especially where there has been massive expansion of irrigated agriculture based on groundwater from aquifers (for example the Ogallala Aquifer, stretching from southern South Dakota to south-eastern New Mexico). In many cases aquifers are being rapidly depleted as extraction rates exceed recharge rates, and farmers are already being forced to abandon irrigation as pumping lowers the level of the water table (Postel, 1999). Only rarely, if at all, is pricing used to limit groundwater extraction rates. Without such pricing, aquifers are certainly being depleted too rapidly. Pricing the water would encourage more economical use of it, allowing irrigated agriculture to be sustained for a longer period and supporting a higher level of farm output over the longer term by encouraging the substitution of other inputs for water.

Overuse is often due to the structure of property rights, but inappropriate government action can exacerbate such problems. Examples of this can be found in California, where heavy use for irrigation has considerably depleted groundwater supplies. In response to the difficulties faced by farmers dependent on groundwater for irrigation, both federal and state programmes have been introduced to supply *subsidised* water for irrigation and for aquifer recharge. This provides quite the wrong incentives in a water -short area and where other users – industrial and household consumers – are prepared to pay high prices for water (implying, *ceteris paribus*, a higher return to its use); heavy use of river water can also damage ecosystems, as in the San Francisco Bay delta.[92]

Property rights in respect of water are quite complicated. There exist two different bases for attribution of surface water rights – "riparian" and "prior use"[93] –

while groundwater rights generally accrue to the surface owner. Broadly speaking, prior use rights are enshrined in the constitutions of most western states, while riparian rights apply in the majority of eastern states.[94] Overlying these legal rights, however, is the common-law principle that owners of water resources hold them in trust for the community. Where water is scarce, its efficient use requires some means of allocating it to its most productive uses, and water trading provides, in some cases, a convenient way to accomplish this. In some parts of the United States active water-trading markets have existed for some time (on the Upper Snake River, Idaho, since the 1930s, for example), but they are rare.[95] In California, one of the few areas possessing very limited surface water resources, with a dynamic economy whose shifting structure suggests that a market in water would be beneficial, putting together a scheme to satisfy all the competing interests is proving very difficult (Box 10).

Revenue from the use of water pricing for demand management, in areas where the overall supply of water is the principal constraint (rather than charges for the construction or maintenance of physical infrastructure), would largely constitute a resource rent. Not charging appropriate resource rents can lead to over-use, as in the example of groundwater mentioned earlier, but also in other cases. The management of federal lands – that make up almost one-fifth of the country – is often criticised for under-charging for grazing and mining rights, leading in the former to serious over-grazing and consequent soil deterioration. It may be felt that the federal government should not be profiting from its ownership of land held in trust (though it is hard to see who other than the federal government should profit from such ownership). The consequence is that the economic rents are appropriated somewhat arbitrarily (from an economic point of view) by those who first registered the rights to graze, mine or extract water. Although this may represent a significant transfer payment, it need not mean an inefficient use of resources, provided the relevant rights are tradable. With a large number of leases on federal land currently expiring, this issue may be important during their renewal period.

Dealing with toxic waste

The programmes for cleaning up past contamination and for regulating the generation and handling of toxic waste (CERCLA, the Comprehensive Environmental Response, Compensation and Liability Act, commonly known as "Superfund", and RCRA, the Resource Conservation and Recovery Act, respectively) have frequently come in for criticism on the grounds of excessive cost. Superfund is particularly notorious, given its reputation for generating long and expensive litigation and other transactions costs, which have apparently absorbed one fifth of its expenditure on compliance.[96] High costs have arisen partly from the law's insistence, and the EPA's interpretation of the law, that sites be cleaned up to very high

Box 10.   Water in the San Francisco Bay delta area

Water resources are treated in the United States as being held in trust for society. Although extraction and use rights can be granted and, once granted, cannot be rescinded except under specific circumstances,[1] state governments therefore maintain the right to influence how the water is used.[2] They may therefore intervene in trading, since unrestricted trading may very well change the use of the water. Furthermore, although prior appropriation rights are well defined and farmers may not even be limited in the quantity they extract, they may lose the rights if they do not make "beneficial use" of the water themselves, for example if they sell it. This obviously makes trading hardly ever worthwhile and encourages farmers to use excessive amounts. During the 1987-92 drought the practical absence of trading in California became untenable, and a temporary trading ("banking") scheme was introduced. Even though the California Water Bank acted as the intermediary in all trades (selling and buying at fixed prices), the efficiency of water use, at least in agriculture, improved markedly (OECD, 1999b, pp. 81-82).

Putting in place more permanent trading arrangements in California appears to be very difficult. This is partly a result of the nature of water trading, where the physical infrastructure and variability of supply (annual flow through the Sacramento/San Joaquim delta into San Francisco Bay can vary by a factor of ten, for example) constrain the kinds of trading that can take place. It is also a function of the large number of agencies that need to be involved in any comprehensive agreement on water strategy.[3] It is likely that property rights and a conflict between established users (mainly agriculture) and newer industries are at the root of this. This makes it unlikely that a market can simply direct water to where its marginal productivity appears to be highest, since the state of California must also take into account non-market interests (such as fish and wildlife). Individual water districts also have some power and may argue against the "export" of water, even if the holder of the water rights would benefit; such arguments might be on externality grounds, for example, since water used for one purpose is frequently available for subsequent reuse.

The Bay-Delta Accord of 1994 was intended to work towards a more rational use of water in the Sacramento/San Joaquim watershed (which drains into San Francisco Bay) and to improve the aquatic environment in the delta, damaged by the much reduced flow of fresh water as a result of increased upstream uses. The CALFED Bay-Delta Program is still in the process of development – though it was intended to begin operation in 1999 – through a process of stakeholder consultation and, while in the long run it may lead to a system of water trading, use of market instruments seems to have been accorded a rather low priority in the ongoing discussions.[4]

---

1. As mentioned earlier, unused extraction or diversion rights can lapse.
2. See the California State Water Resources Control Board website for a discussion of this: http://www.waterrights.ca.gov/application/forms/infobook.htm. Permits to extract or divert water state for which uses the water is intended.
3. The CALFED Bay-Delta Program, which has been attempting "to address the tangle of complex issues that surrounds the [Sacramento/San Joaquim] Delta", lists fifteen federal and state agencies that have direct management or regulatory responsibilities in the area.
4. The revised (June 1999) Phase 2 report of this programme uses the term water transfers rather than trading and, while mentioning the need for cost-efficient sources of water supply, does not discuss water pricing as a demand-side measure.

standards, regardless of the cost or benefit, and partly from the liability provisions, under which even people or companies that had had only a minor connection with a contaminated site could, in principle, be held liable for the entire costs of cleaning it up, unless other "potentially responsible parties" could be identified. Liability is also strict, in the sense that parties are liable for cleanup costs even if they met legal requirements at the time.

This "joint and several" liability provision followed partly from the reluctance of the federal government to finance cleanups from general taxation,[97] even though using general taxation might be thought to be the "fair" approach for rectifying damage done by activities that were often not illegal when they occurred. This reluctance to tax may thus be responsible for imposing considerable costs on the economy. On the other hand, the threat of being found liable for environmental damage under the Superfund legislation has probably had a big effect in pushing companies into internalising the potential environmental costs of their activities.

The requirement under Superfund that sites meet high standards (often much higher than surrounding areas that were not contaminated) has certainly led to unnecessary costs. After 1990 procedures were implemented that allow cleanups to be limited to containing health hazards rather than fully eliminating them. This has reportedly improved the cost-effectiveness of the programme during the 1990s. Another innovation in the early 1990s was the "brownfield" programme. Here the idea was to reduce the supposed burden on potential developers of contaminated land posed by possible Superfund liability. This was thought to be a factor impeding urban regeneration, particularly in poorer districts; improving this situation would represent progress in wider sustainable development goals. Some regeneration projects have subsequently succeeded, though take-up has been less than hoped. Some critics argue that, rather than the costs of environmental clean-up, it is the low incomes, poor infrastructure and social problems, often characteristic of the neighbourhoods of such sites, that are the real barriers to urban regeneration.

While Superfund and its costs have been subjected to intense scrutiny and criticism, the RCRA has been less closely analysed. Although Superfund has played a role in frightening potential polluters into "better" behaviour in their current operations, it is the RCRA that actually sets the constraints they face. OECD (1996) argued, along with other commentators, that RCRA is over-complicated and burdensome and could be reformed to improve cost-effectiveness without compromising environmental standards.

One of the interesting innovations in toxic waste policy is in the provision of information. Under 1986 legislation, industrial sites are required to report all releases of listed chemicals, whether accidental or otherwise, as well as information on off-site transfers for disposal, information that is then recorded in the Toxic

Release Inventory (TRI). This can be thought of as lowering the cost (the Inventory covers substances that are regulated anyway under the RCRA and some other statutes) of enforcing regulations – the availability of information encourages enterprises to make sure they have a "clean" image and makes it easier for concerned members of the public to take legal action against violations as well as adjust their own behaviour if they wish, even when there are no violations. The effectiveness of the TRI is difficult to judge. In practice it covers only a small proportion of all environmental problems and could thus be criticised for drawing attention to these at the expense of less spectacular but perhaps more pervasive problems.

Climate change: rational transport and energy policy?

Many argue that the issue of climate change is currently one of the most important on the environmental agenda in the United States. US emissions of greenhouse gases (GHGs)[98] in general, and carbon dioxide in particular, are much higher than those of any other country, both per capita and in total (Figure 33). Under the terms of the Kyoto Protocol to the United Nations Framework Convention on Climate Change (UNFCCC), the United States is committed (once the Protocol is ratified by the United States and a sufficient number of other countries) to reduce its average emissions of greenhouse gases for the years 2008-12 to a level 7 per cent below that of 1990. Since carbon dioxide emissions in 1997 were some 11 per cent above the 1990 level and projections are that, on unchanged policies, emissions by the year 2010 might rise to as much as 30 per cent above the targeted level, this will be a difficult objective to meet.

One of the options under the Kyoto Protocol is to purchase emission permits from other countries. The United States is one of the principal supporters of the use of such mechanisms.[99] OECD simulations show that the annual cost to the United States, in terms of GDP foregone, of meeting the Kyoto targets would be some 0.27 per cent with no emissions trading but only 0.16 per cent with unrestricted trading among the so-called Annex B countries.[100] The same simulations show that the target would be met with the price of an emission permit (or implicit carbon tax) of $228 per tonne (at 1995 prices) without trade or $94 with full Annex B trading. Terms-of-trade changes associated with financing acquisitions of emissions permits and changes in world energy prices are likely to reduce the theoretical gains from trade measured in terms of real incomes, but the adjustment to output and employment patterns would certainly be less difficult with trade.

If trade in GHG emissions permits were to include developing countries, however, the carbon price would be lower. US Department of Energy officials give credence to a scenario in which a sufficient number of developing countries participate to allow a permit price as low as $20.[101] Compared with prices in the second quarter of 1999, this would imply an increase of over 40 per cent in the delivered price of coal to power stations, or of 20 per cent for oil. It would correspond to

Figure 33. **Carbon dioxide emission intensities, 1997**

Total emissions
Million tonnes

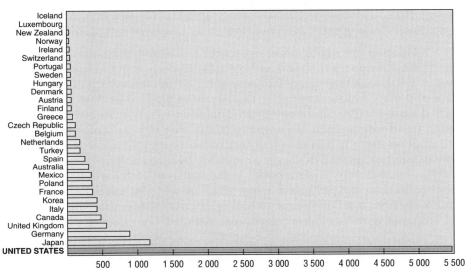

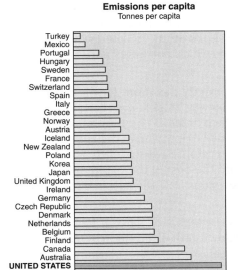

Emissions per capita
Tonnes per capita

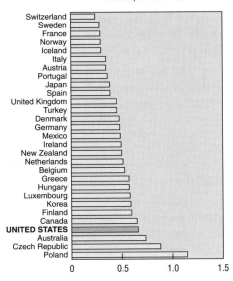

Emissions per unit of GDP
Tonnes per 1 000 US$

Source: OECD.

around 5 cents per gallon of gasoline, well under 5 per cent of the current gasoline price.[102] However, under a more likely scenario, with emissions trading were restricted to Annex B countries, the increase would have to be nearly five times higher. This explains the importance to US policy-makers of convincing developing countries to enter into emission limitation commitments, of minimising restrictions on emissions trading and developing the Clean Development Mechanism.

Meeting the Kyoto target even with a substantial amount of trading will nevertheless require a renewed and quite rapid decline in the use of fossil fuels, since, even though the energy intensity of US output fell substantially during the 1970s and early 1980s, continuing a rather more gradual decline since the mid-1980s (Figure 34), per capita energy consumption has risen steadily since then. A similar trend can be seen in European OECD Member countries, but per capita consumption there is less than half that of the United States. Fossil fuels can to some extent be replaced in energy production by renewables,[103] though the scope for this is limited, or by nuclear power. In the transport sector, where fuel consumption is growing most rapidly, technological advances to increase the scope for switching away from fossil fuels (e.g. to fuel cells), or considerable improvements in fuel economy, or reductions in transport activity, will be required.

Fuel economy in private vehicles has been tackled largely through regulations on average fuel consumption for new car sales – the so-called CAFE standards. But these are not very effective in reducing fuel consumption when the price of fuel itself provides no incentive. Although average fuel efficiency of cars in use improved through the 1980s, there has been little change since 1991, either for cars or for vehicles classed as pickups and sports utility vehicles, which have a less stringent standard on new sales and towards which purchases appear to have shifted in recent years (Figure 35).

At the federal level, road users currently pay more for the facilities they use than the narrowly defined costs: the Highway Trust Fund (HTF), into which the gasoline and diesel taxes are paid and which finances the federal road construction programme, was in surplus until recently.[104] However, at the sub-federal level, and probably overall, such costs exceed revenue extracted directly from road users. Moreover, it is generally agreed that the cost of the externalities imposed by road users also significantly exceeds revenues from the gasoline tax, though the size of the excess is disputed.

One recent estimate, perhaps on the high side since it included costs of accidents which are probably mostly already internalised through insurance, puts the costs as the equivalent of $1.60 per US gallon of gasoline consumed (see Cobb, 1999).[105] Delucchi (1996), on whose data Cobb (1999) is partly based, warns against this kind of calculation and the false inference that a tax at this level would be optimal – many costs are only loosely related, if at all, to fuel consumption. According to Delucchi (1996), external environmental costs of road users in 1991 were

Figure 34. **Energy intensity and consumption**

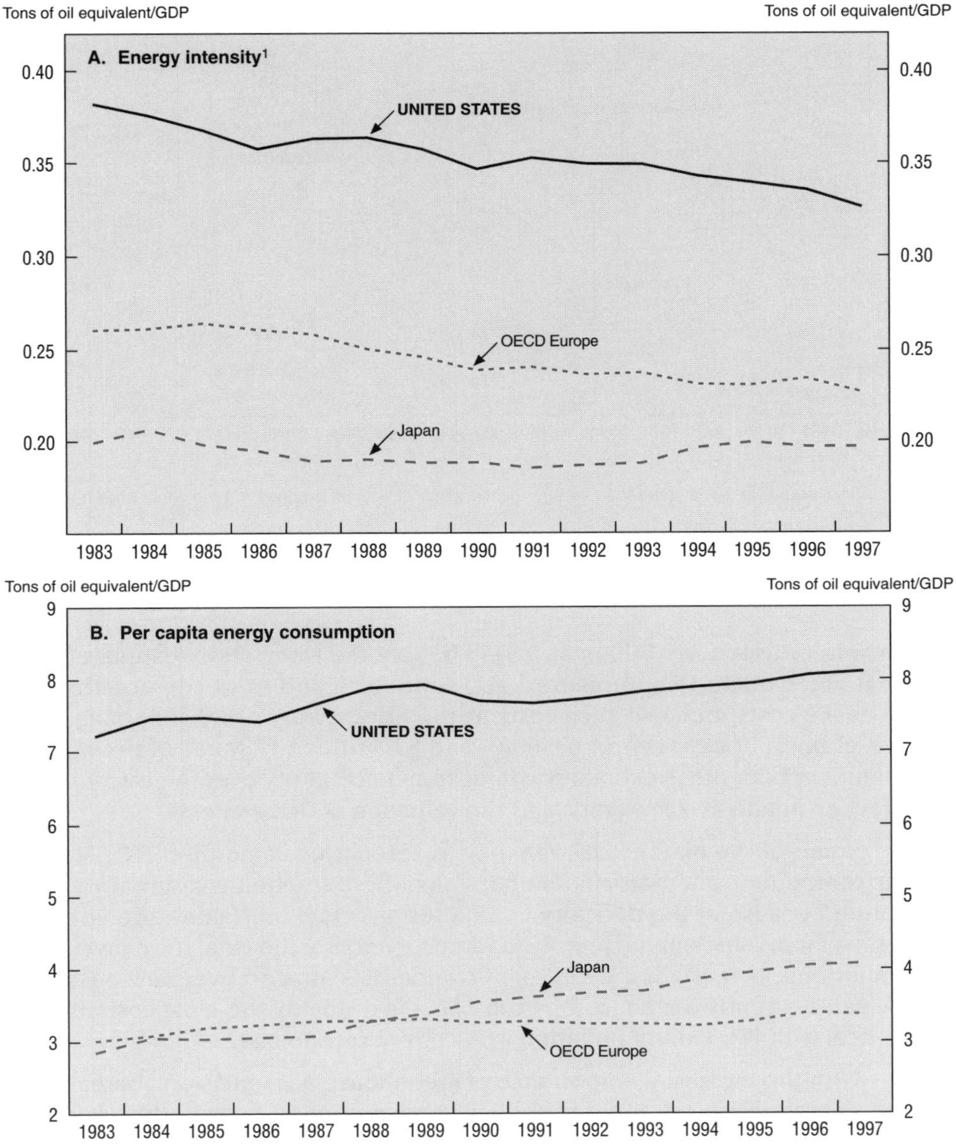
Tons of oil equivalent/GDP
Tons of oil equivalent/GDP
A. Energy intensity[1]
UNITED STATES
OECD Europe
Japan
0.40
0.35
0.30
0.25
0.20
1983 1984 1985 1986 1987 1988 1989 1990 1991 1992 1993 1994 1995 1996 1997
Tons of oil equivalent/GDP
Tons of oil equivalent/GDP
B. Per capita energy consumption
UNITED STATES
Japan
OECD Europe
9
8
7
6
5
4
3
2
1983 1984 1985 1986 1987 1988 1989 1990 1991 1992 1993 1994 1995 1996 1997

1. Total energy consumption per unit of GDP, tons of oil equivalent, 1990 $, 1990 purchasing power parities.
Source: OECD.

Figure 35. **Average fuel consumption of light vehicles**

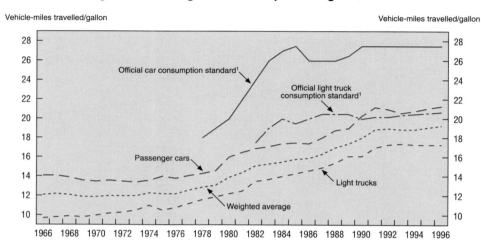

Vehicle-miles travelled/gallon   Vehicle-miles travelled/gallon

1. The official standard is the weighted average for the sales of vehicle producers, commonly known as "cafe" standards.
Source: Federal Highway Administration.

somewhere between $69 billion and $755 billion; the same study estimated total external costs (including uninsured accident costs and road construction and maintenance costs, but also such costs as the opportunity costs of parking space and travel time) at between $1.6 trillion and $3.3 trillion.[106] Much of the range of uncertainty in both these estimates comes from uncertainty over the calculation of the effect on health and mortality, and the valuation of those effects.

Some of the major road transport externalities come from NO_x, volatile organic compounds and particulate emissions where taxation is not really a feasible option because of the difficulty of monitoring actual emissions; the approach taken thus far of imposing technical standards – notably the catalytic converter for NO_x emissions, or the tailpipe emission standards averaged over new passenger vehicle sales recently announced by the EPA – is probably the most cost effective way to deal with this kind of pollution with current technology.

With the increasing importance of greenhouse gas emission abatement in environmental policy, the need to reduce consumption of hydrocarbon fuels will become more pressing and almost certainly necessitate higher fuels prices.[107] Since increasing taxation tends to be particularly difficult politically in the United States, the tendency may be to seek to improve fuel economy by subsidising research into more efficient engines;[108] however, without direct incentives to reduce fuel consumption itself, much of the potential for reductions could be absorbed, for example, in increased vehicle weights, power or distances travelled.

A phenomenon related both to the relatively high per capita energy consumption and to the resistance to higher gasoline taxation is the combination of spreading suburbanisation and the predominance in rural, suburban and nearly all urban areas of private over public road transport. Since mass-transit systems can never be efficient in low population-density areas, once such areas have been built, residents are dependent on cars and will resist proposals to increase the cost of driving. This also contributes to low short -run price elasticities of demand for fuel; thus, taxes have to be set quite high to get significant effects on consumption over such a horizon. Conversely, low fuel costs do nothing to discourage the continuing development of low-density housing. To break this circle would probably require a concerted effort in urban planning to restrict low-density development, something which is unlikely given the clear preference of many to live further from metropolitan centres.[109]

Overall, the likelihood is that US greenhouse gas emissions will substantially exceed its Kyoto target in the period 2008-12, and compliance with the Protocol will require emission allowances to be purchased from other countries. Despite the popular aversion to raising gasoline prices, if full international emission allowance trading is implemented with some participation by developing countries, it should be feasible to impose the necessary price increases to pay for these allowances. If only limited international permit trading is permitted,[110] as currently proposed for example by the European Union, the permit price might be so high that general government revenues might be required to buy permits on the world market, allowing a gap between the world price and domestic price, if it were infeasible to impose the whole cost directly on domestic fuel prices.

Efficiency and implementation: cost-benefit analysis and the reinvention of regulation[111]

In the three decades since the major pieces of environmental legislation were enacted, the approach to this aspect of policy has gone through a number of phases, already outlined in the Introduction. The 1970s legislation generally concentrated on the environmental benefits of regulation, with cost considerations accorded only secondary importance. Much of the legislation included provisions for "citizen suits" allowing private citizens – in practice, environmental pressure groups – to take court action to require government agencies to enforce the law, reducing the ability of the EPA and other agencies to implement policies which take into account costs *de facto*, a practice prohibited *de jure* in certain cases; this prohibition was often intended to prevent the "capture" of the regulator by those being regulated.

The constant involvement of the courts on both "sides" has meant that the practical application of environmental law has evolved continuously. There is a considerable degree of variation in detail among the different states. This is partly because federal law generally specifies target levels for certain indicators, such as aspects of air or water quality, but leaves it up to individual states to decide how to implement these goals. In the case of the Clean Air Act, states must produce Plans (SIPs). The EPA has to agree to the SIPs, after which states are responsible for enforcing them, with the EPA empowered to move directly or through the courts where states appear not to be taking adequate enforcement action; if states do not produce a SIP, the EPA is supposed to develop one itself, a situation which the EPA tries to avoid. In a current court case a set of environmental pressure groups[112] is trying to force the EPA to do this in the context of a number of urban areas that have not introduced anti-smog programmes in conformity with EPA requirements, but against whom EPA has not yet taken any action.

Some states have a more rigorous "compliance culture" than others. It is hard to quantify this, but there is indirect evidence that the degree of inter-state variation may be declining. A recent study (Levinson, 1999)[113] into the costs to enterprises of meeting environmental regulation in different states shows that variation across states was narrowing somewhat up to 1994, although not continuously (Figure 36). It may be speculated that actions in federal courts, creating precedents valid in all states, the wide availability of information,[114] as well as aspects of legislation designed to prevent internal "environmental dumping",[115] have all been part of the process bringing this about.

Opposition to proposed regulations is often based on claims that, even where benefits appear to exceed costs, their instigators underestimate the costs of implementation faced by the private sector. There are examples of regulations for which cost underestimates have been very large, often going hand in hand with overestimates of the benefits, but available evidence does not in fact suggest that this is a systematic tendency. A report by the Office of Management and Budget notes a road-safety case, the fitting of "center high-mounted stop lamps", where the costs are now estimated to be nearly twice the estimate in the Regulatory Impact Analysis (RIA), undertaken in 1983, whereas the number of crashes avoided is estimated to be only between 2 per cent and 10 per cent of that in the RIA; aggregate benefits nevertheless substantially exceed the costs, even when only property damage is considered. But in other cases costs have been overestimated by up to a factor of three or four.[116]

Another recent study (Harrington, Morgenstern and Nelson, 1999) concludes that *ex ante* overestimates of the costs of compliance are actually more frequent than cost underestimates; however this is partly due the fact that compliance with regulations is rarely complete, so that even if per unit abatement costs were overestimated, actual costs could be underestimated. In fact, the study

Figure 36. **Variation in compliance costs across states**[1]
1977-1994

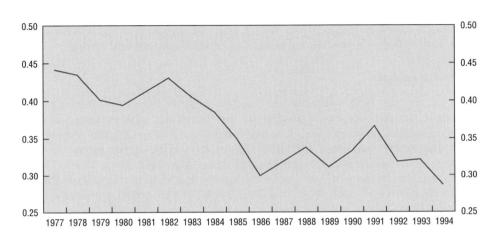

1. Coefficient of variation of industry-adjusted index of compliance costs.
Source: Levinson (1999).

concludes that costs per unit of abatement for EPA and Occupational Safety and
Health Administration regulations are as often over – as underestimated.[117] An
interesting property of the examples covered in this paper is that in cases where
economic incentives were used, it was always the case either that costs were overestimated or that total abatement achieved was underestimated. It was also frequently the case that cost underestimates were associated with unpredicted
technical changes. While the rather small number (25, including three examples of
non-US regulations) of cases in this study limits the weight that can be attached to
these observations, they are consistent with the idea that economic instruments
generate incentives to search for least-cost solutions.

Detailed comparisons of *ex post* with *ex ante* cost estimates are infrequently
available, and it is not clear whether the trend is towards improvements in cost
estimation or not. Although estimates made in the 1980s tended to be more accu-
rate than those of the 1970s, there is little evidence of change since then – see also
OECD, (1999*e*, pp.153-55).

Whether or not costs are being estimated more accurately than earlier,
concern that they may be too high has motivated a series of measures designed to
ensure that excessively costly regulations (not only those in respect of environment and natural resources, but in practice these are often the most important) are

not implemented. Regulatory Impact Assessments (RIAs) have their origin in the year 1978, having been modified under successive presidencies since; they are currently being operated under Executive Order 12866 of 1993.[118] This Order requires any economically significant regulatory act[119] to be accompanied by an RIA, including a cost-benefit analysis, which is to be subjected to an inter-agency review, under the co-ordination of the Office of Management and Budget.

Cost-benefit analysis

The result of this requirement is that, despite the earlier-noted prohibition on the use of cost-benefit analysis in the formal decision-making process for certain aspects of policy, a great deal of it is carried out. The Office of Management and Budget (OMB) has since 1997 published tables showing the monetised costs and benefits of "economically significant" rules (OMB, 1997; 1998; 2000).[120] However, these tables come with many caveats, mostly spelt out in the reports themselves (see, in particular, OMB, 1998 and OMB, 2000). The principal warnings are to do with valuation – some major benefits are not quantified in RIAs, and for some which are, valuation is subject to substantial uncertainty. In addition, the aggregate cost-benefit analysis used generally takes no account of who receives the benefits or pays the costs, meaning distributional consequences are ignored.

Uncertainty in valuation comes from many sources. In valuing, for example, a measure designed to reduce emissions of particulate matter one needs to estimate the reduction that will actually be achieved and what its effect will be on atmospheric concentrations (and where). The effect of that on people's health then has to be estimated, and those effects valued along with possible benefits from improved visibility. The OMB does not carry out any cost-benefit analysis itself, but, in OMB (1998), it has completed valuations that the originating agency did not. For example, OMB applies a value to a "statistical life" when an agency submitting a RIA quantifies the number of lives saved but does not itself value them. Some ideas of the range of uncertainty can be seen in Table 20.

Generally speaking, even when figures at the low end of ranges of uncertainty are used, the OMB finds that the quantified benefits of the regulations covered in its report exceed the quantified costs in aggregate. Overall the calculated benefits exceed the costs by a large margin, largely because of two sets of regulations – restrictions on tobacco sales and part of the acid rain programme.

Although this kind of exercise is extremely valuable and shows that, in the case of the regulations surveyed, monetised benefits exceed monetised costs,[121] this is still a long way from showing that the policies are efficient – it may be that benefits could exceed costs to an even greater extent. This requires calculations of the marginal costs and benefits of different policies or instruments. The inherent advantage of taxes and charges is that the marginal costs can be seen very easily in the level of charges themselves (adjusted for private and public administration

Table 20.   **Valuation ranges**
1996 dollars

Value of life:	
A "statistical life"	2.5 million-5 million
A "life year"	116 500-368 000
Emission reductions, value of one ton of:	
Hydrocarbons	519-2 360
Nitrogen oxides	519-2 360
Sulphur dioxide	3 768-11 539

Note: The value of a statistical life is the value attached to a reduction of one in the expected number of deaths in one year; the value of a life-year is the average value attached to an additional year of life.
Source: Office of Management and Budget (1998).

costs), leaving the task (still by no means an easy one) of calculating marginal benefits.

Just as Regulatory Impact Analyses are intended to give information on the economic costs of regulations, so Environmental Impact Statements (EIS) (originating in the 1969 National Environmental Policy Act) list the environmental consequences of planned federal government policies or investments. The sponsoring agency is required to look at alternative actions and assess which would have the least damaging effects. The environmental impacts are not valued in the EIS, however. Generally, only if an outsider, such as an environmental pressure group, takes legal action, is some comparison of the economic benefits and environmental costs likely to be made.

Project XL

While the notion of cost-benefit analysis leads naturally to a preference for economic instruments, these are frequently difficult to design for real world problems, though perhaps not as often as many claim.[122] Part of the "Reinventing regulation" programme, Project XL (for Excellence and Leadership) is an experiment in trying to make existing approaches more flexible and therefore to lower costs. Regulatory programmes are frequently criticised for not taking sufficient account of local conditions; under Project XL the EPA is empowered to waive regulations on particular sites, for example on technologies required to clean up air pollutant emissions, provided that the firm or facility concerned comes up with a plan that improves its environmental performance (which must already be in compliance with existing regulations). The plan must be drawn up between the facility and the EPA and be developed through a process of stakeholder consultation – with local government and communities.

Project XL was launched in March 1995. As of March 1999 only ten projects had been implemented, with another 14 at various stages of development, but by October these figures were 15 and 28 respectively. A study (Blackman and Mazurek, 1999), looking at progress up to March 1999, suggests that these initial experiments have been rather expensive, with discussions between the firms involved and the regional and central EPA offices absorbing a lot of resources. Costs averaged over $450 000 per firm.

Although it seems that better co-ordination within the EPA, and between its regional offices and headquarters, could reduce costs, the prospect that this approach could produce substantial improvements in regulatory cost-effectiveness seems doubtful at the moment. On the one hand, as Blackman and Mazurek (1999) report, the more a scheme tries innovative and potentially cost-reducing approaches, the more costly it is to get actual approval. On the other, EPA officials feel that many of the Project XL plans, while being effective in local terms, are so site-specific that the gains to be made from learning-by-doing may be small: implementation costs may not decline very much as experience grows, and the lessons for regulation more generally may be limited.

The limits of cost-benefit analysis

Formal cost-benefit analysis has many limitations, and some legislation appears to have ruled out using it for fear that manipulation of the assumptions required for its use might lead to worthwhile policies not being carried out. This may have some foundation in the sense that where policies give a small benefit to many, but the costs are borne by few, the few are more likely to be able to organise themselves to lobby against the policy than the many are to lobby for it. However, the situation described earlier, where a federal court rules that legislation (and court precedent) prevents the EPA from using a rule (a cost-benefit criterion) that the court itself considers would otherwise be acceptable, makes little sense. On the other hand, while it seems unnecessary to prevent agencies from using cost-benefit analysis, it should not be the only criterion for decision-making: for example, the political process may judge some issues to involve rights (for example, to clean air, or at least to not having one's health threatened by air pollution) whose value – if they can be valued – does not necessarily correspond to the sum of individuals' willingness to pay or to accept compensation.

Conclusions

Because of the range and complexity of both the legislation and the underlying problems, this survey is not in a position to recommend comprehensive solutions across a whole range of issues. However, certain general points do stand out, or are at least suggested by some of the examples discussed.

US environmental policy appears to be evolving in a direction which will allow a greater integration of environmental costs into economic decision-making, which should in turn promote growth which is more sustainable. The increasing use of economic instruments is one aspect of this, and another is the amount of environmental information in the public domain. Where economic instruments are not used, Project XL marks an attempt to introduce greater flexibility into the "command and control" instruments, even if wider applicability of the approach seems unlikely at present, in large part because of the high costs involved. Nevertheless, the lessons that could be learned from persevering with the programme in the area of experimenting with different instruments and permitting regulatory flexibility in order to achieve a better cost-benefit trade-off in environmental policies seem to argue for its continuation for the time being.

The heavy use made of the courts in both developing and implementing policy has at times been rather costly, in some cases, perhaps – as for the Superfund legislation – because of the drafting of the laws, but, where it results from the establishment of legal liability for environmental damage, it makes a direct contribution to better integration of environmental consequences into economic decisions. However, since this is a desirable aim, it becomes increasingly anomalous that cost-benefit considerations – largely inescapable in an economic decision-making context – are given inconsistent treatment in different parts of the law. It may be true that preventing the use of cost-benefit analysis in some circumstances may help to defend valuable environmental interests that would otherwise be too weak. It is also true that the resulting ambiguity and inability of the EPA and other agencies to explicitly prioritise on cost-benefit grounds may have helped to create the situation where many of the priorities of those agencies are set by the courts.

Restrictions on cost-benefit analysis should therefore be removed. The fact that valuations are uncertain, and that it may be impossible to value certain effects, does not mean that such analysis is useless. Legislative clarity should be improved, so that the courts are not forced to develop case law on what lawmakers intended. Use of cost-benefit analysis should be the norm, but provide for a "reasoned" rejection of the results of a cost-benefit analysis if non-quantifiable benefits or costs are judged to be more important than these quantified. Provision for reassessment after a certain period of time would also be useful. Renewed attention should also be paid to the analysis of risk, as recommended in the 1991 OECD *Economic Survey* and as planned in the risk management budgeting exercise in 1992.

The OECD *Regulatory Performance Review of the United States* (OECD, 1999e) noted that US regulations were generally excessively complex and that litigation resulting from their implementation and enforcement absorbed considerable resources. This is certainly true of that subset of regulations, a large subset, concerning environmental and natural resource issues, and the inflexibility of many of these regulations further implies that environmental aims are often pursued in inefficient ways, while other policies have significant damage to the environment as side effects. The Review's further observation that a majority of regulations appeared to have costs which exceeded their quantified benefits does not appear to be true for environmental regulations. However the fact that the quantified costs of a regulation may exceed benefits does not imply that it is not worthwhile: this requires a judgement as to the importance of non-quantified benefits. Nevertheless, there is obviously substantial room for changes in environmental and natural resource legislation that would allow for further improvements in environmental performance without large costs, or for reductions in the cost of meeting existing standards.

The wide variety of pollutants and pollutant sources that affect water quality means that improving it requires action on a number of fronts, and maintaining consistency of treatment among them is not always easy. However, the special treatment of agriculture appears increasingly anomalous, in the United States as in many other countries. It is difficult to justify its exemption from most of the regulations faced by other economic activities. In a sector already in receipt of prodigious subsidies, often tending in themselves to increase aggregate amounts of pollution, it is especially important that externalities be internalised where possible. A tax on the excess nutrient content of fertiliser and feed use would be one important step towards this aim, as already argued in the OECD *Environmental Performance Review* (OECD, 1996). A flat tax would be the easiest to implement, though ideally its level could be set as a function of likely environmental damage, which would vary according to location. A substantial tax would of course be costly for agriculture, but justified under the polluter pays principle. The initial effect could be softened in various ways, through tax credits equivalent to the tax payable on a certain level of fertiliser application, for example, or by introducing the tax at a low level (this would reduce the burden but also reduce the initial effect on incentives, unlike tax credits). If taxes are not politically feasible, this is another area where tradable permits (to apply fertiliser) could be used.

The Total Maximum Daily Load programme appears to offer valuable flexibility in achieving water quality objectives. It should be pursued, wherever possible using economic instruments (for example by making discharge permits marketable, already possible under existing legislation) and linking them to measures of damage (provided this does not lead to excessive complexity). These should of course be consistent with measures taken in other domains (for example, incentives to reduce nitrate discharges should be similar in agriculture to those in industry or waste water treatment plants). Because of the local, one-off nature of many TMDL programmes, full valuation studies and cost-benefit analysis may be too expensive to undertake in every case. Evaluations of a sample of programmes should be carried out, with a view to assessing how well they succeed in aligning costs and incentives.

The example of water supply in one area of California discussed in this chapter is too limited in scope to be able to draw clear and general lessons. However, it is certainly suggestive of the conclusion that the structure of water rights is frequently an obstacle to the rational allocation of water use. This is particularly true of rules whereby rights to water lapse if they are not exercised directly by the holder, so that trading implies permanent transfer of the rights. Some of these rules have their origin in the idea that water rights cannot be absolute, being held in trust for the community; it is surely possible to respect this tradition without making it so difficult to allocate scarce water resources to their most beneficial uses. The general subsidisation of agriculture and in particular the huge subsidies to irrigation water are clear examples of policies that do not take sufficient account of environmental externalities.

Superfund and its costs have been subjected to intense scrutiny and criticism, although even now it seems that there is disagreement about how litigation and other transactions costs add to its burden. In any case, reforms in Superfund operation introduced in the 1990s seem to have resulted in lower costs. The Resource Conservation and Recovery Act (RCRA), though pre-dating the Superfund legislation, has been subject to less searching examination. Since the RCRA sets the constraints on the handling of potential pollutants, (while Superfund deals with sites once they are contaminated), such scrutiny is overdue; indeed, the OECD Environmental Performance Review argued in 1996 that RCRA is over-complicated and burdensome and could be reformed to improve cost-effectiveness without compromising environmental standards.

The introduction of the Toxic Release Inventory is a potentially important innovation, providing information about the environment and what may affect it that would not otherwise be available on a systematic basis, although the number of people who can make effective use of the information may be relatively small. By concentrating attention on a certain, admittedly potentially acute, set of risks, disproportionate public attention may focus on these, to the partial exclusion of other environmental or non-environmental risks. The experiment should thus be pursued by expanding the range and nature of the risks covered in such publicly provided data bases.

Many countries consider that the United States has a particular responsibility, as by far the largest current emitter of greenhouse gases, to show that it is taking the threat of climate change seriously by taking concrete steps to curb its emissions. Under favourable circumstances, in particular if there is widespread participation by developing countries in GHG emissions allowance trading, the increase in the gasoline tax needed to meet the Kyoto target may not be very large (though the proportionate increase in oil and coal prices would be considerable).

The US negotiating position on the Kyoto Protocol is based on efforts to encourage such participation by developing countries, but it is not clear that these efforts will be fully successful, particularly if it implies substantial cuts in developing country emissions relative to a "business as usual" baseline. Furthermore, the example of the abandoned BTU tax from 1993 suggests that public resistance (and pressure from heavy energy-using industries) to even these relatively small price increases might be considerable.

However, to meet its commitments under the UN Framework Convention on Climate Change (UNFCCC), and under the Kyoto Protocol to this convention, the United States will have to take steps to accelerate the reduction in its fossil energy consumption per unit of GDP, especially as it now seems likely that its trend output growth rate has increased in recent years. Automobile users probably do not pay their full external cost, even when climate change is ignored. Certainly, a number of other OECD countries are increasing their already relatively high levels of gas taxation, on environmental grounds. The current set of US measures – the CAFE standards – do not establish the right incentives for fuel economy and seem to have reached the limit of their effectiveness at their current levels. Some gasoline price increase will be necessary, whether through taxation or through the cost of buying emissions allowances on the international market, and now is the time to think about implementing this. It would be feasible, for example, to set up a domestic cap-and-trade system for CO_2 emissions in advance of the international arrangements under the Kyoto Protocol. Action in this area would also serve to increase the chances of successful agreement, on detailed measures to implement the mechanisms agreed at Kyoto in 1997, at the next Conference of the Parties to the UNFCCC in November 2000.[123]

The United States has successfully introduced SO_2 trading on a large scale, after a number of smaller scale experiments in different areas. The NO_x scheme among north-eastern states also appears to have started successfully, and will be enlarged to a number of other states (logically, the inclusion of some Canadian provinces would also yield cost-effective environmental benefits). The success of these schemes has been such as to win over many people who would earlier have opposed them, and it is to be hoped that other countries will recognise their attractions.

Permit trading schemes have certain advantages over tax-based schemes: notably, in a society suspicious of taxation, that they are not taxes. However, the equivalence is very close, especially over time when quantitative targets are likely to be revised in the light of the costs of achieving them, just as taxes would be revised in the light of their effects on quantities. In particular they do not avoid the question of redistribution. Even at relatively low prices for GHG emission permits under the Kyoto Protocol, the notional tax revenue corresponding to the implicit carbon tax will be quite large (about $30 billion with a "low" permit price of $20 per

---

Box 11. Summary of conclusions and elements of a reform package

US *environmental policy*

- Has worked to increase flexibility under the reinvention of regulation programme, although results are disappointing so far.
- Has increased its use of economic incentives, especially in the form of tradable quotas, though recourse to the command and control approach remains pervasive, frequently in the form of regulations that are complicated and expensive to administer.

The role of the courts

- Is a valuable part of the process of establishing, or enforcing, acceptable environmental standards.
- But it sometimes produces rather bizarre results, especially where the underlying legislation is unclear or incomplete; and can be expensive.

Cost-benefit analysis

- Is widely but not consistently used, often because different laws set different restrictions on its use and because the OMB is not strong enough to enforce consistent rules for its use.

Despite the increasing emphasis on economic instruments, which are often the ideal method for internalising environmental incentives, some sectoral interests are unjustifiably protected. This Survey is not comprehensive, but notable examples are:

Agriculture

The United States has particularly perverse incentives for water use in agriculture. The sector also benefits from an effective exemption from most clean water legislation and, as in most OECD countries though less than in many, a high level of overall subsidy. This is ironic since a number of agricultural programmes successfully use quite sophisticated means to maximise environmental benefits.

Climate change

The United States is the most important per capita contributor to greenhouse gas concentrations (overwhelmingly deriving from fossil-fuel consumption) and a signatory to an agreement to cut emissions significantly compared with what they would otherwise be by 2008-12. But it seems reluctant to explain to the public the implications of this commitment: meeting its objectives will require considerable increases in carbon-based energy prices, and no steps to bring this about have been contemplated.

Road transport

Quite apart from its importance as a contributor to greenhouse gas emissions, the road transport sector has many other externalities. The costs of reducing some of these is borne by the sector itself (*e.g.* accident insurance and safety regulations, catalytic converters and emission regulation); but where the externality is closely related fuel consumption, increases in fuel taxation are likely to be both more effective and less costly than the existing CAFE standards.

Box 11.   Summary of conclusions and elements of a reform package *(cont.)*

Elements of a reform package

Accordingly, a reform package in the areas touched on in this chapter should include:

- the early introduction of a CO_2 (GHG) trading scheme;
- an increase in fuel taxes, in lieu of the CAFE standards;
- a rationalisation of the treatment of cost-benefit analysis;
- implementation of a system of charging resource rents on water extraction and the removal of impediments to trade in water rights; and
- a careful evaluation of the environmental costs of agriculture to ensure that the subsidies it enjoys are set in full recognition of these costs.

---

tonne of carbon equivalent). If the permits are issued free of charge, then trading will result in a redistribution of income from those with high to those with low abatement costs; the latter would include, for example, operators of coal-fired power stations whose capital stock is fully amortised. While issuing permits free of charge may be necessary initially, it would make sense for the government to collect some revenue from what essentially becomes a resource rent, allowing some of the rent to be returned to consumers (taxpayers), rather than being retained within the affected industry. This applies to all resource trading schemes, from water use to greenhouse gas emissions.

Notes

1. Based on data available in June 1999 (the last complete data set based on the old system of national accounts), the average growth of hourly productivity in the whole economy between 1972 and 1995 was 0.9 per cent.

2. The Bureau of Labor Statistics (BLS) does not publish figures for productivity in the whole economy. The OECD has calculated its own measure of such productivity. This estimate uses the expenditure measure of GDP together with the establishment data for employment augmented by household survey data for the self-employed and family workers. The average work week in the whole economy was assumed to move in line with that in the non-farm economy.

3. These estimates are based on a perpetual inventory estimate of the stock of software capital. The OECD has assumed that this stock of software capital was zero in 1959. Since then the gross investment in software has been cumulated assuming a depreciation rate of 16 per cent per quarter that corresponds to a service life of four years. As the aggregate capital stock is a chain-weighted series, the stock of real capital invested in software and other goods cannot be added. Rather the aggregate growth rate of capital has been calculated by weighting together the growth rates of the two components using as weights the share of the two components in the nominal capital stock of the previous year.

4. Capital service data measure the flow of services from the capital stock. Items with a high depreciation rate (such as computers) receive a greater weighting in this series than in a measure based on their net worth.

5. Gordon (1999) has argued that all of the actual acceleration in productivity outside the computer sector has been cyclical.

6. The figures are based on the national accounts before the recent comprehensive revision, which included substantial upward revisions to banking services output and better output measures for some other services.

7. These estimates do not use national estimates for the prices of computer equipment as not all countries make the appropriate hedonic price correction for the investment goods deflator. Instead, a hedonic price index has been calculated for each country based on the US price index.

8. It should be noted though that hedonic price indices have not been used to measure the impact of electrification on output. Nordhaus (1997) argues that the use of hedonic price indices for lighting would substantially increase the growth of output in the early years of the 20th century.

9. In March 2000, the Bureau of the Census issued its first estimate of electronic retail sales. For the fourth quarter of 1999 E-commerce represented $5.3 billion of turnover,

equivalent to 0.6 per cent of total retail sales and 25 per cent of mail order sales in the same period.

10. Most industry analysts suggest that retail electronic commerce sales will grow by between 35 and 75 per cent annually for the next five years. Such a growth rate would be similar to the 68 per cent average annual growth rate achieved by the Sears Home Catalogue between its introduction in 1895 and 1900. Growth in the following five years fell to 20 per cent and dropped further (to 10 per cent) between 1907 and 1925 (Merrill Lynch, 1999).

11. The data are taken from the Statistical Annex to *Digital Economy* II, Department of Commerce(1999).

12. This research estimates that the increase in the share of temporary employment reduced the NAIRU by about ¼ percentage point between 1979 and 1993, and it suggests an even larger drop in the NAIRU occurred over the rest of the 1990s due to the large run-up in the share of employment at temporary help agencies after 1993.

13. This figure (of 2½ per cent) is higher than the previous OECD estimate of potential growth in the early 1990s because of the recent upward revisions to the historical data in the national accounts.

14. Household debt rose 9½ per cent in 1999, compared with 8¾ per cent in 1998 and 6½ per cent in 1997.

15. In 1998, the proportion of families that owned equities, either directly or indirectly through mutual funds, retirement accounts and other managed accounts, rose to nearly 50 per cent from 40 per cent in 1995 and 32 per cent in 1989. Increases in ownership were particularly large for middle-class families (Kennickell *et al.*, 2000).

16. Assuming a marginal propensity to consume out of stock market wealth of 0.04, consumption has been boosted by an average of 1.3 percentage point per year in the past three years by rising stock market wealth (Greenspan, 2000 and Ludvigson and Steindel, 1999). While 3 to 4 per cent are widely used estimates for the marginal propensity to consume out of wealth, some researchers have found larger effects. Boone *et al.* (1998) found marginal propensities to consume for the United States that range from 0.04 to 0.07. They also found that wealth effects for other G7 countries were not as well determined and were generally weaker due to more limited and less equally distributed stock ownership and later financial liberalisation.

17. The labour force participation rate for prime-age workers is 77.8 per cent, one of the highest rates in the OECD.

18. But with carryover of 2.1 percentage points, the slowdown will not be apparent in the annual average figures. On a fourth-quarter to fourth-quarter basis, real output growth in 2000 and 2001 is projected to be 3.5 and 2.8 per cent, respectively.

19. This period was chosen in order to avoid the extremely high apparent real interest rates seen in the early 1980s when inflation slowed. The coefficients used in the calculations were –0.108 for the federal funds rate less the overall CPI inflation rate; –0.306 for the ten-year Treasury note interest rate less long-run inflation expectations measured by the Livingston Survey; 0.012 for the level of overall stock prices (measured by the Wilshire 5000) relative to GDP and, finally –0.033 for the real broad effective exchange rate, as measured by the Federal Reserve.

20. Since the last *Survey*, gross and net government debt have been raised by two factors. Government pension funds are now allocated to the private sector and the statistics

on the debt of state and local governments were increased by the inclusion of trade credit.

21. The data here are drawn from tax returns. However, at all but the lowest income levels there is a very close linkage between family income and income declared on tax returns (Sailer and Weber, 1997).

22. According to CBO estimates each 0.1 percentage point additional growth generates around $3 billion of extra revenues.

23. The deficit in December 1998 was affected by a shift of social security payments from January 1999 to December 1998, as the January payment date fell on a weekend.

24. The individual interest coupons of a number of low-priced bonds could be recombined in a different fashion, so that the individual components of off-the-run bonds become the same as the components of on-the-run (benchmark) bonds.

25. Estimates that take an even longer time frame (Auerbach, 1999a and Auerbach and Gale, 1999) suggest that the gap may be slightly greater.

26. This is the difference between the current 2½ per cent trend and the measurement adjusted trend of 1.5 per cent used in the 2000 Trustees report.

27. The Technical Panel agreed with the assumption of a slowdown in decline of mortality at young ages. Such a movement seems well established internationally. The Panel, however, felt that the assumed decline among the elderly was too low.

28. Household income includes earnings, interest and dividends, and other money income received (including pensions, public assistance and other cash transfers, but excluding capital gains) before any deductions are made (for taxes and items such as pensions). Income in the official statistics is deflated by the consumer price index. If instead, the new research (current-methods) CPI were used for deflation, real income would have risen more rapidly – 5½ per cent since 1989, compared with 2½ per cent using the official CPI (Bureau of the Census, 1999).

29. Although income inequality clearly worsened in the early 1990s, these measures overstate the magnitude of change. Revisions to data collection methodology in 1993 included increasing the maximum amount of reported income from $299 999 to $999 999, thus boosting measured relative to actual income for the highest income groups. This change raised the income share for the top 5 per cent of household by a full percentage point and accounted for about one-third of the increase in the Gini index between 1989 and 1993 (Ryscavage, 1995).

30. These include health insurance and pension contributions and in-kind benefits some families receive from the government, such as food stamps, Medicare, Medicaid and subsidised housing.

31. In 1998, 4.3 million people, including 2.3 million children, were lifted out of poverty by the EITC (Council of Economic Advisers, 2000).

32. After peaking in March 1994, welfare caseloads dropped 48 per cent through March 1999 to 7.3 million people, or 2¾ per cent of the population (Council of Economic Advisers, 1999a).

33. The study found that during the 1993-96 period one-quarter to one-third of the caseload reduction was due to declining unemployment.

34. In general, minimum wage increases tend to redistribute income among low-income families rather than redistributing income to low-income families. While the minimum wage raises incomes for workers that retain their jobs, displacement effects of the

minimum wage cause reductions in the incomes of other low-wage families (Neumark and Wascher, 1997; Neumark, Schweitzer and Wascher, 1998).

35. While some analysts consider a minimum wage hike likely, prospects for the current bills are uncertain. The congressional bills include a number of other proposals including business tax cuts, which are not supported by Democrats and have been threatened with a Presidential veto.

36. The minimum wage now covers 2½ million workers, but the proposed increases (of nearly 20 per cent) would directly affect nearly 12 million (Bernstein, 1999). With this expansion in coverage, individuals searching for minimum wage employment are likely to face a slowdown in labour demand. A 10 per cent increase in the minimum wage is thought to cause a 1 to 2 per cent decline in employment of teens and young adults (Neumark and Wascher, 1994) and larger employment losses for young, low-skilled individuals (Neumark and Wascher, 1996).

37. A study based on the 1990-91 minimum wage increases also found a negative effect on welfare caseloads, but concluded that recent welfare reforms may have reduced the effect higher minimum wages have on encouraging welfare-to-work transitions (Turner, 1999). Other studies, covering different time periods, have found a positive effect (Brandon, 1995; Page et al., 1999).

38. Chapter III of OECD (1992) covered this topic in depth.

39. In 1998, 62 per cent of health insurance was provided by employment-based private plans.

40. The National Education Goals Panel, an independent federal agency made up of federal and state officials, is charged with monitoring and speeding progress toward the national goals for education.

41. In 1995, among OECD countries, US students scored above average in mathematics in fourth grade but well below average in eighth grade (OECD, 1998).

42. In 1995, pupils (in eighth grade) in 15 states scored higher on average on science achievement examinations than their peers in every country tested except Singapore.

43. The Wisconsin Supreme Court ruled that vouchers for religious schools are constitutional, while the Vermont Court overturned a Vermont law providing vouchers for religious schools. The Maine Supreme Court allowed the state to continue providing vouchers to some private school while denying them to religious schools.

44. In 1998, AT&T's share of long-distance carrier revenues was 43 per cent, compared with 26 for MCI and WorldCom, and 11 per cent for Sprint. However, AT&T's share of the residential market – at 58 per cent – is larger than its overall market share (Federal Communications Commission, 2000).

45. The Bell operating companies were precluded from providing long-distance service to their local subscribers as part of the 1982 settlement between the government and AT&T. This agreement was replaced by the Telecommunications Act of 1996, which outlined specific requirements that the Bell operating companies must meet before they could obtain FCC authorisation to provide long-distance service in their local service areas.

46. In 1996 ILECs' share of the long-distance market in their local service areas varied considerably across the country, from 3.6 per cent in California to nearly 56 per cent in South Dakota (Eisner and Wynns, 1998).

47. The Telecommunications Act of 1996 established three methods of entry into the local phone market. Competitors can purchase telecommunications services from ILECs at

wholesale rates and resell the services to end users; they can lease unbundled elements of the ILEC's network; or they can build and use their own facilities. In mid-1999, about 2 per cent of ILEC lines were being resold to competitors and only 0.4 per cent were leased as unbundled network elements. Information is not available on the number of customer lines provided by competitors that provide their own equipment, but indirect evidence suggests that facilities-based competition for local service is becoming more common (Council of Economic Advisers, 1999b). By mid-1999, competitive local exchange carriers that provided their own facilities were in every state and in over 90 per cent of local operating areas (Federal Communications Commission, 1999).

48. While differences in technical standards and relatively high prices for "roaming" may have held back the spread of mobile telephones in the past, the introduction of nationwide digital networks and rate structures that lower the cost of "roaming" has largely eliminated this as an issue in recent years.

49. AT&T plans to eventually provide telephone services over a vast network of cable systems it has acquired, and other cable systems have been upgrading their systems to be able to market telephone services to their cable customers.

50. This ruling added the high-frequency portion of the local loop to the list of unbundled network elements that incumbent local exchange carriers must make available to competitors.

51. Certain West-coast refiners are dependent on Alaska crude oil and have little short-term ability to switch suppliers.

52. Prices for WTI crude oil traded in Cushing serve as a benchmark for pricing many other crude oils and for crude oil futures trading on the New York Mercantile Exchange.

53. In detail, 38 per cent of corn, 57 per cent of soybeans and 65 per cent of cotton were modified to be either resistant to herbicide or insects (United States Department of Agriculture, 1999).

54. It is noteworthy that price discrimination within nations may not only be tolerated – perhaps network industries like electricity and telecommunications are the most obvious examples – but may even be welfare-improving under certain conditions – see Anderson *et al.* (1995).

55. It is well documented in the economic literature that the mere filing of anti-dumping complaints has a persuasive "threat" effect. For example, Prusa (1999) showed that the value of US imports falls sharply, even for those cases that are rejected.

56. Messerlin and Reed (1995) argue that policies and practices across the major economies have been converging, resulting in increasing use of such duties by these trading partners. Prusa (1999) shows that "new" users have accounted for half the world total in recent years.

57. Leidy (1996) showed the close relationship between the number of antidumping and countervailing duty *petitions* per year and the economic cycle (proxied by the unemployment rate) and competitive pressures (proxied by the real effective exchange rate). The series used in that study is no longer updated. Using the series for *initiations* that is currently available and extending the sample through 1998 substantially weakens the aforementioned relationships, although they remain marginally significant in statistical terms.

58. There were 122 anti-dumping duty orders and 30 countervailing duty orders applying to iron and steel and products thereof in effect on 1 January 1999, 41 and 59 per cent, respectively, of all such orders.

59. Thus the US definition refers to a process, whereas in Europe the phrase is generally seen as referring to a financial institution: "a merchant bank" that engages in investment banking, counselling and negotiating mergers and acquisitions.

60. The Community Reinvestment Act imposes certain obligations on banks to lend in geographic areas where they have branches. The objective of the legislation is to enhance credit availability in less-favoured areas, especially urban areas inhabited primarily by minorities.

61. The assets of LTCM were held in an offshore company.

62. When two banks merge, or one buys another, the resulting bank has choice of two methods of accounting for the changes flowing from the merger. The first is *pooling of interest*. In this case, the assets, liabilities and equity of the two companies are combined as if the two companies had always been operating together. However, using such a procedure requires that the banks be of comparable size and means that there are post-merger restrictions on assets sales and share repurchases. For these reasons a growing proportion of bank mergers have used the second method: *purchase accounting*. In this method, assets and liabilities are marked to market and combined in the new balance sheet. The difference between net worth and the price of the acquisition becomes an intangible asset that has to be written off over a period of time, thereby raising costs.

63. While there is a considerable degree of agreement on the kinds of indicators that are relevant in assessing sustainable development, there is no consensus on the quantitative comparison of indicators in different areas, economic versus social, for example. See U.S. Interagency Working Group on Sustainable Development (1998) for a qualitative assessment of a range of different indicators. While most "economic" indicators represented in that report were judged to be developing favourably, of 16 selected environmental indicators, six were judged to be developing unfavourably (most prominently those related to climate change), five (including urban air and surface water quality) favourably, while five were uncertain. See also OECD (2000a).

64. See Portney (1998) for a brief discussion of the influence of these incidents. The discussion in this section draws heavily on Portney (1998) and OECD (1996).

65. Others include: the Endangered Species Act (1973), the Safe Drinking Water Act (1974), the Resource Conservation and Recovery Act (1976), the Comprehensive Environmental Response Compensation and Liability Act ("Superfund", 1980). See OECD (1996, pp. 32-34) for a comprehensive list.

66. The Toxic Substances Control Act and the Federal Insecticide Fungicide and Rodenticide Act, for example.

67. Their origin can be traced back at least to 1978 or earlier, but Executive Orders 12291 of 1981 and 12866 of 1993 defined them in their present form. OECD (1999e) discusses Regulatory Impact Assessments in some detail.

68. OECD (1996, pp. 27-31) has more details.

69. 1992 Budget documentation showed that the amount spent to save a "statistical life" under different regulatory programmes ranged from under $100 000 to over $20 000 000 (1992 prices). See OMB (1991), pp. 367 *et seq.* and OECD (1991).

70. In the case of interpretation see, for example, Melnick (1983, p. 113 *et seq.*) for a discussion of the courts' role in the development of the Clean Air Act.

71. In another aspect of this issue, high legal costs under the "Superfund" and toxic waste legislation may be partly attributable to the fact that whereas much legislation specifies the Washington D.C. circuit court of appeals as having jurisdiction over regulatory challenges in the first instance, this legislation increases the potential for long series of actions and appeals by allowing plaintiffs the possibility of taking action in state courts.

72. The choice of issues raised here is considerably influenced by the views of administration officials, expressed during Secretariat discussions with them, on what are currently the major challenges for environmental policy.

73. OECD data show that in the mid-1990s the United States generated 720 kg of municipal waste per capita, more than half again as much as the typical OECD Member country (461 kg per capita). Also in 1996 the recycling rates for paper and cardboard and glass were 41 and 26 per cent, respectively, in the United States, while the simple average rates for OECD Member countries were 41 and 51 per cent, respectively.

74. Secondary standards are also set for pollutants' impact on crops, property, etc., subject to a cost-benefit test.

75. SO_2, particulate matter and ozone standards were promulgated in 1971; that for lead in 1978; and those for carbon monoxide and NO_x in 1985.

76. After promulgation, up to three years are allowed for designation of non-attainment areas and up to a further three years for submission of a State Implementation Plan for meeting the new standards. The CAA allows up to ten years, plus two one-year extensions for attainment of the new standards. Thus it allowed up to 2015 for full implementation of the 1997 standards.

77. This can be found in http://www.epa.gov/ttn/oarpg/gen/97-1440a.txt of 2 September 1999.

78. The constitutional issue is that while Congress cannot delegate too much policy-making legislative power to an agency, and the D.C. Circuit Court of Appeals believed that neither the statute nor the agency identified a determinate principle that would make the delegation permissible.

79. For example, regulatory impact assessments were carried out, as required.

80. A number of important government agencies – the Commerce Department, the Council of Economic Advisers and the Office of Management and Budget – in fact believed that the cost-benefit analysis showed that tightening the ozone standards did not have net benefits. Inter-agency discussion did not resolve this disagreement, and the issue was decided by the President.

81. The head of the EPA, appointed by the President, is known as the Administrator.

82. For example, it was allowed under the phase-out of lead in gasoline in the 1980s and of production of chlorofluorocarbons (CFCs) in the 1990s. It was also already used, though with many and evolving restrictions, in California's implementation of the Clean Air Act (the "Offset" scheme) from 1976 onwards, leading to the present "RECLAIM" scheme.

83. Emitters trading under the SO_2 scheme remain nevertheless subject to other health-based regulations on their emissions.

84. In equilibrium, marginal abatement costs are equal to the permit price, since only at that price are buyers and sellers indifferent as to whether they should cut their pollu-

tion levels or buy the needed permits. Although there was wide variation in expectations about permit prices before trading began, $400-500 per ton was generally thought to be a reasonably guess.

85. However, the actual outcomes have entailed smaller reductions than implied by the capped emissions, partly since these represent only one source of SO_2. Acidity in surface water – the main target of the programme – has not noticeably improved even though deposition rates have fallen.

86. Other administrative law requires that regulations should not be introduced without a study of the costs of alternative means to achieve the same ends, which should show that feasible alternatives are more expensive.

87. The 1996 National Water Quality Inventory surveyed conditions in about half of the bodies of water that flow all year round.

88. Agriculture is not generally subject to the Clean Water Act; concentrated animal feeding operations (where the definition in terms of the number of animals varies by species) are an exception. Environmental Impact Statements are not required for agricultural policies generally, though large projects, such as irrigation schemes, might require them under the National Environmental Policy Act.

89. In the Netherlands, such a tax is applied to phosphates. See de Haan *et al.* (1997).

90. So-called abstractions per capita in the mid-1990s were 1880 cubic metres per year, more than double the OECD population-weighted average (930 cubic metres), triple the simple average (618 cubic metres) and ten times the levels in those counties with the lowest intensity of use (Luxembourg, Denmark and the United Kingdom).

91. According to OECD figures, intensity of use, *i.e.* total consumption as a percentage of available resources, in the mid-1990s averaged 19.9 per cent in the United States., similar to Japan's 20.8 per cent. France, 23.9 per cent, Germany 24.4 per cent and Italy, 32.1 per cent, had rather higher intensities. But the weighted average across all OECD countries was only 11.8 per cent.

92. A report by the General Accounting Office to the Senate (US General Accounting Office, 1996) detailed how federal subsidies to agricultural users of federally-sponsored irrigation projects have often amounted to almost 100 per cent of the costs attributed to irrigators.

93. Riparian rights are vested in the owner of a body of water or neighbouring land, whereas prior use rights depend on historical usage. In both cases, the rights tend not to be absolute: water resources are treated as being held in trust for the wider community.

94. Riparian rights for some – basically non-extractive – purposes are also recognised in California, for example.

95. Howe (1997) (quoted in OECD, 1999*b*, p.78) refers to the "long but narrow history" of water markets in the United States. For more detail, see OECD (1999*b*).

96. Sometimes these costs are exaggerated. For example, opponents of the Superfund legislation often refer to RAND research that shows that three-quarters of costs are absorbed by litigation. However, according to Probst *et al.* (1995), this referred to only part of total costs and covered non-representative sites. They estimate that about 20 per cent of total costs are absorbed by transactions costs, including litigation.

97. Tax revenue is generally used to finance initial cleanups, with the liability provisions used to recover costs from responsible parties. About three-quarters of these federal revenues are provided by specific taxes introduced under CERCLA: a chemical tax, a

petroleum tax and an environmental income tax, intended to cover unrecoverable costs. These taxes expired in 1995 following Congress's refusal to reauthorise them.

98. Water vapour is the most important greenhouse gas, but its atmospheric concentration is little affected by human activity. Among GHGs whose presence is due to human activity, carbon dioxide is quantitatively the most important, followed by methane and nitrous oxide. Many other gases in the atmosphere have warming effects, but they are small compared with those of carbon dioxide and methane. See IPCC (1996).

99. There are two in addition to straightforward permit trading: Joint Implementation, where an emitter in one country invests in emissions reduction in facilities in another country participating in the Protocol, earning credits for use at home, and the Clean Development Mechanism, which is similar except that the reduction takes place in a developing country without an overall ceiling on its own emissions. See OECD (1999*c* and 1999*d*).

100. Annex B to the Protocol lists the countries accepting emissions targets, along with their targets. These figures are derived from the OECD's GREEN climate change model, assuming that labour markets adjust flexibly.

101. Simulations with the OECD's GREEN model suggest that if *all* non-Annex B countries participated in the Kyoto Protocol, with their assigned amounts of emission permits based on a "business as usual" baseline, then the permit price could be as low as $10 per tonne in 2008-12.

102. This may not sound very much, especially in view of recent variations in oil prices, but a 1993 Clinton administration proposal to increase the gasoline tax by a similar amount was abandoned in the face of vociferous opposition, and it is now received wisdom in the US political realm that gasoline tax hikes are politically suicidal.

103. Windmills are a growing – though up to now costly – source of electricity in Denmark, for example see OECD (2000*b*).

104. Extra spending on highways, and on mass transit programmes, was agreed in 1998 in order to absorb this surplus, while some had proposed reducing taxation. The Transportation Equity Act of 1998 now prevents funds in the HTF being spent on anything other than transport projects. Something under 20 per cent of the HTF revenue is allocated to mass transit projects, the rest to highway construction and maintenance.

105. The 1999 price of gasoline averaged around $1.20 per gallon (32 cents per litre), with the Federal gasoline tax at 18.4 cents (the diesel tax is 24.4 cents) per gallon. The EPA does not have an official estimate of the external costs of road transport.

106. By way of comparison, in that year, the federal gasoline excise tax was 14.1 cents per gallon (21.1 cents for diesel), raising $14.5 billion.

107. Other externalities, such as the cost of accidents, are related to frequency and distance of travel, which is obviously correlated – though not perfectly – with fuel consumption, so some improvement here could be expected as an ancillary benefit to higher prices.

108. For example, $240 million per annum of public funds is spent on a programme of research into new-generation vehicles.

109. One potential problem in constraining low-density development could be court action by frustrated landowners. Since the value of land would be dependent on whether development permission was given or not, those refused permission could argue that this amounted to a government "taking". Originally intended to prevent uncompensated expropriation of private land by the government, the constitutional

prohibition on "takings" has been interpreted by the courts to include action that very significantly reduces the value of land, even if the land itself is not expropriated. Few examples of successful takings litigation against the government occur in this area however; see Congressional Budget Office (1998). A recent New Jersey programme to develop "green belts" surrounding urban areas is to be implemented by purchasing the relevant land, for which state borrowing of $1 billion was recently authorised.

110. In fact, in such circumstances Congress may refuse to ratify the Kyoto Protocol, in which case it will probably not enter into force and its targets will not be legally binding.

111. For a discussion of regulatory reform more generally, see OECD (1999e).

112. The groups are the Clean Air Council, the Conservation Law Foundation, the Environmental Defense Fund, the Natural Resources Defense Council, the Natural Resources Council of Maine and the Sierra Club.

113. The industrial census figures on environmental compliance expenditures used in this study have not been collected since 1994. In any case, the figures are unlikely to show the full economic cost of environmental regulation, since they are based on actual expenditures and would therefore not have included, for example, output lost through choice of production technique.

114. Official information on discharges and emissions by individual enterprises and on compliance of particular localities with clean air and water standards is available on the Internet.

115. The 1977 Clean Air Act, for example, included "prevention of significant deterioration" language which ensured that the clean parts of the country did not attract polluting manufacturers from the more stringently regulated dirty parts of the country on the basis of their weaker standards.

116. See OMB (1998, p. 36 et seq.), and OECD (1999e, p. 159).

117. Of course, a cost overestimate is no better than an underestimate – both (for given benefits) will lead to misallocation of resources.

118. They can also be traced further back to a requirement for "Inflation Impact Assessments", which dealt with more than effects on inflation, introduced during the Nixon administration.

119. Executive Order 12866 defines such action to include not just proposed regulations but advance notice of, or inquiries into, proposed regulations. "Economically significant" means anything with "an annual effect on the economy of $100 million or more or [which] adversely affect[s] ... a sector of the economy, productivity, competition, jobs, the environment, public health or safety, or State, local, or tribal governments or communities ...".

120. Although Congress discontinued collection of statistics on expenditures by enterprises in meeting environmental regulations (see footnote 107), the Act governing the OMB's cost-benefit publications extended the OMB's remit in 1999 to include investigating the impact on State, Local and Tribal governments. Executive Order 13132 ("Federalism") of August 1999 reinforces the requirement for federal agencies to consult with lower levels of government.

121. There remain some doubts. On the benefit side, researchers at Resources for the Future argue that the value of a life saved is often over-stated (perhaps by an order of magnitude) because the techniques used for eliciting subjective valuations (willingness to pay, or willingness to be compensated) do not take proper account of people's tendency to believe that unlikely events occur more frequently than they really

do; nearly all the benefits of the major pieces of environmental legislation are linked to lives saved. On the cost side, while cash expenditures on monitoring, abatement and administration can be accurately measured (though no longer officially recorded, see footnote 107), it is doubtful whether the cost of a choice of technology constrained by legislation can be easily assessed.

122. It is often noted that firms who may be subject to restrictions say they prefer a regulatory approach over the use of taxes or charges on the grounds that this gives them greater certainty. One possible explanation for this is that the regulators' interlocutors in enterprises are often not those within an enterprise who are most concerned with its profitability: it may make their lives easier to argue for "command and control" even though that is not necessarily in the best interests of the enterprise. Even when it is in an individual enterprise's interest, this may be because it hopes to use the regulation as a way to reduce competition, for instance as a barrier to entry.

123. Any agreement would then be submitted to national legislatures in all countries for ratification, in the US case early in the new Administration.

Bibliography

Achieve (1999),
   The 1999 National Education Summit Briefing Book.

Anderson, Simon P., Nicolas Schmitt and Jacques-François Thisse (1995),
   "Who Benefits from Antidumping Legislation?", *Journal of International Economics*,
   Volume 38, No. 3-4, May, pp. 321-327.

Auerbach, Alan J. (1999a),
   "On the Performance and Use of Government Revenue Forecasts", *National Tax Journal*,
   Volume 52, No. 4, December, pp. 767-788.

Auerbach, Alan J. (1999b),
   "Formation of Fiscal Policy: the Experience of the Past 25 Years", Paper presented
   to the Federal Reserve Bank of New York Conference on Fiscal Policy in an Era of
   Surpluses.

Auerbach, Alan J. and William G. Gale (1999),
   "Does the Budget Surplus Justify Large-Scale Tax Cuts? Updates and Extensions", *Tax
   Notes*, 18 October, pp. 369-376.

Bank for International Settlements (1999),
   Market Liquidity: Research findings and Selected Policy Implications, Basle, May.

Bernstein, Jared (1999),
   "The Next Step: The New Minimum Wage Proposal and the Old Opposition", EPI *Issue
   Brief*, Economic Policy Institute, 27 April.

Bettelheim, Adriel and Alan K. Ota (2000),
   "Governing the Internet", CQ *Weekly*, Volume 58, No. 4, Congressional Quarterly,
   pp. 110-111.

Blackman, Allen and J. Mazurek (1999),
   "The Cost of Developing Site-Specific Environmental Regulations: Evidence from EPA's
   Project XL", Resources for the Future Discussion Paper 99-35, Washington, DC, April.

Board of Trustees (1999),
   The Annual Report of the Board of Trustees of the Federal Old Age and Survivors Insurance Fund,
   Washington, DC, May.

Boone, Laurence, Claude Giorno and Peter Richardson (1998),
   "Stock Market Fluctuations and Consumption Behaviour: Some Recent Evidence", Economics Department Working Paper No. 208, OECD, Paris, December.

Boston Consulting Group (1999a),
   "The State of Online Retailing 2.0", Shop.Org, Silver Spring, MD, July.

Boston Consulting Group (1999*b*),
"The State of Online Retailing", Q3 1999 Update, Shop.Org, Silver Spring, MD, 30 November.

Brandon, Peter (1995),
"Jobs Taken by Mothers Moving from Welfare to Work And the Effects of Minimum Wages on This Transition", Employment Policies Institute, February.

Brynjolfsson, Erik and Lorin Hitt (1998),
"Beyond the Productivity Paradox", *Communications of the* ACM, August.

Bureau of Labor Statistics (1999),
Employee Benefits in Medium and Large Private Establishments, 1997, Bulletin 2517, US Department of Labor, September.

Bureau of the Census (1999),
Money Income in the United States: 1998, Current Population Reports, P60-206, US Government Printing Office, Washington, DC, September.

Burkhauser, Richard V., Kenneth A. Couch and Andrew J. Glenn (1996),
"Public Policies for the Working Poor: The Earned Income Tax Credit versus Minimum Wage Legislation", *Research in Labor Economics*, Volume 15, pp. 65-110.

Burniaux, Jean-Marc, Thai-Thanh Dang, Douglas Fore, Michael Förster, Marco Mira d'Ercole and Howard Oxley (1998),
"Income Distribution and Poverty in Selected OECD Countries", Economics Department Working Papers No. 189, OECD, Paris, March.

Burtless, Gary (1999),
"Growing American Inequality: Sources and Remedies", *Brookings Review*, winter, pp. 31-35.

Calomiris, Charles W. (1997),
The Post-Modern Bank Safety Net: Lessons from Developed and Developing Countries, American Enterprise Institute, Washington, DC.

Calomiris, Charles W. (1999),
"Building an Incentive-Compatible Safety Net", *Journal of Banking and Finance*, Volume 23, No. 10, October, pp. 1499-1519.

Campbell, Jennifer (1999),
Health Insurance Coverage: 1998, Current Population Reports,Series P60-208,US Census Bureau, US Government Printing Office, October.

Carrington, William J. and Bruce C. Fallick (1999),
"Minimum Wage Careers?", Finance and Economics Discussion Series 1999-60, Board of Governors of the Federal Reserve System, August.

Clark, Todd E. (1999),
"A Comparison of the CPI and the PCE Price Index", *Economic Review*, Federal Reserve Bank of Kansas City, Third Quarter, pp. 15-29.

Cobb, Clifford (1999),
"The Roads Aren't Free", *Challenge*, Volume 42, No. 3, May-June, pp. 63-83.

Cohen, Darrel S. and Glenn R. Follette (1999),
"The Automatic Fiscal Stabilisers: Quietly Doing Their Thing", Finance and Economics Discussion Series 1999-64, Board of Governors of the Federal Reserve System, December.

Congressional Budget Office (1991),
Controlling the Risks of Government Sponsored Enterprises, Congress of the United States, Washington, DC, April.

Congressional Budget Office (1998a),
Projecting Federal tax Revenues and the effect of Changes in Tax Law, Washington, DC, December.

Congressional Budget Office (1998b),
Regulatory Takings and Proposals for Change, Washington, DC.

Congressional Budget Office (1999),
Maintaining Budgetary Discipline: Spending and Revenue Options, Washington, DC, April.

Congressional Budget Office (1999),
The Budget for Fiscal Year 2000: An End of Year Summary, Washington, DC, December.

Congressional Budget Office (1999),
The Long-term Budget Outlook: An Update, Washington, DC, December.

Congressional Budget Office (1999),
The Economic and Budget Outlook: An Update, Washington, DC, July.

Congressional Budget Office (2000),
The Economic and Budget Outlook: Fiscal Years 2001-2010, Washington, DC, January.

Congressional Budget Office (2000),
"Monthly Budget Review", Washington, DC, various issues.

Council of Economic Advisers (1998),
"Good News for Low Income Families: Expansions in the Earned Income Tax Credit and the Minimum Wage", Executive Office of the President of the United States, December.

Council of Economic Advisers (1999a),
"The Effects of Welfare Policy and the Economic Expansion of Welfare Caseloads: An Update", Executive Office of the President of the United States, August.

Council of Economic Advisers (1999b),
"Progress Report: Growth and Competition in US Telecommunications 1993-98", Executive Office of the President of the United States, February.

Council of Economic Advisers (2000),
Economic Report of the President, Executive Office of the President of the United States, February.

Council of Economic Advisers and the Office of the Chief Economist, US Department of Labor (1999),
"20 Million Jobs: January 1993-November 1999", Executive Office of the President of the United States, 3 December.

Council on Environmental Quality (1997),
Environmental Quality Along The American River, Executive Office of the President of the United States.

Counter Party Risk Management Group (1999),
"Improving Counterparty Risk Management Practices", Goldman Sachs and JP Morgan, New York, June.

Cox, W. Michael and R. Alm (2000),
Myths of Rich and Poor, Basic Books, January.

Dalaker, Joseph (1999),
Poverty in the United States:1998, Current Population Reports, Series P60-207, US Census Bureau, US Government Printing Office, September.

David, Paul (1999),
> "Digital Economy and the Productivity Paradox: After Ten Years What has been Learned", Paper presented to the Conference, Understanding the Digital Economy Data, Tools, Research, US Department of Commerce, May.

Davies, Terence (1988),
> "The Environmental Protection Act", The Conservation Foundation, Washington, DC, mimeo.

De Haan, Cees, Henning Steinfeld and Harvey Blackburn (1997),
> *Livestock and the Environment. Finding a Balance*, Food and Agriculture Organisation, available at http://www.fao.org/WAICENT/FAOINFO/AGRICULT/aga/LXEHTML

De Young, Robert (1999),
> "Mergers and the Changing Landscape of Commercial Banking", Chicago Fed Letter Number 145, September.

Delucchi, Mark (1996),
> "The Annualised Social Cost of Motor-Vehicle use in the US, 1990-1991: Summary of Theory, Data, Methods and Results", Davis, California: Institute of Transportation Studies.

Department of Commerce (1999),
> *The Emerging Digital Economy* II, Washington, DC, June.

Eisner, James and Peyton Wynns (1998),
> *Historical Patterns of Entry into Long Distance by Local Exchange Carrier*, Federal Communications Commission, September.

Eissa, Nada and Jeffrey G. Liebman (1996),
> "Labor Supply Response to the Earned Income Tax Credit", *Quarterly Journal of Economics*, Volume 112, Issue 2, May, pp. 605-637.

Environmental Defense Fund (2000),
> "Environmental Impacts of Hog Factories in North Carolina", available at http://www.hogwatch.org/getthefacts/factsheets/enviroimpacts.htm/.

Feather, Peter, Daniel Hellerstein and LeRoy Hansen (1999),
> "Economic Valuation of Environmental Benefits and the Targeting of Conservation Programs: The Case of the CRP", Agricultural Report, No. 778, US Department of Agriculture.

Federal Communications Commission (1999),
> *Local Competition*, Washington, DC, August.

Federal Communications Commission (2000),
> *Trends in Telephone Service*, Washington, DC, March.

Federal Reserve System Study Group on Subordinated Notes and Debentures (1999),
> *Using Subordinated Debt and an Instrument of Market Discipline*, Staff Studies No. 172, Board of Governors of the Federal Reserve System, Washington, DC, December.

Fiorino, Daniel J. (1995),
> *Making Environmental Policy*, University of California Press.

Fleming, Michael J. (1999),
> "The Benchmark Performance of the US Treasury Market: Recent Performance and Possible Alternatives", Paper presented to the Federal Reserve Bank of New York Conference on Fiscal Policy in an Era of Surpluses.

Forrester (2000), "States Lose Half a Billion in Taxes to Web Retail", Forrester Research Inc.,
    Cambridge, MA, February.

General Accounting Office (1996),
    "Bureau of Reclamation. Information on Allocation and Payment of Costs of Constructing
    Water Projects", GA/RCED -96-100.

Giorno, Claude, Pete Richardson, Deborah Roseveare and Paul van den Noord (1995),
    "Potential Output, Output Gaps and Structural Budget Balances", OECD *Economic Studies*,
    No. 24, 1995/I, OECD, Paris, pp. 167-209.

Goolsbee, Austan (1999),
    "In a World without Borders: The Impact of Taxes on Internet Commerce", Submission to
    the Advisory Commission on Electronic Commerce, Washington, DC.

Goolsbee, Austan and Jonathan Zittrain (1999),
    "Evaluating the Costs and Benefits of Taxing Internet Commerce", *National Tax Journal*,
    Volume 52, No. 3, September, pp. 413-428.

Gordon, Robert (1999),
    "Has the New Economy' Rendered the US Productivity Slowdown Obsolete?", paper
    presented at OECD Workshop on Productivity Growth, OECD, Paris, 6 December.

Greenspan, Alan (1999),
    "Mortgage Markets and Economic Activity", speech before a Conference on Mortgage
    Markets and Economic Activity sponsored by America's Community Bankers, Washington,
    DC, 2 November.

Greenspan, Alan (2000),
    "Technology and the Economy", Speech before the Economic Club of New York, New
    York City, 13 January.

Guyer, Jocelyn, Matthew Broaddus and Michelle Cochran (1999),
    "Missed Opportunities: Declining Medicaid Enrollment Undermines the Nation's
    Progress in Insuring Low-Income Children", Center on Budget and Policy Priorities,
    21 October.

Harrington, Winston, R.D. Morgenstern and P. Nelson (1999),
    "On the Accuracy of Regulatory Cost Estimates", Resources for the Future, Washington,
    DC.

Hawke, John D. (1998),
    Testimony Before The Senate Committee On Banking, Housing, And Urban Affairs On
    Financial Regulatory Relief And Economic Efficiency Act of 1997, 10 March.

Hellerstein, Walter (1999),
    "The Law of Sales Tax in a Cyber Economy", Submission to the Advisory Commission on
    Electronic Commerce, Washington, DC.

Hollenbeck, S.M. and M.K. Keenan Kahr (1999),
    "Individual Income Tax Returns, 1997 Early Tax Estimates", Bulletin of the Internal Rev-
    enue Service, Washington, DC, November.

Howe, Charles W. (1997),
    "Increasing Efficiency in Water Markets: Examples from the Western US", in
    Anderson, Terry L. and Peter J. Hill (eds.) *Water Marketing – the Next Generation*,
    Larham, Rowman and Littlefield.

Intergovernmental Panel on Climate Change (IPCC) (1996),
    Climate change 1995: the science of climate change. Contribution of the Working Group 1 to the Second

Assessment Report of the IPCC, J.J. Houghton, L.G. Meiro Filho, B.A. Callander, N. Harris, A. Kattenberg and K. Maskell (eds.), Cambridge University Press, Cambridge.

Jayartne, Jith and P.E. Strahan (1997),
"The Benefits of Branching Deregulation", *Economic Policy Review*, Volume 3, No. 4, Federal Reserve Bank of New York, December, pp. 13-29.

Jorgenson, Dale W. and Kevin J. Stiroh (1995),
"Computers and Growth", *Economics of Innovation and New Technology*, Volume 3, No. 3-4, pp. 295-316.

Kambhu, John, Paul Bennett and Kenneth Garbade (1999),
"Enhancing the U.S. Treasury Securities in an Era of Surpluses", Paper presented to a New York Federal Reserve Bank Conference on Fiscal policy in an Era of Surpluses, New York, December.

Kasten, Richard, David J. Weiner and G. Thomas Woodward (1999),
"What Made Receipts Boom and When will they go Bust", *National Tax Journal*, Volume 52, No. 3, September, pp. 339-347.

Katz, Lawrence and Alan B. Krueger (1999),
"The High-Pressure US Labor Market of the 1990s", *Brookings Papers on Economic Activity*, 1:1999, pp. 1-87.

Kennickell, Arthur B., Martha Starr-McCluer and Brian J. Surette (2000),
"Recent Changes in US Family Finances: Results from the 1998 Survey of Consumer Finances", *Federal Reserve Bulletin*, Volume 86, No. 1, January, pp. 1-29.

Kete, Nancy (1991),
"The Acid Rain Control Allowance Trading System: Case Study", paper delivered to OECD Workshop on Tradable Permits to Reduce Greenhouse Gas Emissions, June.

Kiley, Michael T. (1999),
"Computers and Growth with Costs of Adjustment: Will the Future Look Like the Past ?", Finance and Economics Discussion Series 1999-36, Board of Governors of the Federal Reserve System, July.

Kwan, Simon H. (1998),
"Securities Activities by Commercial banking Firms' Section 20 Subsidiaries: Risks, Returns and Diversification Benefits 34 Annual conference on Bank Structure and Competition", Federal Reserve Bank of Chicago, May.

Kwan, Simon H. and J.A. Wilcox (1999),
"Hidden Cost Reduction in Bank Mergers: Accounting for more Productive Banks", Working Papers in Applied Economic Theory, No. 99-10, July.

Lebow, David, Louise Sheiner, Larry Slifman and Martha Starr-McClure (1999),
"Recent Trends in Compensation Practices", Finance and Economics Discussion Series 1999-32, Board of Governors of the Federal Reserve System, July.

Leidy, Michael (1996),
"Macroeconomic Conditions and Pressures for Protection Under Antidumping and Countervailing Duty Laws: Empirical Evidence From the United States", International Monetary Fund Working Paper WP/96/88, August.

Levinson, Arik (1999),
"An industry-adjusted index of state environmental compliance costs", National Bureau Of Economic Research Working Paper No. W7297, August.

Liang, Nellie and Steven Sharpe (1999),
"Share Repurchases and Employee Stock Options and their Implications for S&P 500 Retirements and Expected Returns", Finance and Economics Discussion Series 1999-59, Board of Governors of the Federal Reserve System, November.

Litan, Robert E. and Jonathan Rauch (1997),
American Finance for the 21st Century, US Government Printing Office, Washington, DC.

Ludvigson, Sydney and Charles Steindel (1999),
"How Important is the Stock Market Effect on Consumption?", Federal Reserve Bank New York, *Economic Policy Review*, Volume 5, No. 2, July, pp. 29-51.

Melnick, R. Shep (1983),
Regulation and the Courts: The Case of the Clean Air Act, Brookings Institution, Washington, DC.

Mendelsohn, Robert (1999),
"The greening of global warming", paper presented to OECD Climate Change Modelling Workshop, June.

Mendelsohn, Robert, William D. Nordhaus and Daigee Shaw (1994),
"The impact of global warming on agriculture: a Ricardian analysis", *American Economic Review*, Volume 84, No. 4, September, pp. 753-71.

Merrill Lynch (1999),
e-Commerce: Virtually Here, Special Report, April.

Messerlin, Patrick and Geoffrey Reed (1995),
"Antidumping Policies in the United States and the European Community", *Economic Journal*, Volume 105, No. 433, November, pp. 1565-1575.

Meyer, Bruce D. and Dan T. Rosenbaum (1999),
"Welfare, the Earned Income Tax Credit, and the Labor Supply of Single Mothers", National Bureau of Economic Research Working Paper No. W7363, September.

Meyer, Lawrence (2000),
"Sustainability and Monetary Policy", speech before the National Economists Club and the Society of Government Economists, Washington, DC, 20 January.

Mitchell, Michael J. (1999),
"The Benchmark U.S. Treasury Market: Recent Performance and Alternatives", Paper presented to a New York Federal Reserve Bank Conference on Fiscal policy in an Era of Surpluses, New York, December.

Moulton, Brent R., Robert P. Parker and Eugene P. Seskin (1999),
"A Preview of the 1999 Comprehensive Revision of the National Income and Product Accounts: Definitional and Classification Changes", *Survey of Current Business*, Volume 79, No. 8, US Department of Commerce, August.

Moulton, Brent R. and Eugene P. Seskin (1999),
"A Preview of the 1999 Comprehensive Revision of the National Income and Product Accounts: Statistical Changes", *Survey of Current Business*, Volume 79, No. 10, US Department of Commerce, October.

National Association of State Budget Officers (1999),
"The Survey of States", National Association of State Budget Officers and the National Governors Association, Washington, DC, June.

National Education Goal Panel (1999),
The National Education Goals Report: Building a Nation of Learners 1999, US Government Printing Office, Washington, DC.

National Federation of Independent Businesses (2000),
"News Releases", 14 January.

National Telecommunications and Information Administration (1998),
Falling Through the Net II: New Data on the Digital Divide, US Department of Commerce.

National Telecommunications and Information Administration (1999),
Falling Through the Net: Defining the Digital Divide, US Department of Commerce, November.

Neumark, David and William Wascher (1994),
"Employment Effects of Minimum and Subminimum Wages: Reply to Card, Katz and Krueger", Industrial and Labor Relations Review, Volume 47, No. 3, pp. 497-512.

Neumark, David and William Wascher (1996),
"The Effects of Minimum Wages on Teenage Employment and Enrollment: Evidence from Matched CPS Surveys", Research in Labor Economics, Volume 15, pp. 25-64.

Neumark, David and William Wascher (1997),
"Do Minimum Wages Fight Poverty?", National Bureau of Economic Research Working Paper No. W6127, August.

Neumark, David, Mark Schweitzer and William Wascher (1998),
"The Effects of Minimum Wages on the Distribution of Family Incomes: A Non-Parametric Analysis", National Bureau of Economic Research Working Paper No. W6536, April.

Nordhaus, William D (1997),
"Do Real Output and Real Wage Measures Capture Reality? The History of Lighting Suggests Not", In The Economics of New Goods, eds. Timothy F. Bresnahan and Robert J. Gordon, Chicago: University of Chicago Press, pp. 26-69.

OECD (1991),
OECD Economic Surveys, United States, Paris, November.

OECD (1992),
OECD Economic Surveys, United States, Paris, November.

OECD (1996),
Environmental Performance Reviews: the United States, Paris.

OECD (1997),
OECD Economic Surveys, United States, Paris, November.

OECD (1998),
Education at a Glance: OECD Indicators 1998, Paris.

OECD (1999a),
The Economic and Social Impact of Electronic Commerce, Paris.

OECD (1999b),
Regulatory Reform in the United States, Paris.

OECD (1999c),
OECD Economic Surveys, United States, Paris, May.

OECD (1999d),
Regulatory Performance Review: United States, Paris.

OECD (1999e),
Action against Climate Change: the Kyoto Protocol and Beyond, Paris.

OECD (1999f),
  Implementing Domestic Tradable Permits for Environmental Protection, Paris.

OECD (1999g),
  The Price of Water: Trends in OECD Countries, Paris.

OECD (1999h),
  "International emissions trading under the Kyoto Protocol", OECD Information Paper, ENV/EPOC (99)18, FINAL, Paris.

OECD (2000a),
  "Cellular Mobile Pricing Structures and Trends", OECD DSTI Working Paper, Paris, March.

OECD (2000b),
  Frameworks for measuring sustainable development, papers from a workshop on sustainable development indicators, Paris, forthcoming.

OECD (2000c),
  Economic Surveys: Denmark, Paris, forthcoming.

Office of Management and Budget (OMB) (1991),
  Budget of the United States Government, Fiscal Year 1992.

Office of Management and Budget (OMB) (1997),
  Budget of the United States Government, Fiscal Year 1997.

Office of Management and Budget (OMB) (1998),
  Report to Congress On the Costs and Benefits of Federal Regulations 1998.

Office of Management and Budget (OMB) (2000),
  Report to Congress On the Costs and Benefits of Federal Regulations 2000, forthcoming; available in draft for public comment.

Oliner, Stephen D. and Daniel E. Sichel (2000),
  "The Resurgence of Growth in the Late 1990s: Is Information Technology the Story?", *Journal of Economic Perspectives* (forthcoming).

O'Neill, June E. (1998),
  "Remarks to the Conference on Appraising Fannie Mae and Freddie Mac Essential Information", Washington, DC, May.

Or, Zeynep (2000),
  "Determinants of Health Outcomes in Industrialised Countries: A Pooled Cross-Country, Time-Series Analysis", OECD *Economic Studies* No. 30, 2000/1, pp. 53-78.

Ota, Alan K. (1999),
  "Rural, Tech Interests Connect on Broadband Battleground", *CQ Weekly*, Volume 57, No. 48, Congressional Quarterly, pp. 2967-2970.

Otoo, Maria Ward (1999),
  "Temporary Employment and the Natural Rate of Unemployment", Finance and Economics Discussion Series 1999-60, Board of Governors of the Federal Reserve System, November.

Oxley, Howard, Jean-Marc Burniaux, Thai-Thanh Dang and Marco Mira d'Ercole (1997),
  "Income Distribution and Poverty in 13 OECD Countries", OECD *Economic Studies* No. 29, 1997/II, pp. 55 -94.

Oxley, Howard, Thai-Thanh Dang and Pablo Antolin (2000),
  "Poverty Dynamics in Six OECD Countries", OECD *Economic Studies* No. 30, 2000/1, pp. 7-52.

Page, Marianne, Joanne Spetz and Jane Millar (1999),
"Does the Minimum Wage Affect Welfare Caseloads?", Public Policy Institute of Califor-nia.

Petska, Tom and Mike Strudler (1998),
"Income Tax and Progressivity: An Examination of Recent Trends in the Distribution of Individual Income and Taxes", Statistics of Income Research Paper, Internal Revenue Service, Washington, DC, November.

Petska, Tom and Mike Strudler (1999),
"The Distribution of Individual Income and Taxes: A New Look at an Old Issue", Statis-tics of Income Research Paper, Internal Revenue Service, Washington, DC, May.

Portney, Paul R. (1998),
"Counting the Cost: the Growing Role of Economics in Environmental Decision Making", *Environment Magazine*.

Postel, Sandra (1999),
"When the World's Wells Run Dry", World Watch, Washington, DC.

President's Council for Sustainable Development (1999),
Towards a Sustainable America, May.

President's Working Group on Financial Markets (1999a),
Hedge Funds, Leverage, and the Lessons of Long-Term Capital Management, Washington, DC, April.

President's Working Group on Financial Markets (1999b),
Over-the Counter Derivatives Markets and the Commodity Exchange Act, Washington, DC, November.

Probst, Katherine N., Don Fullerton, Robert E. Litan and Paul R. Portney (1995),
Footing the Bill for Superfund Cleanups, Brookings Institutional Resource for the Future, Washington, DC.

Prusa, Thomas J. (1999),
"On the Spread and Impact of Antidumping", National Bureau of Economic Research Working Paper No. W7404, October.

Rector, Robert E. and Sarah E. Youssef (1999),
"The Determinants of Welfare Caseload Decline", A Report of the Heritage Center for Data Analysis, The Heritage Foundation, May.

Reifschneider David, Robert Tetlow and John Williams (1999),
"Aggregate Disturbance, Monetary Policy and the Macroeconomy: The FRB/US Perspec-tive", *Federal Reserve Bulletin*, Volume 85, No. 1, January, pp. 1-19.

Ryscavage, Paul (1995),
"A Surge in Growing Income Inequality", *Monthly Labor Review*, Volume 75, No. 8, August, pp. 51-61.

Sailer, Peter and Michael Weber (1997),
"Household and Individual Income Data from Tax Returns", mimeo, Statistics of Income Division, Internal Revenue Service, Washington, DC.

Sailer, Peter and Michael Weber (1998),
"Household and Individual Income Data from Tax Returns", Statistics of Income Research Paper Internal Revenue Service, Washington, DC, April.

Schreyer, Paul (2000),
   "The Contribution of Information and Communication Technologies to Output Growth: A Study of the G7 Countries", STI Working Paper, 2000/2, OECD, Paris, March.

Schwenk, Albert E. (1999)
   "Trends in Health Insurance Costs", *Compensation and Working Conditions*, Bureau of Labor Statistics, spring.

Seskin, Eugene P. (1999),
   "Improved Estimates of the National Income and Product Accounts for 1959-98: Results of the Comprehensive Revision", *Survey of Current Business*, Volume 79, No. 12, US Department of Commerce, December.

Short, Kathleen, John Iceland and Thesia I. Garner (1999),
   Experimental Poverty Measures: 1998, US Census Bureau, US. Government Printing Office, Washington DC, September.

Sichel, Daniel (1997),
   The Computer Revolution: An Economic Perspective, Brookings Institution, Washington, DC.

Sichel, Daniel (1999),
   "Computers and Aggregate Economic Growth", *Business Economics*, Volume XXXIV, No. 2, April, pp. 18-24.

Smith, Anne E., Jeremy Platt and A. Danny Ellerman (1998),
   "The Cost of Reducing SO_2 (It's higher than you think)", *Public Utilities Fortnightly*, 15 May 1998.

Stewart, Kenneth J. and Stephen B. Reed (1999),
   "CPI research series using current methods, 1978-98", *Monthly Labor Review*, Volume 122, No. 6, June, pp. 29-38.

Sullivan, D. *et al.* (1999),
   "The Need for a Real Time Sales Tax", Submission to the Advisory Commission on Electronic Commerce, Washington, DC.

Taylor, Lori L. (1998),
   "Does the United States Still Overinvest in Housing?", *Economic Review*, Federal Reserve Bank of Dallas, Second Quarter, pp. 10-18.

Technical Panel on Assumptions and Methods (1999),
   "Report to the Social Security Advisory Board", Washington, DC, November.

Tevlin, Stacey and Karl Whelan (2000),
   "Explaining the Investment Boom of the 1990s", Finance and Economics Discussion Series (2000-11), Board of Governors of the Federal Reserve System, March.

Terrile, Jeanne G. (1999),
   "e-Commerce: Virtually Here: An Overview" in *e-Commerce: Virtually Here*, Merrill Lynch, April.

Turner, Mark (1999),
   "The Effects of Minimum Wages on Welfare Recipiency", Urban Institute and Johns Hopkins University, June.

United States Department of Agriculture (1999),
   "Crop Production: Farmer Reported Genetically Enhanced Varieties", PCB-BB, October.

US Interagency Working Group on Sustainable Development Indicators (1998/99),
   "An Experimental Set of Indicators", Washington, DC.

Wenner, Lettie M. (1982),
   The Environmental Decade in Court, Indiana University Press.

Whelan, Karl (2000),
   "Computers, Obsolescence, and Productivity", Finance and Economics Discussion Series (2000-6), Board of Governors of the Federal Reserve System, February.

Zolnierek, James, Katie Rangos and James Eisner (1999),
   Long Distance Market Shares, Federal Communications Commission, March.

Annex I

Government-sponsored enterprises

Government-sponsored-enterprises enable the federal government to pursue a number of social and economic policy objectives through the issuance of debt. Currently, three enterprises are engaged in housing finance (Federal Home Loan Bank System, Fannie Mae and Freddie Mac);[1] two provide farm credit (Farm Credit System and Farmer Mac);[2] and one finances education (Sallie Mae). In exchange for agreeing to specific limits and requirements on their activities, these privately-owned institutions enjoy some privileges denied to other private firms. As government-sponsored enterprises, they can raise funds in the private market more cheaply than can similarly capitalised private firms and have standby credit lines with the Treasury. Even though no explicit guarantee exists, private investors believe the federal government will not allow these institutions to default on their debt obligations. In addition, specific laws treat their securities in some respects like Treasury debt, and they enjoy a number of tax advantages (see Table A1). In the past twenty-five years the market in the debt of these institutions has come to equal that of the total Treasury debt. Their role in financial markets continues to grow despite the disappearance of many of the initial conditions that led to their creation.

Federal Home Loan Banks

Perhaps the least well-known of the three institutions involved in housing finance is the Federal Home Loan Bank System. By September 1999, the gross assets of this system had grown to $477 billion – a 240 per cent increase in the previous five years – considerably faster than the best known of the institutions (Fannie Mae). Indeed, in 1998, the System was the largest seller of debt in the world, issuing $2.6 trillion of securities – more than the US Treasury (though much of this was re-financing of short-term bills). The System consists of 12 regional banks that are owned by savings and loans institutions (S&Ls) and commercial banks that are members. They are supervised by the Federal Housing Finance Board whose chairman is appointed by the President. Current law requires federally chartered savings and loans to be members of the System, while state-chartered thrifts may join voluntarily. In 1989 Congress allowed commercial banks and credit unions to join if they held at least 10 per cent of their portfolio in residential mortgages. In practice any bank can join the System. It suffices to be holding 10 per cent of total assets in tradable mortgage-backed securities that can be sold once the bank becomes a member. The Banks make secured advances to their members so that they can offer, in principle, new home loans. They also help member institutions manage interest-rate risk. Indeed, they are the only large source of long-term funds that the member institutions can use to match the duration of mortgages they hold in their portfolios. Advances with maturity greater than five years, however, are only a small portion of the System's total advances by 1998, they accounted for only 20 per cent of total assets.

Table A1. **Government-sponsored enterprises**

	Fannie Mae	Freddie Mac	Federal Home Loan Bank System	Farm Credit System	Farmer Mac	Sallie Mae[5]
Status	Privately owned by shareholders	Privately owned by shareholders	12 regional banks owned by member deposit institutions	6 Farm Credit Banks, 1 Bank for Cooperatives and 1 Agricultural Credit Bank owned by borrowers	Privately owned by shareholders	Privately owned by shareholders. Due to lose GSE status by 2008
Purpose	Improve access to housing by holding mortgages in portfolio or securitise and guarantee timely payment of securities	Same as Fannie Mae	Make advances to member banks to encourage more housing loans	Make direct loans to farmers through co-operatives or purchase assets held in portfolio	Guarantee securities backed by farmer loans and purchase farm mortgages directly	Purchase insured student loans and make secured loans to lenders
Federal Regulator	Office of Federal Housing Enterprise Oversight	Office of Federal Housing Enterprise Oversight	Federal Housing Finance Board	Farm Credit Administration	Farm Credit Administration	Treasury Department.
(Department)	Housing and Urban Development	Housing and Urban Development	Independent Agency	Independent Agency	Independent Agency	
Presidential board appoint.	5/18	5/18	6/14	None	5/15	7/21[1]
GSE Benefits[2]						
Auth. Treasury lending	$ 2.25 billion	$ 2.25 billion	$ 4.0 billion	None	$ 1.5 billion	$ 1.0 billion
Exempt from SEC registration	Yes	Yes	Yes	Yes	No	Yes
Profits exempt from federal taxes	No	No	Yes	Yes	No	No

Table A1. **Government-sponsored enterprises** (*cont.*)

	Fannie Mae	Freddie Mac	Federal Home Loan Bank System	Farm Credit System	Farmer Mac	Sallie Mae[5]
Profits exempt from S&L taxes	Yes	Yes	Yes	Yes	No	Yes
Interest on secs. exempt from S&L taxes	No	No	Yes	Yes	No	Yes
1998			*$ billion*			
Assets	485	321	434	84	1.9	37.2
Profits	3.4	1.8	2.8	1.3	0.006	0.49
			Per cent			
Capital to assets ratio	3.4	3.7	5.3[3]	14.8	4.2	2.3
Return on equity[4]	22.5	22.6	8.6	10.8	7.4	5.6

1. The President also appoints the chairman.
2. In addition the securities of all the GSEs are eligible for open-market purchases and are eligible as collateral for public deposits. The GSEs can use the Federal Reserve as a fiscal agent and trade their securities through the payments system.
3. May not adequately reflect risk to the government as most of the assets are financed by the deposit insurance fund; see text.
4. Return on equity is measured as the ratio of profit to period average equity capital.
5. The data refer to the Sallie Mae and not its holding company: the SLM Holding Corporation.
Source: Konstas (1995), Nitschke (1998) and annual reports.

The System provides two additional benefits to the public. The Federal Home Loan Banks (FHLBs) also direct housing credit to under-served households and areas. The Community Investment Program provides low-cost advances to member institutions for loans to low-income persons and community development and rehabilitation projects in low and moderate-income neighbourhoods. The Affordable Housing Program subsidises institutions that rehabilitate rental housing, part of which is affordable to very low-income families. These programmes are small, however; total contributions through 1997 were only 9 per cent of outstanding advances. Second, the System helps fund the aftermath of the S&L cleanup. The 1989 Financial Institutions Reforms, Recovery, and Enforcement Act saddled the FHLBs with an obligation to pay $300 million a year through 2030 to fund a portion of the interest on bonds floated by the Resolution Funding Corporation (REFCORP).

The System, however, has evolved in ways Congress never intended. Rather than providing long-term finance, most advances are short term and so are substitutes for deposits or money-market funds. Because of their GSE status the Banks can raise money cheaply in the securities market, paying only about 20 basis points above Treasury securities (Congressional Budget Office, 1993). As a result, it is cheaper for all but the most efficient thrifts to raise loanable funds from the FHLBs than it is from retail deposits or other sources. Furthermore, because deposit insurance rates are based on insured deposits, substituting advances for retail deposits can lower an institution's deposit insurance premium. Moreover, while the System's objective was to aid small banks in regions that were short of loanable funds, it actually lends primarily to large banks. Thus, although there were 7 226 banks that were members in September 1999, over 31 per cent of the System's loans went to the ten largest borrowers, with one company (a unitary thrift) taking over 14 per cent of all advances. As well as the cost advantage, these advances benefit from being completely fungible within a financial institution. Thus, a bank can use mortgages on its balance sheet as collateral for advances from a FHLB and then invest the proceeds in whatever assets it chooses. For example, the accounts of the largest borrower from the System show that its principal business line was consumer banking and that company was able to finance the entire growth of its balance sheet in the year to September 1999 through advances from the System.[3] One of the largest banks in the world is also the second largest borrower from another FHLB.

Besides making advances to their members, the FHLBs invest in market securities to exploit their funding advantage. Their low borrowing costs generate a spread that the Banks can arbitrage even after controlling for risk. In 1989, at the height of the savings and loans shakeout, demand for advances fell, and the Banks began investing in securities. The share of assets in securities zoomed from about 20 per cent to about half between 1989 and 1991. Since then, the fraction has gradually fallen back to 30 per cent by September 1999. At the end of 1997, 37 per cent of these financial investments were in mortgage-backed securities;[4] the rest were in Treasury obligations, the federal funds market or other securities. The FHLBs rebate their profits from these investments and advances to their member banks; they hold very little of them as retained earnings.[5] Some of the dividends to the member banks are in the form of new capital stock with the System, thereby allowing member banks to defer taxation on their dividends until this capital stock is liquidated. The Banks pay no federal or state or local income, corporate or property taxes, nor SEC registration fees on their debt issues.

Some analysts argue that the reason why the FHLBs borrowing costs are so low is because the System is very safe. No member institutions has ever defaulted on an advance, which are heavily collateralised with mortgages the members hold in their portfolios. Other financial assets held by the Banks are for the most part in safe assets. In addition, the System appears well capitalised, at least compared to the other housing-related GSEs. From the perspective of the federal government, however, this level of capitalisation is illusory. Ninety-eight per cent of the banks' capital in 1997 was outstanding stock; retained earnings were only 0.1 per cent of all assets. Moreover, insured deposits fund most of the stock bought by member banks. Banks have to put up only 1.6 cents of their own equity for each dollar of stock they own, given their debt-equity ratios (Congressional Budget Office, 1993). Thus the effective rate of return on equity earned by member banks easily exceeds the apparent rate of return on equity of the FHLB system, which was only 8.6 per cent in the first nine months of 1999. Taken as a whole, private equity in the System is minute, and the deposit insurance funds and the federal government hold the majority of the risk. It is obvious that the member banks are drawing some advantage from membership they cannot obtain elsewhere. In spite of the substantial obligation in the form the REFCORP payment, interest in System membership remains strong. Between 1992 and September 1999, the number of voluntary members – commercial banks, insurance companies and credit unions – grew from 1 693 to 6 297 institutions, and even though state-chartered thrifts have been allowed to leave the system since 1995, their numbers increased from 589 to 684 between 1992 and September 1999.

The Administration had opposed piecemeal reform of the FHLB system. In its view, such a process could preclude real reform. Thus, devolving management authority from the regulator (the FHLB Board) to the individual banks and liberalising borrowing and membership terms for small banks would entrench the existing system. Moreover, switching the REFCORP payments from a flat-rate to an income-related payment might generate incentives for Congress to expand the remit of the System, as increased payments would allow increased discretionary spending in other areas on current pay-as-you-go budgetary rules. More fundamentally, the Administration had argued for tightly linking advances to public objectives and for setting strict limits on the investments of the System, other than advances, and finally, it had opposed the introduction of any form of share structure other than the current system for raising capital. The Congressional Budget Office (1993) went further, questioning whether the System is needed at all.

In the event, the 1999 Financial Modernization Act did not make provision for fundamental reform of the FHLB System. Rather it appears to have allowed a further expansion. First, relatively weak capital-adequacy standards have been introduced. The existing capital of the System will be converted to Class A shares that are redeemable on six months notice. A new type of Class B stock will be issued that can only be redeemed with five years notice. Class B shares and retained earnings will be classed as "permanent" capital. The FHLBs will be required to hold capital of 5 per cent, a floor that can be reduced to 4 per cent if there is a sufficient amount of Class B stock or retained earnings. These constraints are unlikely to be binding as the Banks currently have 5.6 per cent capital. However, capital will also be judged against market risk measured through stress testing. Second, the system will be free to admit small banks (under $500 million of assets) even if they do not hold 10 per cent of their assets as mortgages. Moreover, the system will be free to advance money to these banks against the collateral of non-residential loans. Third, the special restrictive limits on lending to non-qualified thrifts were abolished. Finally, the REFCORP payment was converted to a payment of 20 per cent of earnings, representing a one-third increase in the annual payment that will speed up the eventual repayment of the outstanding debt.

Fannie Mae and Freddie Mac

Two other institutions involved in housing finance, Fannie Mae and Freddie Mac, purchase mortgages from originating lenders and either pool them into securities for open-market sales or hold them in their portfolios.[6] Purchasing mortgages from originators lowers the interest and credit risks these institutions bear, and it provides funds to make new loans. These two institutions were instrumental in developing the secondary market for conventional mortgages, which they dominate.[7] This market is now large and mature. Trading in these securities is one-third that of Treasurys, and studies show that prices now move to suggest that they are fully integrated with the Treasury market (Department of Housing and Urban Development, 1996). The private sector has developed an active secondary market in larger mortgages. The charters of the two GSEs prohibit them from trading in this market.

Congress last considered major legislation concerning these two GSEs in 1992 when it passed the Federal Housing Enterprises Financial Safety and Soundness Act. This law established the Office of Federal Housing Enterprises Oversight (OFHEO) within the Department of Housing and Urban Development (HUD) to regulate them and establish risk -based capital standards to guarantee their soundness. To date, however, the Office has not made these regulations final. In addition, the law mandated that HUD (1996), the Department of Treasury (1996), the General Accounting Office (GAO) (1996b) and the Congressional Budget Office (1996) each report on the feasibility of privatising the two GSEs. To a large extent, the four reports agree on five important points:

- The two GSEs provide HUD some opportunity to further policy goals. Following the 1992 Act, HUD developed credit targets for the two GSEs, and available evidence suggests that they are raising the amount of credit given to the targeted groups. Nonetheless, their performance in the past has been poor when compared to government and even non-government lenders that are deposit institutions subject to the Community Reinvestment Act (Table A2). Recently issued data suggests that this differential may have increased by 1998.

- The GSEs enjoy several statutory advantages over other private financial firms. Their securities receive similar treatment to Treasury debt. Federal Reserve Banks can hold them, as can the Board of Governors of the Federal Reserve System, and the Board of Governors can trade them in open market operations. The securities have favourable risk weights for calculating risk-based capital standards. The GSEs are exempt from paying state and local taxes other than property taxes. They are also exempt from Securities and Exchange Commission registration requirements, and each has a $2¼ billion credit line with the Department of the Treasury. The General Accounting Office (1996b) estimates the value of the registration and state and local tax exemptions to be worth $300 to $400 million per year.

Table A2.   **FHA-eligible mortgage funding borrower and area characteristics**

1994 figures in per cent

	Portfolio share			Market share		
	FHA	GSE	Other	FHA	GSE	Other
Low income	42.2	28.5	32.5	32-34	26-28	38-42
African-American	13.3	4.5	5.9	48-49	18-20	31-34
Hispanic-American	11.5	6.1	6.0	41-42	24-26	33-35
Underserved areas	38.6	26.6	30.4	34-35	26-29	36-40
Total FHA-eligible				27-28	31-34	38-42

Note: The data are taken from the Home Mortgage Disclosure Act.
Source: Department of Housing and Urban Development (1996).

Table A3.   **Estimated value of implicit government guarantees for Fannie Mae
and Freddie Mac**

	HUD	GAO	CBO	Treasury
	Basis points			
Debt	30-75	30-106	70	55
Mortgage-backed securities	30-35	5-35	40	35
Consumer mortgage rates	25-40	15-35	35	30
	Billions of dollars			
Before-tax subsidy value		2.2-8.3	6.5	6
Borrowers			4.4	4
Shareholders			2.1	2

Source: Studies from the federal organisations on privatising the two GSEs.

- *Investors do not believe the government would let a sponsored enterprise fail.* This implicit guarantee provides the GSEs with their large funding advantage. They are automatically rated better than AAA, whereas if they were private firms and held a similar capital-debt structure they would be rated AA- or A. Midpoints of estimates of this funding advantage across the four studies range from 50 to 70 basis points (Table A3). While there is no explicit law that backs GSE debt, the government did bail out another GSE, the Farm Credit System, with a $1.26 billion loan package when it ran into trouble in 1985.

- *Some of this funding advantage is passed to consumers through lower mortgage rates.* Midpoints of estimates of the effect on mortgage rates range from 25 to 35 basis points. Presumably most of this would be lost if the two firms lose their GSE status.

- *Nonetheless, shareholders of Fannie Mae and Freddie Mac do reap some benefits from their GSE status.* The Treasury and the CBO estimated that the total subsidy is between $6 and $6½ billion, with about $2 billion accruing to GSE shareholders. Their after-tax return on equity averaged 26.8 and 22.1 per cent, respectively, between 1990 and 1995, which is significantly higher than those of other financial firms.

Despite their agreement on some of the analysis, the reports came to different conclusions. HUD recommended no change in the status of these GSEs because consumer mortgage rates are lower than they otherwise would be and because the two firms are fulfilling specific credit goals HUD developed to encourage more lending to disadvantaged groups. The CBO, on the other hand, concluded, "In sum, scant evidence exists of public benefits from the GSEs that would justify a retained taxpayer subsidy that is more than $2 billion annually". The Treasury found that the secondary markets would work well without the institutions having GSE status, but that there was not a strong case to privatise them (McKinley, 1997), while the GAO made no recommendations.

Other GSEs

Two GSEs serve the agriculture sector. The Farm Credit System, created in 1916, is now a network of six Farm Credit Banks, a Bank for Cooperatives and an Agricultural Credit Bank.

The System makes short- and long-term loans to farmers through a set of credit associations.. Its borrowers own the institutions of the System. Like the other GSEs, the Farm Credit System raises funds by issuing bonds and other obligations and enjoys several privileges from its GSE status.

Farmer Mac (Federal Agriculture Mortgage Corporation) was created in 1987 and originally only guaranteed farm-based securities other institutions pooled. In 1996 Congress gave this GSE, which had lost money in recent years, the power to purchase loans and issue asset-backed securities. It also demanded that Farmer Mac increase its capital base from $12 to $25 million within two years or face closure. When Farmer Mac's share price rose 515 per cent in 1996, it marketed new shares and raised sufficient capital.

Unlike the secondary housing market, rural credit markets are not well developed, and the case for privatising these institutions is not as strong. Farmer Mac is tiny compared to other GSEs, and it has had problems carrying out its mission to develop secondary markets for farm loans. No secondary markets for rural business loans exist. Moreover, financial innovation and liberalisation have led to some disintermediation out of rural areas. Rural community banks need other sources of loanable funds besides deposits. A conference on the state of rural credit in the United States found "... that rural businesses and consumers have a smaller menu of financial products and often pay more to access capital" (Drabenstott and Meeker, 1997, p. 3).

The last GSE, Sallie Mae, purchases government-guaranteed student loans from originators. It sells some of them to a subsidiary that securitises them, while it holds the rest – currently about one-third of all guaranteed student loans. Unlike the other GSEs, Sallie Mae has chosen to go fully private;[8] at its request Congress included language in a 1996 omnibus appropriations bill that dissolves its charter by 2008. It may privatise sooner, because it wants to expand its business into student loan origination, an opportunity that its current charter denies. The firm also believes its primary mission as a GSE is complete. But, in going private, Sallie Mae will give up its advantages of a GSE, including lower borrowing costs.

Federal credit agencies

Besides its regulation of private credit markets and its sponsored enterprises, the government also directly provides credit through loans and guarantees loans originated elsewhere. About half of its $181 billion in direct loans in 1997 were for agriculture (Table A4), either to assist in rural development (including housing) or to help finance exports. The federal government guaranteed another $17 billion in agriculture loans. Other direct loans and some loan guarantees went to finance other trade through the Export-Import Bank, to finance post-secondary education, or to fund other programmes, such as international development and disaster assistance (Table A5).

By far, the most significant government credit programmes are the housing programmes administered by the Federal Housing Agency (FHA) in HUD and the Veterans' Administration (VA). These agencies guarantee home mortgage loans, subject to a specified limit[9] and other constraints, for a fee paid by originators. The Government National Mortgage Association (Ginnie Mae), which is also part of HUD, pools them for sale as securities guaranteeing the timely payment of interest and principal on pools of these securities. Because these agencies are part of the federal government, their credit guarantees have the full faith and credit backing of the US government. As such, they dominate the low end of the mortgage market. In 1996 the FHA and VA accounted for about 15 per cent of mortgage credit, and in 1997 their outstanding balances were roughly 60 per cent of the outstanding federal credit granted to the private market excluding government-sponsored enterprises (Table A4). Besides aiding lower-income persons, the FHA also targets its lending programmes on minorities and people living in under-served areas (Table A2).

Table A4. **Federal credit programmes in 1997**

Billions of dollars

	Direct loans estimate		Guaranteed loans estimate	
	Value	Losses	Value	Losses
Agriculture/rural[1]	92	13-23	17	1-3
Electrification/telephone	34	3-6		
Other development[1]	47	10-16	12	1-2
Export assistance	11	0-1	5	0-1
Export-import bank	10	3-4	22	4-7
Student loans	21	8-12	99	5-10
Small business	1	0-1	34	2-4
Housing			619	1-16
FHA			449	−4-9
VA			170	5-7
Other	57	10-18	31	2-5
International	21	1-3		
Disaster assistance	10	7-11		
Other	26	2-4	31	2-5
Total	181	34-58	822	15-45

1. Includes rural housing credit assistance not through the Federal Housing Agency or the Veterans Administration.
Source: Office of Management and Budget.

Table A5. **Government insurance programmes**

Billions of dollars

	Total insurance liablities	Estimated liabilities	Fund assets	Net Income	1997 insurance losses
Deposit Insurance Funds	3 039.0	1.4	51.5	4.02	0.00[1]
Banks	2 267.9	0.3	28.6	1.44	0.00
Savings Associations	476.8	0.0	9.6	0.48	0.00
Resolution Trust (FSLIC & RTC)	0.0	1.1[2]	9.6	1.95	0.00
National Credit Unions	294.3	0.0	3.7	0.15	0.00
Pension Benefit Guarantee Corporation	64[3]	11.8	15.3	2.61	0.50
Other					
Flood insurance					
Crop insurance	23.8				0.97

1. One bank failed in 1997 leading to a $4 million loss to the Bank Insurance Fund. No thrifts failed.
2. Does not include accumulated deficit of $127 billion offset by contributed capital of $135.5 billion.
3. Estimated pension underfunding at the end of 1995, the last year available; underfunding has likely declined over the intervening period.
Source: Annual Reports.

Notes

1. Previously known as the Federal National Mortgage Association and the Federal Home Loan Mortgage Corporation, respectively.

2. Federal Agriculture Mortgage Association.

3. A director of this thrift is also a director of a FHLB. This company is the eighth largest financial services company in the United States. In September 1999, it had one-quarter of its assets in higher margin consumer, commercial real estate and consumer finance loans. It intends to raise this proportion to 40 per cent by 2004. At one point, some market participants expected a large technological company to take control of the bank.

4. The Federal Housing Finance Board limits mortgage-backed securities holdings to 300 per cent of the capital base. In 1997 these securities represented 268 per cent of capital. In 1991 the Board raised the authority from 50 to 200 per cent and again to 300 per cent in 1993 (Federal Housing Finance Board, 1998).

5. The same act that required the Banks to make annual REFCORP payments also required the Banks to contribute $2½ billion between 1989 and 1991 to capitalise the Corporation. This taking is one reason why the Banks maintain such a low level of retained earnings. Between 1980 and 1988 retained earnings averaged 1.6 per cent of assets; by 1997 it was only 0.1 per cent.

6. Originally, Fannie Mae only held its mortgages in portfolio, while Freddie Mac only pooled mortgages. About 1980, Fannie Mae began selling mortgage-backed securities, and in the early 1990s Freddie Mac began building a loan portfolio.

7. Mortgage-backed securities are divided into three distinct markets. One market is for Federal Housing Authority (FHA) and Veterans' Administration (VA) loans that the Government National Mortgage Association (Ginnie Mae) guarantees. Ginnie Mae, as a federal agency, operates in this market. The second market, in which Fannie Mae and Freddie Mac operate, is for conventional conforming mortgages. Conforming mortgages are defined as those of a value below a certain ceiling that originated in the private sector and satisfied other underwriting standards. The last market securitises conventional non-conforming private loans, most of which are called jumbo loans because they are above the conforming mortgage limit. Several private firms operate in this market.

8. Prior to its privatisation in 1997, some analysts also considered Connie Lee (College Construction Loan Insurance Fund) a GSE, although this is disputed because it was largely owned by Sallie Mae and the Education Department.

9. The limit for 2000 on FHA loans is $121 246 for most areas and $219 459 for some high-cost areas such as parts of California and New York. For VA loans the maximum is $184 000. For comparison, the nationwide median price of homes sold in November 1999 was $145 000. The limit on Fannie Mae and Freddie Mac conforming loans is $ 252 700 for 2000.

Bibliography

Congressional Budget Office (1993),
   The Federal Home Loan Banks in the Housing Finance System, Congress of the United States, Washington, DC, July.

Congressional Budget Office (1996),
   Assessing the Public Costs and Benefits of Fannie Mae and Freddie Mac, The Congress of the United States, Washington, DC, June.

Department of Housing and Urban Development (1996),
   Studies on Privatising Fannie Mae and Freddie Mac, Washington, DC, May.

Department of Treasury (1996),
   Government Sponsorship of the Federal National Mortgage Association and the Federal Home Loan Mortgage Corporation, Washington, DC, July.

Drabenstott, Mark and Larry Meeker (1997),
   "Financing Rural America: A Conference Summary", *Economic Review*, Federal Reserve Bank of Kansas City, No.82(2), Second Quarter, pp. 89-98.

Government Accounting Office (1996),
   Housing Enterprises: Potential Impacts of Severing Government Sponsorship, Washington, DC, June.

Annex II

Calendar of main economic events

1999

April

The World Trade Organisation (WTO) approves the removal of US trade concessions on EU products worth $191 million after the European Union failed to comply with a WTO ruling against the European Union's system of importation and distribution of bananas.

May

The Federal Open Market Committee (FOMC) begins to announce its policy bias for the inter-meeting period at the same time as it announces its decision on the target federal funds rate, rather than delaying the announcement as had been customary in the past.

The FOMC announces no change to its target for the federal funds rate of 4¾ per cent but adopts a directive tilted toward tightening. The discount rate is left unchanged at 4½ per cent. Both rates were last changed in September, October and November 1998, when they were reduced by ¼ percentage point each time.

June

The FOMC raises the federal funds rate by 25 basis points to 5 per cent and adopts a directive that "includes no predilection about near-term policy action".

July

The WTO approves the removal of US trade concessions on EU products worth $117 million after the European Union fails to comply with a WTO ruling against the European Union's ban on meat from animals treated with hormones.

August

The FOMC raises the federal funds rate by 25 basis points to 5¼ per cent and the Board of Governors approves a 25 basis point increase in the discount rate to 4¾ per cent. The FOMC adopts a directive that is symmetric with regard to the outlook for policy over the near term.

September

President Clinton vetoes a bill that would have cut taxes by $792 billion over ten years.

October

The FOMC leaves its target for the federal funds rate unchanged but adopts a directive biased toward tightening.

MCI WorldCom announces it plans to take over Sprint for $129 billion. The Federal Communications Commission signals that a strong case will need to made that the merger benefits consumers for approval of the deal.

The Supreme Court rejects an appeal of a Maine law that provides tuition for children attending private non-religious schools but denies assistance to those attending religious schools, thus leaving the law in place.

November

The FOMC raises the federal funds rate by 25 basis points to 5½ per cent and the Board of Governors approves a 25 basis point increase in the discount rate to 5 per cent. The FOMC shifts its directive back to symmetric.

A FY 2000 omnibus appropriations bill is passed, which is estimated to exceed the spending caps set in 1997 for this budget year by over $30 billion.

The Gramm-Leach-Bliley Financial Modernization Act, which repeals Glass-Steagall restrictions on cross-ownership within the financial services industry, is passed.

The judge in the Microsoft case concludes in his findings of fact that Microsoft engaged in a pattern of predatory conduct to protect its monopoly power in the market for personal computer operating systems that stifled competition and harmed consumers.

The United States signs a bilateral trade agreement with China associated with its accession to the WTO.

December

The FOMC announces no change to its target for the federal funds rate and adopts a symmetric directive over the inter-meeting period in order to focus on the smooth transition over the century-change date.

The Federal Trade Commission approves Exxon's $81 billion acquisition of Mobil on the condition that the companies divest themselves of a variety of assets.

The World Trade Organisation agrees with the United States in its dispute against Canada's export subsidies for milk.

The Supreme Court refuses to review another case dealing with vouchers. In this case, the Vermont Supreme Court overturned a Vermont law that subsidised tuition for some students attending religious schools.

The Federal Communications Commission approves Bell Atlantic's application to provide long-distance service to its customers in New York State, making it the first local Bell telephone company to win such authority.

2000

January

The FOMC announces modified disclosure procedures effective in February. A statement will be issued to the public immediately following every FOMC meeting rather than only in the event of a policy action or major shift in view. The discussion of the policy bias over the inter-meeting period will be eliminated and new, standardised language will describe the balance of risks to the attainment of the Committee's long-run goals of price stability and sustainable economic growth

The unemployment rate falls to 4.0 per cent, the lowest rate in 30 years.

The $150 billion merger AOL and Time Warner is announced.

The WTO rules against the European Union's claim that Section 301 of the US Trade Act of 1974 does not comply with US trade obligations.

February

President Clinton sends to Congress the Administration's budget proposal for FY 2001, with a projected surplus of $184 billion.

The FOMC raises the federal funds rate by 25 basis points to 5¾ per cent and Board of Governors approves a 25 basis point increase in the discount rate to 5¼ per cent. The FOMC announces that it "believes that the risks are weighted mainly toward conditions that may generate heightened inflation pressures in the foreseeable future".

The Senate votes to confirm Alan Greenspan for a fourth, four-year term as chairman of the Federal Reserve Board.

The Federal Trade Commission announces that it will seek an injunction in federal court to prevent the merger of BP Amoco and Atlantic Richfield Company on the grounds that the merged company will control Alaska oil supplies to the West Coast.

The WTO rules in favour of the European Union's claim that US tax treatment of "foreign sales corporations" constitutes a prohibited export subsidy.

March

The FOMC raises the federal funds rate by 25 basis points to 6 per cent and the Board of Governors approves a 25 basis point increase in the discount rate to 5½ per cent. The FOMC announces that it "believes the risks are weighted mainly toward conditions that may generate heightened inflation pressures in the foreseeable future".

BASIC STATISTICS:

INTERNATIONAL COMPARISONS

	Units	Reference period [1]	Australia	Austria
Population				
Total	Thousands	1997	18 532	8 0
Inhabitants per sq. km	Number	1997	2	
Net average annual increase over previous 10 years	%	1997	1.3	0
Employment				
Total civilian employment (TCE)[2]	Thousands	1997	8 430	3 6
of which:				
Agriculture	% of TCE	1997	5.2	6
Industry	% of TCE	1997	22.1	30
Services	% of TCE	1997	72.7	63
Gross domestic product (GDP)				
At current prices and current exchange rates	Bill. US$	1997	392.9	206
Per capita	US$	1997	21 202	25 5
At current prices using current PPPs[3]	Bill. US$	1997	406.8	186
Per capita	US$	1997	21 949	23 0
Average annual volume growth over previous 5 years	%	1997	4.1	1
Gross fixed capital formation (GFCF)	% of GDP	1997	21.5	24
of which:				
Machinery and equipment	% of GDP	1997	10.3 (96)	8.8 (9
Residential construction	% of GDP	1997	4.4 (96)	6.2 (9
Average annual volume growth over previous 5 years	%	1997	7.3	2
Gross saving ratio[4]	% of GDP	1997	18.4	
General government				
Current expenditure on goods and services	% of GDP	1997	16.7	19
Current disbursements[5]	% of GDP	1996	34.8	4
Current receipts	% of GDP	1996	35.4	47
Net official development assistance	% of GNP	1996	0.28	0.2
Indicators of living standards				
Private consumption per capita using current PPP's[3]	US$	1997	13 585	12 95
Passenger cars, per 1 000 inhabitants	Number	1995	477	44
Telephones, per 1 000 inhabitants	Number	1995	510	46
Television sets, per 1 000 inhabitants	Number	1994	489	48
Doctors, per 1 000 inhabitants	Number	1996	2.5	2
Infant mortality per 1 000 live births	Number	1996	5.8	5
Wages and prices (average annual increase over previous 5 years)				
Wages (earnings or rates according to availability)	%	1998	1.5	5
Consumer prices	%	1998	2.0	1
Foreign trade				
Exports of goods, fob*	Mill. US$	1998	55 882	61 75
As % of GDP	%	1997	15.6	28
Average annual increase over previous 5 years	%	1998	5.6	
Imports of goods, cif*	Mill. US$	1998	60 821	68 01
As % of GDP	%	1997	15.3	31
Average annual increase over previous 5 years	%	1998	7.5	
Total official reserves[6]	Mill. SDR's	1998	10 942	14 628 (9
As ratio of average monthly imports of goods	Ratio	1998	2.2	2.7 (9

* At current prices and exchange rates.
1. Unless otherwise stated.
2. According to the definitions used in OECD Labour Force Statistics.
3. PPPs = Purchasing Power Parities.
4. Gross saving = Gross national disposable income minus private and government consumption.

EMPLOYMENT OPPORTUNITIES

Economics Department, OECD

The Economics Department of the OECD offers challenging and rewarding opportunities to economists interested in applied policy analysis in an international environment. The Department's concerns extend across the entire field of economic policy analysis, both macro-economic and microeconomic. Its main task is to provide, for discussion by committees of senior officials from Member countries, documents and papers dealing with current policy concerns. Within this programme of work, three major responsibilities are:

- to prepare regular surveys of the economies of individual Member countries;
- to issue full twice-yearly reviews of the economic situation and prospects of the OECD countries in the context of world economic trends;
- to analyse specific policy issues in a medium-term context for the OECD as a whole, and to a lesser extent for the non-OECD countries.

The documents prepared for these purposes, together with much of the Department's other economic work, appear in published form in the *OECD Economic Outlook, OECD Economic Surveys, OECD Economic Studies* and the Department's *Working Papers* series.

The Department maintains a world econometric model, INTERLINK, which plays an important role in the preparation of the policy analyses and twice-yearly projections. The availability of extensive cross-country data bases and good computer resources facilitates comparative empirical analysis, much of which is incorporated into the model.

The Department is made up of about 80 professional economists from a variety of backgrounds and Member countries. Most projects are carried out by small teams and last from four to eighteen months. Within the Department, ideas and points of view are widely discussed; there is a lively professional interchange, and all professional staff have the opportunity to contribute actively to the programme of work.

Skills the Economics Department is looking for:

a) Solid competence in using the tools of both microeconomic and macroeconomic theory to answer policy questions. Experience indicates that this normally requires the equivalent of a Ph.D. in economics or substantial relevant professional experience to compensate for a lower degree.

b) Solid knowledge of economic statistics and quantitative methods; this includes how to identify data, estimate structural relationships, apply basic techniques of time series analysis, and test hypotheses. It is essential to be able to interpret results sensibly in an economic policy context.

c) A keen interest in and extensive knowledge of policy issues, economic developments and their political/social contexts.

d) Interest and experience in analysing questions posed by policy-makers and presenting the results to them effectively and judiciously. Thus, work experience in government agencies or policy research institutions is an advantage.

e) The ability to write clearly, effectively, and to the point. The OECD is a bilingual organisation with French and English as the official languages. Candidates must have excellent knowledge of one of these languages, and some knowledge of the other. Knowledge of other languages might also be an advantage for certain posts.

f) For some posts, expertise in a particular area may be important, but a successful candidate is expected to be able to work on a broader range of topics relevant to the work of the Department. Thus, except in rare cases, the Department does not recruit narrow specialists.

g) The Department works on a tight time schedule with strict deadlines. Moreover, much of the work in the Department is carried out in small groups. Thus, the ability to work with other economists from a variety of cultural and professional backgrounds, to supervise junior staff, and to produce work on time is important.

General information

The salary for recruits depends on educational and professional background. Positions carry a basic salary from FF 318 660 or FF 393 192 for Administrators (economists) and from FF 456 924 for Principal Administrators (senior economists). This may be supplemented by expatriation and/or family allowances, depending on nationality, residence and family situation. Initial appointments are for a fixed term of two to three years.

Vacancies are open to candidates from OECD Member countries. The Organisation seeks to maintain an appropriate balance between female and male staff and among nationals from Member countries.

For further information on employment opportunities in the Economics Department, contact:

Management Support Unit
Economics Department
OECD
2, rue André-Pascal
75775 PARIS CEDEX 16
FRANCE

E-Mail: eco.contact@oecd.org

Applications citing ''ECSUR'', together with a detailed *curriculum vitae* in English or French, should be sent to the Head of Personnel at the above address.

For more information about all OECD publications
contact your nearest OECD Centre, or visit
www.oecd.org/bookshop

Pour plus d'informations sur les publications de l'OCDE,
contactez votre Centre OCDE le plus proche
ou visitez notre librairie en ligne :
www.oecd.org/bookshop

Where to send your request:
Où passer commande :

In Central and Latin America / En Amérique centrale et en Amérique du Sud

OECD MEXICO CENTRE / CENTRE OCDE DE MEXICO
Edificio INFOTEC
Av. San Fernando No. 37 Col. Toriello Guerra
Tlalpan C.P. 14050, Mexico D.F.
Tel.: +525 528 10 38   Fax: + 525 606 13 07
E-mail: mexico.contact@oecd.org   Internet: www.rtn.net.mx/ocde

In North America / En Amérique du Nord

OECD WASHINGTON CENTER / CENTRE OCDE DE WASHINGTON
2001 L Street N.W., Suite 650
Washington, DC 20036-4922
Tel.: +1 202 785-6323
Toll free / Numéro vert : +1 800 456-6323   Fax: +1 202 785-0350
E-mail: washington.contact@oecd.org   Internet: www.oecdwash.org

In Japan / Au Japon

OECD TOKYO CENTRE / CENTRE OCDE DE TOKYO
Landic Akasaka Bldg.
2-3-4 Akasaka, Minato-ku
Tokyo 107-0052
Tel.: +81 3 3586 2016   Fax: +81 3 3584 7929
E-mail : center@oecdtokyo.org   Internet: www.oecdtokyo.org

In the rest of the world / Dans le reste du monde
DVGmbH
Birkenmaarsstrasse 8
D-53340 Meckenheim
Germany
Tel.: +49 22 25 9 26 166/7/8   Fax: +49 22 25 9 26 169
E-mail: oecd@dvg.dsb.net

OECD Information Centre and Bookshop/
Centre d'information de l'OCDE et Librairie
OECD PARIS CENTRE / CENTRE OCDE DE PARIS
2 rue André-Pascal, 75775 Paris Cedex 16, France
Enquiries / Renseignements : Tel: +33 (0) 1 45 24 81 67
E-mail: sales@oecd.org

ONLINE BOOKSHOP / LIBRAIRIE EN LIGNE : **www.oecd.org/bookshop**
(secure payment with credit card / paiement sécurisé par carte de crédit)

OECD PUBLICATIONS, 2, rue André-Pascal, 75775 PARIS CEDEX 16
PRINTED IN FRANCE
(10 2000 02 1 P) ISBN 92-64-17502-4 – No. 51209 2000
ISSN 0376-6438